"Chynoweth and Adams remind us that the cure for fascism is democracy—not as an abstract set of institutions but as direct participation and human agency. The problems that seem so hopeless they recast as contradictions, and every contradiction is an opportunity, a point of leverage. These authors, who've devoted their lives to seeking points of leverage and acting to make change, offer a practical framework and techniques any and all of us can take up, to change and save the world and ourselves one step at a time, in community with one another."

  —Steve Randy Waldman, computer programmer
  and writer at interfluidity.com

"Rooted in twenty-first-century local struggles, experienced activist and theoretician Danielle Chynoweth has written a timely, insightful, and practical guide for melding together different oppressed communities into united struggle against the US empire."

  —Sundiata Keita Cha-Jua, professor, University of Illinois,
  Urbana-Champaign

I0117242

REMAKING DEMOCRACY

HOW WE MAKE
THE WORLDS
WE WANT

"We need to know how to do the work of social change, and how to build structures to sustain our values of care, justice, and respect for the Earth and all its inhabitants. The guidebook for this change is *Remaking Democracy*."

—**Safiya U. Noble,** author of *Algorithms of Oppression*

"Now is the time to put forward bold, people-centered solutions. To do so, we need to learn from past movements, not rehash them. We need organizers who have been on the frontlines training a new crop of leaders that can see beyond their own time. *Remaking Democracy: How We Make the Worlds We Want* is a training manual for our future."

—**Carol Ammons,** Illinois State Representative, co-chair of the Illinois Black Caucus

"For the first time in human history, a connected, just, and equitable global society is possible. What we lack is mass participation in imaging and creating that world. *Remaking Democracy: How We Make the Worlds We Want* helps us think beyond the reality of our current existence to forge a radically inclusive, global community."

—**Alfredo Lopez,** founder of May First Movement Technology

"A love letter to past, present, and future change makers, *Remaking Democracy* is the antidote to techno-authoritarianism—and all projects used to truncate human connectedness—that we have been waiting for. With savvy, accessible prose, Chynoweth and Adams have composed an indispensable volume for theorists, organizers, and creative practitioners that speaks to the resilient power and promise of collective imagineering and community-sung desire and play at every scale."

—**Anita Say Chan,** author of *Predatory Data*

"Danielle Chynoweth has kept her eyes on the prize for decades, shepherding institutions that have withstood outside pressure from fascists and funders alike—while building the organic community leaders and durable community-building policies that are the bedrock of transformation. This book will be a gift to anyone else hoping to do the same at this pivotal moment."

—**Hannah Sassaman,** Executive Director, People's Tech Project

"A truly remarkable book loaded with ideas and strategies for reimagining society and building community."

—**C.T. Lawrence Butler,** co-founder of Food Not Bombs

"Finally, after many years and much searching, I have found a book for all ages that can be used as a response to the question: what to do? I will use it in my lifelong learning courses on democracy."

—**Larry Richards,** cybernetician

"This book is a tour de force offering a clear and deep analysis of capitalism and its inherent contradictions through which we can organize and bring this beast to its feet. Danielle Chynoweth and Elizabeth Adams brought me real hope that defeat of capitalist vicious greed can be done."

—**Faranak Miraftab,** professor, University of Illinois, Urbana-Champaign

"My creative journey has become inseparable from community, social responsibility, and care. The teachings of Danielle Chynoweth and Elizabeth Adams further deepened my understanding of approaching individual and collective harmony. [This] holistic approach has taught me to hold both in balance, affirming that a society flourishes only when the individual and the collective are equally seen, nurtured, and respected."

—**Koushalya Jeganathan,** filmmaker

"This book comes at the perfect time, when people everywhere are anxious about the new world order and citizen activism matters more than ever."

—**Keiko Sei,** media activist

"This is a book I've been waiting for, even when I didn't know it consciously. Chynoweth and Adams provide a timely and urgent call to participation in imagining the world we want to live in. Drawing on their decades of experience, they offer a message of hope and possibility. Anyone who looks at the world around them and sees reasons to despair should pick up this book and learn how to hope again."

—**Dr. Andrew Ó Baoill,** lecturer, University of Galway

"*Remaking Democracy* is a rallying call to transform a world in crisis. Urgent, practical, and fiercely hopeful, this book equips readers to imagine boldly, act collectively, and build the equitable futures our movements demand. Blending theory, real-world case studies, and actionable exercises, it invites us to envision—and create—the futures we deserve. In a time of democratic erosion, climate catastrophe, and rising authoritarianism, *Remaking Democracy* provides a radically hopeful and deeply practical approach to collective transformation."

—**Tish Stringer,** visual anthropologist

"This book serves as a curriculum that invites us to become active collaborators in reimagining, revolutionizing, and reconstructing new equitable democratic practices that accompany futurist thinking, participatory joy, advancing praxis, promotional healing, and equitable democracies."

—**Stacey A. Robinson,** multimedia artist

"This is the cookbook we need when democracy is in crisis. These are the recipes—and the stories behind the recipes—that will allow every local activist, line cook, and renowned chef alike to build their own local recipes for democracy; to improvise the exact ingredients and spices for their own communities. Democracy should be delicious."

—**Dr. Kate McDowell,** professor, University of Illinois, Urbana-Champaign

"In an era of harrowing ecological, economic, and authoritarian crises, *Remaking Democracy* is an optimistic yet realist approach to building a more thoughtful and civil society."

—**Sascha Meinrath,** policy activist and educator

"This invaluable and timely book provides actionable plans and essential tools for transforming our world from the ground up. Inspiring hope and courage to confront the daunting challenges facing us today, *Remaking Democracy* is mandatory reading for anyone working towards a more just society."

—**Victor Pickard,** professor, University of Pennsylvania

"Blending experimental art, systems thinking, and grassroots organizing, *Remaking Democracy* offers an urgently needed toolkit for designing participatory, just futures. Chynoweth and Adams bring theory and practice together with originality, clarity, and care."

—**Keith Moore,** composer, artist-organizer, and educator

REMAKING DEMOCRACY

HOW WE MAKE THE WORLDS WE WANT

Danielle Chynoweth
Elizabeth Adams

COMMON
NOTIONS

PHILADELPHIA, PA

ISBN: 978-1-94533-551-8 | eBook ISBN: 978-1-94533-573-0
Library of Congress Control Number: 2026930550

10 9 8 7 6 5 4 3 2 1

Common Notions
PO Box 18823
Philadelphia, PA 19119

commonnotions.org
info@commonnotions.org

Discounted bulk quantities of our books are available for organizing,
educational, or fundraising purposes. Please contact Common Notions at
the address above for more information.

Cover design by Josh MacPhee
Edited by Erika Biddle
Layout design by Copenhaver Cumpston
Typeset by Kirsten Dennison
Editorial support from Alice Boone
Illustration by Christopher A. Evans

Printed on acid-free paper

This book is dedicated to

Susan Rose Parenti

composer, playwright, teacher, feminist,
player of attention to language,
virtuoso performer in everyday life.

Preface

Since the US presidential election of 2024, my phone and email have been blowing up, and people are lining up at microphones during my talks on the harms inflicted by the tech industry on our society and selves. They are all asking the same questions: "What do we do to make change—how do we respond to this moment?" *Remaking Democracy: How We Make the Worlds We Want* by Danielle Chynoweth and Elizabeth Adams has become part of my answer. We all feel like we are drowning in bad news; this book reminds us of the power of everyday people to drop anchor and make a difference right where we are, right now, on very big problems.

Remaking Democracy is an essential tool for this moment. We are being beckoned, locally and globally, to build alternative systems to the antidemocratic, fascist, and neofeudalist desires of billionaires who are profoundly unimaginative. Their products, projects, and politics show an acceptance of the disposability of others for their own gain. We need to know *how* to do the work of social change, and *how* to build structures to sustain our values of care, justice, and respect for the Earth and all its inhabitants. The guidebook for this change is *Remaking Democracy*.

We are struggling with not just the collapse of democracies around the world, but with difficulties in sharing knowledge—even among educators, organizers, and facilitators—and teaching how to make democracy real in our lives. Democracy is not a word that belongs just to electoral politics and politicians; it's an approach to creating societies that make space for everyone to live, in communities (large and small) that are empowered, healthy, and socially just.

We live in worlds hyperconnected by social media and the internet, but we are simultaneously disconnected from each other and our ability to problem solve the major crises our communities face. Instead of artificial intelligence, don't we really want *authentic* intelligence—intelligence that deepens our spiritual and intellectual sense of self, and our interconnectedness? This book collects the wisdom of elders, organizers, scientists, and artists—the makers and dreamers who can help us reimagine and realize the worlds we want. I am in awe of what an incredible feat it is to write a book that can marry imagination and possibility with everyday actions. You are indeed holding such a book.

The gift of this work is that it can truly help us transform self and society simultaneously. If you don't know where to start, read on.

I was inspired by the authors' critiques of superiority in all its forms, and the way they connected these critiques to action that forge radical inclusivity through participation. They provide an analysis of power, capitalism, and oppression along with step-by-step strategies for designing more socially just, multiracial, democratic, and sustainable ways of being. This book will give you ideas about how to remake relationships and systems, and you can try these ideas out with friends, family, coworkers, neighbors, classmates, union members, faith-based groups, associations—any configuration of people imaginable. However much we value justice, equity, and respect for all people, we also need strategies to manifest these in action. *Remaking Democracy* is a guide to remind us that *we* can dismantle policies of hate and harm and build practices and systems of love, care, and inclusion.

No matter your politics, let us witness that around the world, millions of people want a world that reflects the highest, best version of us—one that demonstrates universal care rather than a reckless disregard for humanity. In our most trusted relationships, we experience the fullness of being accepted and offering acceptance. Many of us yearn to live, work, play, and love in community with others, despite the structures that impede us. We yearn to have workplaces, organizations, and institutions that are aligned with our values and demonstrate respect and awareness.

The collapses of democracy, and our civil and human rights, have been a long time in the making. Our rights are much more fragile and easier to take down than we could have guessed. Few imagined the abuses of power that are now unfolding, and the overwhelming consequences of chaotic policies that have been fueled by dark money and ethnonationalism for decades. We see the legal system responding, but we cannot just watch from the sidelines. It will take all of us. We need to coordinate legal, political, and cultural strategies to resist these policies. While people may have previously relied upon others—policymakers, organizers and activists, and those in power—to create some semblance of stability, the truth is that change must be enacted and sustained by both grand political gestures and millions of small, localized decisions. We are the change we need. We must not abdicate our power when the world so desperately needs new dreams of hope and possibility.

We can turn to Chynoweth and Adams' *Remaking Democracy* for tools and ways of approaching our problems, such as with the Spiral of Change. The authors provide numerous examples from their organizing to model this approach. Of course, we know that a few powerful people may have diametrically opposing agendas and ideas about how to organize the world—but *we* constitute a majority who can bring the art and science of experimentation, and the heuristics of systems theory, to dismantle the structures that oppress. Using the framework of intersectionality, our authors remind us that the stakes are different for many people based on their historical and contemporary identities, and their experiences of uneven and unfair exercises of power. When we see the contradictions inherent in abuses of power, we find opportunities for leverage and change "so that those affected by systems can become their creators," as the authors argue. By analyzing systems, we can see problems, but we can also see promises that beg us to reflect on "what do we want instead" and how can we realize these desires? Alongside the courage and effort you bring, *Remaking Democracy* teaches the strategy and reflection needed to dream up new worlds and make effective, sustainable change.

We have incredible challenges before us. Our global internet has been turned into a propaganda machine. Big Tech and Silicon Valley threaten to remake democracies into authoritarian regimes. Two-party national politics and voter suppression leave more than half of Americans without representation. Climate change is here, and exacerbating inequality harming those in the Global Majority, and those vulnerable to corporate power in the Global North. Poverty is on the rise, pushing up eviction rates, and Black women's unemployment is increasing. The list of problems is long. But even in the face of it, this book is full of inspiring stories and thinkers who we can learn from as we forge our own paths. And as we work we can build a shared analysis that reveals our struggles as linked: from support for Palestine and Sudan, to calls for gun and nuclear weapons control; from defunding the prison industrial complex and corrupt policing, to divestment from surveillance technologies; from cleaning up environmental disaster to reversing climate change.

We have wisdom to inherit and share with one another. We need not be paralyzed and overwhelmed. We can make the change we want to see in the world. We can take the best our systems have to offer and reinvent the parts that fail us. We can do it. We are world-makers. Now is our time. Let's get going in remaking democracy.

Safiya U. Noble
Los Angeles, September 2025

"What time is it on the clock of the world?"

Our responsibility, at this watershed in our history, is to face the past honestly and do the things necessary to heal ourselves and our planet. Healing our society will require the patient work not primarily of politicians, but of artists, ministers, gardeners, workers, families, women, and communities. It will require new forms of governance, work, and education that are much more participatory and democratic than those collapsing around us. It will require enlarging our vision and decolonizing our imaginations.

—Grace Lee Boggs, *The Next American Revolution: Sustainable Activism for the Twenty-First Century*

This book began to take shape in 2016 when I, Danielle, like many organizers I knew, started receiving a torrent of messages like this one: "I wanted to reach out to you for guidance and leadership. You have been a shining example of putting ideas into action for the longest time; and I feel a great weight and shame that I have not. I believe now has to be the beginning of the fight to reclaim our nation, and that the struggle will be real, hard fought, and will require active participation. Can you please help me identify some meaningful ways to get involved?"[1] As more and more people reached out, I realized: I have much to say . . . in fact, I have a book-length amount of things to say about how to participate in making change.

At the time, I was working as the Organizing Director for Media Justice, a network of over a hundred social change organizations across the United States. We were celebrating a winning streak with our efforts to mobilize and expand connection and participation. In 2010, we pushed the Local Community Radio Act through Congress, opening up the airwaves for millions of local voices.[2] In 2016, we won the Prison Phone Justice campaign so families could connect with incarcerated loved ones. That same year, we won Lifeline support for rural and poor communities to connect to jobs and resources through the internet.[3] We were mobilizing people impacted by harmful policies to rewrite them.

I was a single mother to five-year-old Ezra Shine, who crisscrossed the country with me, his little body bear-hugging my roller bag as we sped through airports. As corporate and state power consolidated, contradictions long embedded in our social systems were erupting. My reaction was to work harder, organize more people, and produce more events. I remember saying to my colleague: "If I don't get out from under this stress, I am going to get cancer." Two months later I learned of the five-pound malignant tumor growing inside my ovary. I did not know whether I would live or die—whether my child would lose his only parent. As my body was knitting itself back together, my mother, father, aunt, uncle, baby cousin, and a number of friends and colleagues were also diagnosed with cancer.[4]

At this difficult time, I sought the wisdom of my intellectual mentors whose reproductive tissue had also mutated as they struggled to articulate a society in which what was happening to them would not happen to others: Audre Lorde, Rachel Carson, Susan Steingraber. I filled notebooks with formulations: *Cancer is the personal consequence of pollution from deregulated industry combined with toxic stress of overwork. Fascism is the political consequence of the disillusion and dissolution of democracy as corporate power overtakes public institutions.*

Both cancer then fascism originate many years before their visible manifestation. In each, a part of the body, or body politic, mutates and grows until it is stopped, or kills its host. They threaten to overwhelm our capabilities to respond, and yet we do—with analysis (diagnosis), strategy (plan of care), and tactics (health care intervention). Coordinating a diversity of tactics that address mind, body, soul, and community creates the highest chances of survival.

I watched from my recovery room as millions of people participated in the largest protests in US history during the Women's March of 2017. The vast majority of people across the planet did not want wars, displacement, discrimination, famine, and environmental destruction, but we were unable to steer our systems of governance away from producing violence. I felt the contradiction of the moment—both its terrible weight, and the way it was cracking open spaces for creating new systems and new ways of being.

I wondered: we know *why* we need democracy, but where do we learn *how* to make it? Given the exclusive structures of power established by our history of colonization and forced labor, how do we *remake* democracy to include everyone's participation? How do we make authoritarianism unimaginable and organize to meet human needs unconditionally?

As I considered my next steps, I wrote out these intentions: *Come home. Meet direct needs while organizing to address root causes. Learn from those ensnared in the biggest contradictions we face. Build structures of participation to alter power relations.* I ran for the elected position of Cunningham Township Supervisor to redesign our local public aid office around the goal of ending local homelessness. While reducing harm through direct service, I saw the need for a guidebook for social change to help people from all walks of life build their participation, confidence, and collective power. So I reached out to Elizabeth Adams, wizard collaborator and public artist, inviting her to co-create this book with me. We share a decade of experience teaching at the School for Designing a Society (SDaS), a multigenerational, international school that has convened artists and organizers for thirty years to design desirable social futures. We both felt that a book that combined the creative design tools of SDaS with the strategic organizing of our campaign work would be a powerful combination.

When Danielle approached me in the spring of 2017, I, Elizabeth, had just finished my doctorate in music composition. I was teaching music theory but wondering all the while: how can I teach social change? My ongoing politicization through resisting the Iraq War and participating in Occupy Wall Street had led me to organizing interventions in education, housing, and the arts. Building from Occupy's education working group, Free University NYC prefigured a model of horizontal education through pop-up events in public parks where I learned: when everyone has something to teach and everyone has something to learn, participation builds connection, analysis, and movements for justice. Organizing with the Crown Heights Tenant Union, I saw how collaborating with my neighbors could lead to fundamental shifts in power on the scale of building, city, and state. In Julie and Elizabeth's Anti-Capitalist Concert Series, Julie Harting and I created a context in which we can connect our music, audiences, and performers with our political longings for a decommodified, abolitionist future of music-making free from wage slavery.

I was coordinating care for my mother, Constance Carden, a former public interest lawyer who had won wheelchair accessibility for polling places a decade before the Americans with Disabilities Act of 1990, among her many victories for marginalized New Yorkers, and who had survived two brain injuries. And, in the foreboding political environment of this moment, in which all care work is undervalued while motherhood is gendered and commodified, I was trying to figure out how to have a kid. SDaS had radically informed my strategies for both care and movements, so when Danielle, my SDaS mentor and co-teacher, asked me to collaborate on this book, I said yes right away.

We started to write the book that is now in your hands. Danielle buried her father, supported her mother after surgery, and healed from her own cancer. My daughter was born. Six months later, I was stuck in lockdown, sick with COVID-19 in New York City, when every siren signaled another family in distress. As the systems we relied on were shaken, the politically impossible became real: a halt on evictions for twenty-two months; billions of federal and state dollars in rental and utility assistance materialized; a radical drop in global energy consumption; free, universal access to medical support through COVID tests and vaccines; jails emptied of nonviolent suspects. Mutual aid efforts formed all over the country. In Urbana, Danielle and friends launched Solidarity Gardens where volunteers grew and distributed food to neighbors in need, checking in on those isolated during quarantine.

Danielle and I had by this point produced only a rough draft of this book, but we agreed that the urgency of the moment required us to teach from it *now*. With support from Highlander Research and Education Center, Media Justice, and the Siebel Center for Design, we turned the book-in-progress into a seven-week webinar entitled *Democratize This!* We invited movement mentors and artists to be in conversation with the ideas presented here, which synthesize decades of conversation, organizing, and art making. The webinar allowed us to try out these ideas with would-be readers, giving us the opportunity to reflect on and reformulate our strategies for making democratic change.

Strategy: The Spiral of Change

Fast forward to now. We wrote this book because we believe that a livable future relies on everyone participating in making the worlds we want. Inspired by our work with SDaS and the movements we helped grow, we offer you this guide to build participation. *Remaking Democracy* will help you analyze root causes of problems in systems, generate desires, design actions, and reflect on those actions to begin again with renewed wisdom. It aims to proliferate participation and grow democratic practices, so that those affected by systems can become their creators. It does this through formulations, assignments, and stories of successful interventions for change. Rather than arguing for any one solution, we equip you to design the abundant variety of solutions our surviving and thriving requires.

As the contradictions in our social and economic systems intensify, we ask: *how can we empower ourselves and our communities to make lasting social change?* Ours is a time of crisis and possibility. We are in a crucial moment when, in the cracks produced by the current crises, we can plant the seeds of a more fundamentally just and equitable society. Oppression stems from a lack of power, which results from a lack of participation. Because participation builds power, the antidote to rising fascism and rising seas is to build universal participation in remaking democracy.

In this book, we guide our readers through the Spiral of Change, a strategy for making democratic change in oppressive social systems by growing participation on every scale and in every domain. After studying and enacting successful social change efforts in our own work, we developed the Spiral of Change to teach how small groups of people can intervene to change large and complex systems. We use the metaphor of spiral to visualize the revolutionary project of democracy as both repeating and progressing,[5] powered by knowledge gathered in practice. Practicing the Spiral of Change at many scales—from personal to communal to public—enables us to democratize all aspects of life, transforming ourselves as we transform the world. We present the Spiral of Change in six steps:

I   Gather People and Stories
We come to voice, and gather to share our stories, weaving connections between our experiences of harm and hope. We build trust across differences and commit to working together on change.

II   Formulate Problems and Systems
The way we formulate a problem determines its set of solutions.[6] Therefore, we analyze the roots of our problems from many angles, taking care to formulate them in language that illuminates a path toward our desires. The problems we face emerge from dynamic social systems that we can describe, perturb, and reimagine.

III   Generate Desires
We generate desires to wrest our imaginations away from the constraints of our problems and establish new realms of possibility where we can design.

IV   Unearth Contradictions
When a problem is unsolvable in the current system, we work to formulate its underlying contradictions, which require a change of system rather than mere reforms within it. Where

contradictions become visible, we locate points of leverage where strategic actions can have outsized consequences.

V **Design Interventions**

Guided by our desires, we design social interventions at these points of leverage.

VI **Act and Reflect**

As soon as we act, we forage for the consequences of our actions, so that we can reflect, change our minds, and grow in coalition. Together, we envision new desires and designs. Repeating the steps of the Spiral of Change is how we grow participation and remake democracy. Democracy is the act of collectively designing the society in which we live.

The Spiral of Change relies on three core concepts, which we take in turn here: it views systems as dynamic; problems as dialectic; and interventions as heuristic. A view of systems as dynamic regards them as self-regulating and open to influence. This lens, which we develop in Step II, gives us agency no matter our positionality in a system. It releases us from our feelings of powerlessness in the face of problems.

A view of problems as dialectic sees them in their contradiction between two opposing arguments, a thesis and an antithesis, which are resolved into a new synthesis. Broadly used, dialectics asserts a theory of historical evolution where opposing ideas or forces (such as capital and labor, slaveholders and enslaved people) struggle in repeated ways. The progression of the Spiral of Change is dialectic.

A view of interventions as heuristic combines action and reflection in iteration: you take a step, observe consequences, and use that observation as input for your next steps. Rather than a goal-oriented process, the work of the Spiral of Change is a heuristic process of intervention: open-ended, agile, uncertain, and repeated.

Audience for *Remaking Democracy*

If you are reading this book, it is for you. *Remaking Democracy* grew out of decades of conversations; we want it to generate decades more. We invite you to bring *your* expertise, problems, and desires to work—as individuals and groups—to remake democracy. We invite you to design the society you want. You need no training or confidence. The only requirement is that you want to make a change and are willing to do something about it. This book is addressed to anyone who finds themselves in these scenarios:

You have little experience in making change and want to know where to begin.

You have a lot of project-making or organizing experience but feel stuck.

You work inside a system or institution you would like to change.

You want to build a new program or organization.

You are part of a group and want to build your analysis, skill set, and teaching repertoire.

You want to develop yourself in community with others.

As authors, our "we" is aspirational. The "we" in this book invites readers to remake democracy in their everyday lives and work in ways that refuse logics of superiority and are guided by logics of inclusion and equity. Under capitalism, imperialism, patriarchy, ableism, and other systems premised on superiority, this "we" is a functional impossibility. As authors, we acknowledge that we are two white, materially secure citizens of the United States, with all the privileges that entails. We are also female, queer, and navigating trauma and its effects on our bodies and minds. We recognize that an uncritical use of the term "we" opens the door for an uncritical exercise of power and privilege. Throughout this work, we teach formulation and design for participatory systems change through an anti-oppression lens that looks at both who speaks and who is silent, whose experience is centered, and who holds essential knowledge in the margins. The aspirational "we" posited here is not homogeneous, but intersectional. Our "we" seeks to represent a threatened humanity within our shared ecology. Our aspiration is for the equitable participation of all people to build a multiracial, multigendered global democratic community—made of the many worlds we want and represent. Our long-haul commitment is to build this aspirational "we."

Origins of *Remaking Democracy*

This book is the fruit of four generations of SDaS teachings, which draw from critical theory, radical pedagogy, and experimental art. Woven through these teachings is a fierce insistence on the uniqueness of every person and the indispensability of all people. It is our hope that this book will invite and equip a fifth generation to participate in remaking democracy—combining the lessons of our elders with the unique perspective and expertise of each reader.

We trace the lineage of our teaching to another period in human history that felt like the end of the world. Our teachers at SDaS—and their teachers— were artists, thinkers, and organizers who were trying to understand this contradiction: *How had the project of building democratic nations produced two world wars and the Holocaust?*[7] Two of our teachers were refugees of German fascism. Marianne ("Manni") Brün founded the artist-in-residence program at the University of Illinois, where she taught the first-ever "Designing Society" course, carrying forward her work with Bertolt Brecht and other antifascist artists and intellectuals.[8] Herbert Brün, an electronic music pioneer, taught experimental composition for over thirty years at the University of Illinois School of Music, inviting students of all disciplines to participate in his seminar. The Brüns collaborated with critical theorists such as Theodor Adorno, radical educator Ivan Illich, and cybernetician Heinz von Foerster. Von Foerster, who ran the University of Illinois' Biological Computer Laboratory, was aware of the growing tendency for scientific research to be captured and used for the purposes of war and profit. With Margaret Mead, they insisted on the ethical responsibility of the observer in systems[9] which connected cybernetics to critical social research, inspiring experimental arts, and radical education.

In 1968, at the request of students organizing against the Vietnam War, Herbert Brün and von Foerster taught a class entitled "Heuristics," where they first gave the assignment "Right or Wrong, My Desires." Participants were asked to envision and describe, one statement at a time, the society they would prefer to live in. A distinguishing and fundamental method of their teaching was sharing their explorations of "legitimate questions" with their students, inviting students to become teachers. Legitimate questions are questions without known answers, prompting critical conversation. Manni Brün built on the desire assignment in her "Designing Society" course at the University of Illinois in 1981 and 1984. Manni recounts, "The idea, for me, was to make an analysis of the society we live in and then look at what aspects of the present-day society, the status quo, we don't want, and what kind of a society we do want. The image of that society [had] two functions: one, a critique of the society we live in, and [two] the beginning of a path to a new society."[10]

From 1978 to 2004, a group of students from Herbert Brün's composition seminar formed the Performers Workshop Ensemble (PWE), a troupe of musicians and performers who toured throughout the United States and Germany, establishing connections between art and society, performers and audience, with experimental compositions and performances. It was through PWE's touring that we met Herbert Brün's students-turned-collaborators—Susan Parenti, Mark Enslin, and many other teachers and mentors. In a workshop entitled "The History and Future of Political Song," Mark performed "Sonata Quijada," a startlingly complex composition for percussion, chattering teeth, and a jack-in-the-box, in which he enumerates the volume of propaganda the US used to undermine Chilean democracy. This, like many of Mark's compositions, dramatizes contradictions by putting the performer in impossible situations. In Susan's workshop "Acoustic Portraits," we made compositions that used negative dialectics to forever elicit the "not yet." Drawn to working with Susan, Mark, and an ensemble of social change artists, I, Danielle first attended SDaS in 1993, hosted in West Virginia by the Gesundheit! Institute and Dr. Patch Adams, who was soon to be made famous by the 1998 Hollywood movie based on his book.[11] After attending SDaS and collaborating on projects in Florida and Illinois, I relocated to Urbana, Illinois to perform and teach at SDaS, which is where I met Elizabeth.

Originally, we conceived of this project as a book version of SDaS. So many projects have been generated by this idiosyncratic and tenacious project, and so little has been written about it, we wanted to record the concepts and assignments so they could be shared, scaled, and adapted. We have merged what we learned at SDaS with lessons from our organizing successes within social movements for housing justice, media justice, gender justice, and abolition. To these, we add our extensive work in somatic healing from trauma, which provides a precondition for our ability to author this book. We find the anticommunication of experimental arts to have an effective friction with the strategic acumen of organizing, and that both are nurtured and sustained by healing practices.

This book integrates all of these with a number of powerful intellectual threads: the risks taken by experimental art and composition; the understanding of complex and dynamic systems from cybernetics; the use of consensus and facilitation in movements for participatory democracy; the coordination of tactics in policy campaigns; the analysis of intimate and internalized violence offered by feminism; the intersectional analysis of race, class, gender, and ability asserted by Black feminism and the new civil rights movements; and the pivotal roles cultural organizing and transformative justice play in envisioning and practicing our ideas as we work to move them into reality.

Overview of *Remaking Democracy*

The structure of this book models a key principle in social justice organizing: cultivate shared analysis before developing strategy; use strategy to generate tactics. In chapter 1, "Living in Contradiction," we present an analysis of the fundamental problems we face which highlights their contradictions and vulnerabilities. The strategy we propose to address these problems is the Spiral of Change, which teaches how to analyze problems, design strategic interventions, act, and reflect on them, iteratively. Chapter 2 provides an overview of the Spiral of Change, followed by chapter 3, which illustrates all six steps of the Spiral of Change through the story of Indymedia.

This is followed by six sections that each dive deeper into one of the steps on the Spiral of Change. For each step, we provide a chapter of formulation for theorizing about this step; a chapter of assignments for you to try out the theory on your own problem; and a chapter telling the story of an intervention drawn from our own experiences. In chapters 6 and 16, we share our own stories of trauma and healing as feminist praxis, so that through our vulnerability, we can connect to yours. Once we get to the Design Interventions step, we provide a toolbox of design concepts to inform your praxis. The assignments provided throughout are designed to be useful on many scales, in many domains. You or your group could devote a workshop, semester, or years to working through them, and we hope you will return to them as we have many times over decades.

The interventions described in this book are an interconnected set of influences. SDaS (featured in chapter 12) incubated both the Health Care Design Intensives (described in chapter 19) and the Urbana-Champaign Independent Media Center (see chapter 3), which hosted Champaign--Urbana Citizens for Peace and Justice (chapter 21), and played a lead role in the Campaign for Prison Phone Justice (chapter 9). Cunningham Township's campaign to end homelessness (discussed in chapter 15) represents the culmination of the design work embedded in all these projects. These stories of interventions provide concrete examples of successful change-making on a wide range of scales and domains.

Our Invitations to You

We invite you to generate your own ideas and projects.

This book does not offer answers or endpoints. It guides you through a process that is informed again and again by the desires of you and your collaborators. We offer many examples of our own ideas and projects, but our aim is to show you how to make your own. When a new intervention is needed, it's in our shared "not knowing" that our creativity is called forth, and true collaboration begins.

We invite you to work on both self and structure, healing and change.

This book offers tools for transformation in the domains of the personal, the communal, and the public. In social change work, there is often tension between three needs: the need to heal from violence, the need for harm reduction to make a situation "less bad," and the need for systems change to address root problems. We invite you to address each of these needs—for healing, harm reduction, and systems change—to stop cycles of violence and design desirable futures.

We invite you to use design to cure alienation.

This book shows you how to increase the variety of alternatives available in the world with your unique contribution. Responding to alienation requires design that connects our needs with each other's offers and generates many different senses of purpose. We produce liberatory care when we design to accommodate everyone's needs and encourage everyone's offers.

We invite you to collaborate.

Every individual is a designer, but rarely do designers act individually. To design a response to a problem, you likely need a team. These will be people who are aligned with the basic values of the project, add skills and contacts, and offer necessary friction and challenge to sharpen ideas. The assignment chapters can be done alone, but are more pleasurable to engage with as a group.

We invite you to the joy of praxis.

Education revolutionary Paulo Freire defined praxis as the combined force of "reflection and action directed at the structures to be transformed."[12] Whenever we take action, we are intervening in existing systems such that there is a dialectic between our contribution and what already exists, which changes both. In this way, we are collaborating with our forebears while bringing forth the worlds we want. Thinking and doing are pleasurably intertwined.

We invite you to collaborate with us!

Remaking Democracy is a book nested in a series of conversations and connections. We, the authors, would love to connect the ideas here with your communities and projects. Please visit our website, **remakingdemocracy.org**, to engage and share.

What is it that you want?

What do *you* want?

What do you *want*?

What are the premises of the world you want you
and your loved ones to live in?

In what world would we all thrive?

Take a blank notebook and pencil.
Put away your phone, your worries,
and other distractions. Give yourself time.
Go someplace that allows you to think.
Breathe. Then start.

Make a list of desire statements about which you would say:

they are currently false,

you wish they would become true, and

**for them to become true would require a
change of system.**

In each case, write a complete sentence as though it were true
now, like a magician, waving your magic wand. So instead of
"enough food" or "I wish that everyone had enough food" you
would write, "everyone has enough food."

Make the sentences brief.

Do not argue.

Do not assess their feasibility.

These desire statements form the basis of the work of this
book.

Get ready to bring forth visions for a new world.

Spiral of Change

CHAPTER 1

FORMULATION

Analysis:
Living in Contradiction

Contradictions are our hope!

—Bertolt Brecht, *The Film, the Novel and Epic Theatre*

"What time is it on the clock of the world?" This is the question Grace Lee Boggs posed in a historic discussion with economic historian Immanuel Wallerstein on June 24, 2010.[1] I, Danielle, was one of twenty thousand people who had gathered in Detroit for the third US Social Forum to organize for global justice through a decentralized structure of people's assemblies happening all over the world. Ours was part of a growing network of gatherings, starting in 1996 at the First Intercontinental Encounter for Humanity and Against Neoliberalism in Chiapas, Mexico that became a series of regional forums and annual World Social Forums (WSF) in 2001. Organizers on the front lines of social movements were using expanding public access to the internet to convene a broad array of grassroots and civil society organizations. The WSF was designed to provide an open meeting place "for reflective thinking, democratic debate of ideas, formulation of proposals, free exchange of experiences, and interlinking of effective action by groups and movements of civil society."[2] In the WSF "Charter of Principles," we agreed to oppose "domination of the world by capital, and any form of imperialism, and . . . committed to building a planetary society directed towards fruitful relationships among humankind and between it and the Earth."[3] The approach to participatory democracy embodied in the WSF was an early input to the Spiral of Change concept.

I navigated Motor City on an old bicycle, visiting neighborhoods that were no longer reachable by car because the concrete streets had been chewed back into earth by weeds. Whole swaths of the city had been turned into ghost towns, where residents labored every day to meet their basic needs while sleeping in abandoned strip malls and factories. I squeaked along broken streets, through neighborhoods full of collapsed homes and labyrinthine, overgrown parks. I stopped at the foot of a towering brick building, its facade torn off by the force of deindustrialization, its lights still dangling from ceiling tiles, and wondered: "Where am I? Hiroshima? Beirut?" Beyond the rubble was a skyline with three shiny new casinos—a billion-dollar extractive industry in the center of economic despair.

Detroit had been strategically chosen for the 2010 US Social Forum. The city served as a warning of what happens when we acquiesce to an economic system premised on endless growth and exploitation: the bottom falls out.[4] Over half a decade, Detroit lost two thirds of its residents—nearly two million people—as the auto industry moved production overseas to lower labor and production costs. Public officials were in the process of withdrawing services from about a third of the city. Around me, the residents left behind were cobbling together power, water, waste management, and transportation from the detritus that remained. By 2013, Detroit would become the largest US city to declare bankruptcy.

Grace Lee Boggs spoke to us in plain terms: "In times of crisis, you either deepen democracy or go to the other extreme and become totalitarian."[5] Both pathways were present in Detroit, which also serves as a model of the mutual aid and community resilience required to survive these times. Boggs embodied this resilience. Following her talk, we celebrated her ninety-fifth birthday. Boggs and her husband founded the James and Grace Lee Boggs Center to Nurture Community Leadership in Detroit in the 1990s, declaring: "Revolutions are made out of love for people and for place."[6] As part of the Social Forum, the Boggs Center hosted a tour, "From Growing Our Economy to Growing Our Souls," where we traveled by bus to witness how Detroit residents were seeding local democracy in the cracks of economic devastation. Earthworks Urban Farm was feeding whole neighborhoods organic produce from abandoned lots. The Hush House's community radio program was broadcasting the stories of people abandoned by government and commerce.

After our gathering, many participants crossed the border to Toronto to protest at a meeting of the G20, where elites from the most powerful countries and corporations were gathering to cement the dominance of globalized capital. The US Social Forum in Detroit had been strategically timed to coincide with the G20 meetings. As the G20 was sharpening an anti-democratic agenda five hours north, we were designing its antithesis: a people's agenda to globalize solidarity and advance democracy. These protests were just one of hundreds that continue to show up at every major meeting where corporate and government elites attempt to suppress such "barriers to free trade" as unions, environmental protections, and human rights. Toronto invested C$89.2 million in security to shield the G20 representatives from demonstrators calling for Indigenous sovereignty, the recognition of water as a human right, an end to fossil fuel subsidies, and action on world poverty. The police detained over a thousand people in the largest mass arrest in Canadian history.

THE CONTRADICTIONS WE FACE

After touring Detroit and witnessing the suppression of global justice protests in Toronto, we felt the fullness of the moment: will humanity steer toward "everyone for themselves" with deepening poverty, exploitation, and control? Or will we globalize equality, self-determination, and liberation? Boggs expresses this sense of urgency in her book *The Next American Revolution* (2012):

> In our bones we sense that this is no ordinary time. It is a time of deep change, not just of social structure and economy, but also of ourselves. If we want to see change in our lives, we have to change things ourselves. Democracy must become a normal and natural practice of our everyday activities. That is what Detroit is about, and that is how the next American Revolution is beginning.[7]

In this chapter, we respond to Boggs' urgency to analyze the fundamental contradictions we face at this time on the clock of the world. Formulating our problem as a contradiction renders it unstable and thereby assailable. It orients us to multiple points of leverage for action. In an increasingly oppressive and bleak situation, formulating contradictions serves as a pivot from analyzing a problem to designing strategic interventions for change. Our analysis of this historical moment emerged slowly, after many rounds of playing what we call the "Why Game," a process of asking legitimate (unanswered) questions and researching, discussing, and wrestling with the answers. We asked:

Why do we face climate catastrophe?

Must capitalism grow, exploit, and alienate, and if so, *why*?

If capitalism is so terrible, then *why* do we live by it?

17

Why is the global majority—who do not want climate change, inequity, and oppression—being thwarted, and by whom?

Why are we seeing increasing support for autocratic governments?

What resulted from this process was a description of four interlocking contradictions that provide an analysis of *why* we need participation. From this analysis flows our strategy for *how* to build participation through the Spiral of Change, which we outline in the next chapter. We phrase our contradictions in time, starting with the words *"we live at a time when,"* so as to assert that the conditions we face are dynamic and changeable.

Contradiction 1
Meeting Our Needs to Extinction

We live at a time when humans are increasingly able to meet our needs, but the way we do so is producing climate change and mass extinctions, threatening our survival.

One tangible example of this contradiction is the cell phone. It offers us many connections—to family, work, information, and services—but not to the workers exploited in its creation. Instead, we share its benefits with executives, shareholders, app developers, and other service providers. The costs of these devices are spread across vast supply chains and borne by whole communities whose water and soil are polluted by mining and waste, and whose labor and safety are undervalued. Our collective overuse of cell phones has eroded our attention spans and mental health.

If we could, we would choose *not* to exploit others, commodify every aspect of our lives, and disconnect from other people and the planet. We would choose not to contribute to mass extinctions. Without available alternatives to choose among, well-meaning people must participate in these destructive systems to meet our needs. This contradiction creates a pervasive sense of moral injury and powerlessness. Every person we speak to wants alternative systems to support our thriving. So why can't we meet our needs in other ways? Why is capitalism so pervasive, and so hard to quit?

It is both uncomfortable and a big relief to articulate and struggle with these questions. The antidote to feelings of powerlessness is to understand ourselves as elements who have agency within systems; and the first step in that understanding is to learn about the systems we find ourselves in. It's easy to say either that "capitalism is the problem" or to extol its virtues, but how many of us understand how it actually works as a system?

One year at the School for Designing a Society (SDaS), participants learned how to analyze systems in their connectedness through the assignment of making public service announcements about current social conundrums. Mark Enslin created a video about climate change. It uses an atonal soundtrack over one long shot that pans, very close-up, along the outside of his van. The reflections of the cameraperson and phone are faintly visible in the vehicle's pearlescent sheen. The frame moves from the exhaust pipe, around the taillight, to the gas cap where the words "What's driving climate change?" scroll slowly up the screen. The camera continues to pan across the doors, and inside the van to the driver's seat, where a hand grips the wheel. The words "I am" scroll up the screen, and the camera turns abruptly to Mark's face. The piece asks us: "How do you see yourself connected to the systems in which you live?"

What is the system that meets our needs to extinction?

The capitalist system we live in now is driving us to the brink of disaster, yet it has many seductive aspects. It has disrupted social hierarchies—those guided by tradition, religion, caste, gender, ethnicity, and others—to assert its own power structure. The innovations, labor, and extractions of the past two centuries have raised the standard of living for billions of people and connected a growing global middle class. As early as 1848, Karl Marx acknowledged that "the bourgeoisie, during its rule of scarce one hundred years, has created more massive and more colossal productive forces than have all preceding generations together."[8]

Globalized capitalism, which nearly every human now depends upon in some way to meet their needs, brings with it unbearable caveats: it produces and requires exploitation, endless growth, and alienation.[9] It offers endless consumer variety while hiding the costs of production it has foisted on people and our environment. It replaces alternative ways of meeting our needs by being good at producing and concentrating wealth, then uses it to buy out competing alternatives and capture state power to cement its influence. Its reliance on fossil fuels is producing crescendos of environmental and social catastrophe. Capitalism's contradictory logic was summarized more than twenty-five years ago by German ecologist Wolfgang Sachs:

> The only thing worse than the failure of this massive global experiment would be its success, for even at its most optimum level, the benefits of a global economy only go to a small minority of people who sit near the hub of the process, while the rest of humanity is left fighting for fewer jobs, increasingly landless and homeless, living in violent societies.[10]

If there's any hope of preventing this outcome, it begins with understanding why and how the capitalist system must move in this direction of global exploitation of workers and the environment, regardless of the intentions of its actors, including us.

Why must capitalism exploit workers and the environment?

Detroit is hardly alone in suffering the ravages of capitalism as it chews up people and their environment through a process of extraction and abandonment. Since 1994 when the North American Free Trade Agreement was signed, one in three Americans working in manufacturing (about six million people) lost their jobs.[11] This was due to the wholesale export of industry jobs from places like Danville, Virginia; Newton, Iowa; Bruceton, Tennessee; Johnstown, Pennsylvania; and Youngstown, Ohio, leaving hundreds of towns in economic free fall.

In rural West Virginia, where we teach SDaS each summer, the state legislature has gutted labor and environmental protections. West Virginia is consequently the site of high incidences of coal mining disasters, black lung disease and other health problems, chemical spills, mining waste, fracking, and deadly floods. Increasing automation has eliminated nine out of ten mining jobs while increasing coal production. More production means more profit extracted by out-of-state shareholders, more greenhouse gasses exacerbating the climate crisis, and more pollution poisoning West Virginians. Not far from where we gather to design desirable societies, the folk hero John Henry likely died of silicosis after competing with an automated steam drill. But even today, a miner may start working at sixteen, for $19 an hour, work ten hours a day in the mines, get sick, become one of the 20 percent of West Virginians receiving disability payments, and die twenty-five years before their counterparts in other industries.[12]

To grow and survive as a system, capitalism incentivizes these devastating outcomes and pressures the state to keep them legal. Companies compete with one another to produce and sell their product more cheaply to stay in business. To do so, they cut costs by cutting wages, minimizing protections for workers and the environment, and automating jobs. Competition pressures owners to increase exploitation in these ways, and the threat of unemployment pressures workers to tolerate their increasing exploitation.

Why must capitalist economies grow to survive?

Capitalism is "the investment of money to make more money," so the imperative to grow is baked into its definition.[13] This growth is the wealth creation that has supported our increasing ability to meet our needs over the past two and a half centuries, albeit in inequitable ways, while the population has increased sevenfold. Capitalism generates wealth but concentrates that wealth, thereby producing poverty. Private industry extracts the wealth from workers and natural "resources." Governments tax that wealth, in part to redistribute it to things like teacher salaries, unemployment and disability benefits, and superfund site cleanups—but also to subsidize things like oil companies and industrial agriculture. In this process, the profits are privatized while the risks and costs are shifted onto the public. Democratically elected governments manage how much profit can be extracted and reinvested in growth before the public rebels. When the people rebel, their ire is usually directed at the public institutions that promised them some level of control, and not the private corporations driving the mass exploitation. The people's disillusionment and withdrawal from public institutions allows capitalism's power to grow faster.

Capitalism realizes its imperative to grow through four main dynamics: it *must* expand markets, absorb unemployment, use credit, and increase both use and efficiency, or it will perish.[14] Capitalism is so good at meeting needs that it runs out of needs to meet, so it must expand markets to find new people to sell to and grow demand for new products. Planned obsolescence is the practice of designing products to break and be replaced to keep up demand. The increased efficiency of production inevitably forces layoffs and overwork, producing unemployment and poverty, which over time creates disabling health conditions. Laid off workers consume less and may organize around grievances, destabilizing the capitalist state. Governments respond by incentivizing more job creation, offering meager unemployment and disability benefits, and incarcerating people to absorb unemployment and hide homelessness. These subsidies to companies, workers, and the prisons create economic growth.

Capitalist growth is also driven by the expansion of uses of credit. There is a misconception that banks have the money they lend, but they do not; they invent much of it as credit.[15] Banks used to lend mostly to companies, but the capitalist mandate for growth has expanded credit markets into the consumer housing market, credit cards, and student debt. All this credit drives overproduction and growth. Lastly, capitalism perverts efficiency through the Jevons paradox: as we use a resource more efficiently, we use more of it—whether it is boosting coal production as the price drops, or the efficiencies produced by our cell phones leading to us spend more time on them, or highway lane additions increasing traffic jams. On a finite planet, this endless growth is quickly becoming a problem. These four dynamics drive growth and are foundational to the capitalist system. They can be slowed by democratic regulation but cannot be eliminated.

If we allow endless growth to chew through our planet and our people, how will we survive? As we write this, the Alaskan glacial ice shelf has melted completely, nearly half of the Earth's trees have been felled, and incidents of fires and floods have tripled. More than seventy million people worldwide have been forced to leave their homes and migrate to escape violence, poverty, or environmental disasters. Developed nations' actions have wrecked poorer nations while tightening their borders against those fleeing the adverse conditions they helped to create. Migrants who have made it across the border are targeted with violence and expulsion. As the economy slows and dips, we once again see moves toward war over scarce resources and populist support for strong leaders. This is capitalism working perfectly: when the powerful few benefit at the expense of the many who struggle to meet their needs even though there is plenty for everyone.

How does capitalism produce alienation?

Exploitation and endless growth combine to alienate us from our work, each other, and the environment. When we own the means of production and thereby have agency in our work lives, we may see production from start to finish and witness the product in use at a scale we can fathom. This kind of labor gives us a sense of purpose, meaning, and integrity. Conversely, when we are treated like machines, producing and consuming products that contribute to pollution, climate change, and the exploitation of ourselves or others, we are alienated from our labor and each other through these moral injuries. The way we are treated as disposable in the workplace affects behavior outside of it. It becomes normal to treat each other like machines or objects. Health care, teaching, and social work have become mechanized and commodified to do more, faster, with less time to care for one another.

As supply chains stretch across the globe, we can no longer locate, or advocate for, the people involved or the environment impacted by a single product. If you wanted to find out who was exploited by your Amazon purchase, how would you go about it? A system that produces and moves a fidget spinner from a child's labor in China to your toddler's mouth is now spread across a million bits of information such that there appear to be no humans involved at all. Meanwhile, the expansion of markets into the digital economy and the tsunami of social media has sold our attention away from our loved ones, so that we stare at our phones instead of looking at each other.[16] Economist David Harvey describes capitalism's requirement of alienation from nature and our own human potential as its "fatal contradiction":

> Alienation from nature is alienation from our own species potential. This releases a spirit of revolt in which words like dignity, respect, compassion, caring and loving become revolutionary slogans.[17]

Harvey sees the possibility in cracking open this contradiction to find new ways of being—even as he acknowledges how difficult this collective work might be. If we understand that climate change is driven by capitalism, and that capitalism must exploit, grow, and alienate—what makes it so hard for us as a society to choose other ways to meet our needs?

Contradiction 2
Capitalism Versus Democracy

We live at a time when capitalism undermines democracy by requiring the few to exploit the many and concentrating wealth and power, while democracy threatens capitalism by growing participation, refusing exploitation, and distributing power.

It is a fundamental contradiction that we are experiencing climate change because of capitalist growth, and we haven't been able to vote our way out of climate change because capitalist interests have already undermined democracy enough to buy that vote. Let's unpack the fundamental contradiction between capitalism and democracy since, in the neoliberal story, they are conjoined by assertions of "freedom": free markets, free press, and the freedom to vote. So the argument goes, capitalism and democracy cooperate: capitalism creates a surplus of things for human enjoyment and democracy distributes that surplus. However, taken to their logical conclusions, each would make the other impossible. Full democratic participation would end capitalism: workers would insist that the profits made from their labor be shared with them fairly and that their environment not be poisoned. Full exploitation of people by capitalism requires their disenfranchisement: this would end democracy.

As capitalism advances, democracy recedes. Corporations—and the wealthy class of elites they produce—buy policy outcomes that suppress the democratic participation of citizens. In seeking to grow innovation and wealth for the benefit of their voters, governments subsidize corporations. In seeking to grow profits for their shareholders, corporations capture our institutions of government to minimize regulation of their industries, resist redistribution of wealth, and grow and concentrate their power. In this way, forces of capitalism colonize our governance structure before our very eyes. Corporations influence judicial rulings in ways that favor corporations over people, push for wars that compromise national security, and seek dominance by purchasing election outcomes. We feel this domination as poverty, displacement, pollution, unsafe work environments, and poor health. Poverty is thus not a consequence, as is often thought, of lack of resources or education, but of a lack of democratic participation that would redistribute these resources. When the public blames the government for its exclusion and not the collusion of government and corporate power, the resulting disillusionment and withdrawal from democratic participation opens the door to autocratic forces.

Democracy elicits symbiotic relationships between human beings, and therefore lives in contradiction with capitalism, which seeks to commodify everything it touches and alienate all relationships. This contradiction is managed through the collusion of state and corporate power to limit democratic participation. One of the most visible examples of this limitation is the long history of state repression of global justice protests, like the one against the G20 in Toronto described at the beginning of this chapter, and the protests against the World Trade Organization described in chapter 3. To transform our society, we need more democratic participation at every level and in every domain with many groups and movements illuminating many analyses of how we got here and many pathways out. In the words of the Zapatistas, we need "one no and many yeses."

Where democratic movements organize, they mobilize participation to refuse exploitation, build grassroots resilience, and distribute power. We can see this kind of democratic movement building in action with the tenant movement in New York State that I, Elizabeth, organized with, as a member of the Crown Heights Tenant Union, while we were writing this book. In 2015, New York Governor Andrew Cuomo, on behalf of his biggest real estate donors, blocked critical tenant protections at a time of record housing displacements. Rent laws were lavishly rewarding landlords for evicting tenants. By allowing a 20 percent increase in rent every time a lease turned over, the law was incentivizing annual displacements.

In response to Trump's election in 2016, there were huge organizing efforts to register voters, which effectively tripled voter turnout. This massive increase in democratic participation elected a progressive state legislature that was independent of the governor's influence, and more centered on the needs of working people. To make the most of this legislative power, Housing Justice for All formed a statewide tenant coalition to unite behind a slate of nine bills to close loopholes in the rent laws.[18] This coalition gathered and united a movement through political education, voter registration, policy writing, lobbying, and direct action. We shut down the New York State Capitol building in Albany with our bodies in June 2019, which led to a sweeping victory: the passing of seven out of nine bills on the slate. Later that summer, some landlords who had recently purchased buildings tried to back out of their loans because their business plan had been premised not on housing people but evicting them in order to increase rents.

When the COVID-19 outbreak hit New York City in March 2020, our housing rights coalition was already organized. We protested in the streets to demand a moratorium on evictions, accompanied by a media campaign in which affected tenants told their stories publicly and demanded dignity, respect, and compassion. For twenty-two months, we returned to the streets over and over to shut down the housing courts and extend the moratorium. During the moratorium's first year, New York City's eviction rates dropped from 15,000 households to only 10 (not 10,000, just 10!). Thousands of tenants went on rent strike out of necessity, thousands more in solidarity, and this tactic gained popularity and success as a leverage point to force repairs, rent re-stabilization, and sales or even forfeitures that can be leveraged toward tenant control or ownership. This campaign fundamentally shifted the balance of power between housing investors and tenants.

In this six-year snapshot of organizing for housing rights, increasing participation meant tracking our state legislators and organizing voting registration and turnout. It meant tenants organizing against negligent and predatory landlords across different local rent laws in distant parts of New York State. It meant direct action in Albany and at our local housing courts during the pandemic. It meant refusing eviction, and, through rent strikes, withholding profits, and in some instances wresting property from landlords through the courts. Those participatory actions at multiple points of leverage in our political and economic systems resulted in the assertion and recognition that tenant power is a force to be reckoned with, housing is a human right and fits into a much longer and broader history of tenants fighting for decent living conditions. Under capitalism, democratic movements can never rest on our laurels, or merely repeat what worked last time, because capital is regrouping, growing, concentrating, and looking for new ways to disenfranchise people. To effectively counter these forces, we must continue to broaden participation, sharpen our shared analysis, and act strategically.

Contradiction 3
Logics of Superiority Versus Logics of Inclusion

We live at a time when the capitalist state uses logics of superiority—such as racism, patriarchy, ableism, and classism—to justify exploitation and inequality. Meanwhile, democratic movements challenge these logics of superiority with logics of inclusion that refuse exploitation and insist on participation for all.

In the current system, the capitalist state employs logics of superiority to justify inequities within a democracy that its members would otherwise consider inhumane. It is only through dehumanization—based on race or ethnicity, conviction status, gender, disability, or income—that we allow our neighbor to live in a sleeping bag on the street, or a mother to get shackled to the bed as she gives birth to a baby who is then taken from her, or a child to be made an orphan by the deportation of her immigrant parent, or a neighbor with disabilities to be shut in due to lack of accessible spaces and services.

Systems premised on superiority predate capitalism, which is only a few hundred years old. Sexism was a justification for the enslavement of women. Racism was an ideological weapon for imperialism. These have been combined under capitalism as the child of imperialism in what bell hooks refers to as "imperialist white-supremacist capitalist patriarchy," to articulate that these systems intersect and work together to maintain oppression and privilege.[19] Logics of superiority are essential for managing the contradictions of capitalist democracies.

Logics of superiority operate such that if even *one* is allowed, it opens the door to allow others. Similarly, if one is overcome, others will take its place until we refuse *all forms* of superiority. Michelle Alexander argues in *The New Jim Crow: Mass Incarceration in the Age of Colorblindness* that Black Americans were re-enslaved through criminalization which was used to justify racism by another name.[20] Criminalization is used to disenfranchise Black and working-class voters and cements this regime. Taking Alexander's argument a few steps further, we can discuss how criminalization produces lifetimes of underemployment for those marked with felonies; how this lack of work means that formerly incarcerated residents are ten times more likely to be homeless; and how homeless residents end up disabled and die thirty years younger than the general population. In this causal chain reaction, a person can be dehumanized for being Black, a "convict," unemployed, homeless, disabled or any combination. Furthermore, people of all identities can look down on "criminals," who can look down on "squatters," who can look down on "addicts." Just as one liberation movement tears down one logic of superiority, another pops up. We have to unravel the whole logic of superiority, all of its interconnections, to overcome this dynamic.

The assertion of superiority becomes an assumption that reinforces itself. Susan Burton, a national leader in creating re-entry homes and services for women returning from prison, put it succinctly at a public talk delivered in Urbana: "We criminalize women's response to trauma." For example, based on the assumption "she is poor because she made bad choices," support is withdrawn, leading to further deprivation, human reactions to that condition, and further punishment. This cycle—assertion, assumption, action, reality, assertion—strengthens these logics of superiority over many iterations and is used to justify systems of punishment and control. Few will say explicitly, "he deserves to die because he is Black," but the toxic combination of systematically producing misery while blaming and dehumanizing victims is a product of capitalism attempting to reconcile with democracy. We have internalized this reality as implicit bias so that our society acquiesces to Black residents having fewer resources to live, less safety, worse health, and dying younger than their white counterparts.

When we challenge logics of superiority and insist on the participation of all people in their full humanity as equals, we expose the contradiction between capitalism and democracy. Civil rights, Black power, immigrant, Indigenous, feminist, and LGBTQ+ movements are therefore not mere "identity politics" distractions from economic issues. They undercut logics of supe-riority and therefore are central to the democratic project. Consider these messages of protest: "I am a Man." "#BlackLivesMatter." "Pride." "#MeToo." "Full Human Beings." "Standing Rock." "Don't dis my ability." These are all assertions of full equality within a socioeconomic system that would be wholly transformed by equality.

To root society unequivocally in the premise of equality and inclusion will require a re-founding of our democracies. US democracy was built on logics of superiority, in an attempt to justify both the land theft and genocide of Indigenous peoples and the capture and enslavement of Africans. We must acknowledge and repair those harms embedded in the building blocks of our founding as a necessary precondition of making and remaking our democ-racy. The same is true of other imperial powers. If we look at racial justice movements of the last twenty years—embodied in the Movement for Black Lives,[21] the DREAMers,[22] and Indigenous protests at Standing Rock[23]—they assert logics of inclusion with revolutionary practices that are holistic, inter-sectional, restorative, and leader-full.[24]

While gender is used to justify violence, exploitation, and forced child-bearing, the LGBTQ+ movement is actively dissolving the gender binary, confounding exploitation on this basis, and opening the possibility of roles being designed and chosen rather than socially overdetermined by gender. Movements for disability justice reject the premise that productivity deter-mines human worth, instead arguing that humans' functional diversity—with many alternative expressions of physical and mental functioning—should be viewed as a source of enrichment.[25] They fight for accessibility and safety, equal opportunity, and rights protections based on premises of the capability and inherent dignity of all humans, in challenge to the capitalist state. By asserting logics of inclusion and practicing participation, we open up demo-cratic spaces for imagination, desire, and systems change toward a more just and equitable society.

Contradiction 4
Mechanisms of Domination
Versus Mechanisms of Liberation

We live at a time when the capitalist state deploys media and technology for domination and control, while democratic movements develop and repurpose media and technology to grow participation and therefore our collective liberation.

Media and technology work hand-in-hand, amplifying the power of the sys-tems they serve, accelerating the goals of either domination or liberation. The capitalist state uses media to amplify the logics of superiority and uses technology to assert control. This trend toward greater consolidation of state and corporate power through media and technology has historically been met with resistance by democratic movements. As the media justice movement has shown, media and technology are domains that provide many points of leverage for designing at the site of the contradiction between capitalism and democracy. Here, we offer some wisdom and tools learned from three visionary media justice mentors: Malkia Devich-Cyril, Alfredo Lopez, and Safiya Noble. We now have the technological tools at our disposal to build a global society, composed of many democratic communities, and to coordinate together to meet our needs, if only we can protect them from capitalist co-optation.

From Devich-Cyril, we learned about the key role of narrative strategy to shift culture to support more equitable power relations in a deep and lasting way.[26] The capitalist state has continued aspects of the slave system within the criminal justice system, by "manufacturing consent" of the public through a corporate media system that disseminates false narratives of superiority, especially white supremacy.[27] Devich-Cyril locates the wellspring of liberation within the stories of those experiencing the pain and grief of oppressions that are both deeply felt and structural. They have led the Media Justice movement to organize around these stories and develop a shared analysis to push for change. Devich-Cyril offers a vision of "a future where we are all connected, represented, and free."[28]

At a time of a power merger between Big Tech, the military industrial complex, and autocratic governments, it is hard to see where ordinary people have any points of leverage against these giants. We find hope in Devich-Cyril's advocacy for shifts in culture to provide a nonnegotiable foundation for legal and political gains for oppressed groups. The legal and policy changes we make are only as strong as the culture that supports them. A culture that is firmly grounded in the premise that no person is superior to any other will resist domination and division at every turn—from the most ordinary daily activities to extraordinary demonstrations of people power.

From Lopez, we learned the formulation that technology is "the collaborative act of humans using the environment to make tools to meet our needs."[29] In his work as co-director of May First/People Link, an international grassroots technology collective, he has long advocated and designed structures for technosocial cooperation. As members of May First wrote in their original Statement of Unity, "We believe that because technology is the product of collaboration by people all over the world throughout history, it rightfully belongs to all people and all people should control it."[30] In this view, the internet is not the technology itself, but the global connection of billions of people through a technology that is advanced by their desire to communicate and collaborate. The labor of the internet's inventors and funders is a tiny speck compared to the trillions of hours of ordinary people to grow it. Lopez argues that the internet represents our networked movement to create human connection and self-govern. Centering users as the true producers of the internet represents a fundamental shift in frame. Under capitalism, people are objects to be controlled by technology. In a democracy, technology is the object people control. The work of media justice is to develop people's consciousness and ability to use their (already existing) networked power to organize for collective liberation.

We have learned from Noble's work to look under the hood of ubiquitous technologies like the internet and commercial search engines to show how algorithms and artificial intelligence are trained on logics of superiority that exacerbate bias and harm.[31] For example, algorithms that have been trained on a history of racially biased policing are used to determine who is deserving of release from jail and who should remain behind bars. First practiced on the most vulnerable communities, algorithmic use then expands—to determine who is worthy of credit, who is more likely to be successful in college and admitted, who should be allowed to move freely, and who should be overpoliced. Noble's work makes clear the need for public oversight of and accountability for technology given its use in violations of human rights. She calls for liberatory designs of technology that help to disentangle our social systems from the logics of superiority and of colonization. Decolonizing technology, she suggests, incorporates the wisdom of Black and Brown residents long impacted by it and is guided by democratic principles of justice and equity.

Efforts to grow the capitalist state, justifying inequality with logics of superiority, use media and technology in the service of concentrating power and resources. Applying pressure at points of leverage, democratic movements employ logics of inclusion to increase participation and distribute power and resources. There is a rich network of media justice organizers, artists, and theorists engaging in creative interventions, as we will see in chapter 3, "From Indymedia to Media Justice" and chapter 9, "Campaign for Prison Phone Justice."

FASCISM IS THE THREAT

The four interlocking contradictions we have outlined in this chapter live in tension. To stabilize the inevitable crises produced by its contradictions, the capitalist state concentrates power and boosts growth, which deepens the contradictions and accelerates the crises. These crises are exploited by those who benefit, leading to a perverse incentive to continue them. In *The Shock Doctrine: The Rise of Disaster Capitalism*, Naomi Klein analyzes how corporate actors use crises as opportunities to raid public resources and concentrate power.[32] This dynamic produces the insanity we see in accelerating consumption of fossil fuels and deforestation as temperatures climb. At this time on the clock of the world, we find ourselves at a crossroads: toward more participation or more fascism.

Fascism is when corporate and state actors collude to concentrate their wealth and preserve their power at the expense of their constituents under the threat of violence. As Franklin D. Roosevelt explained in his 1938 "Message to Congress on the Concentration of Economic Power," warning against the rise of the capitalist state: "The liberty of a democracy is not safe if the people tolerate the growth of private power to a point where it becomes stronger than their democratic state itself. That, in its essence, is fascism—ownership of government by an individual, by a group, or by any other controlling private power."[33] In a contemporaneous text, Bertolt Brecht refers to fascism as "the nakedest, most shameless, most oppressive, and most treacherous form of capitalism."[34]

When systems' actors stoke fear as a motivation for expulsion; when they target minority groups and women for control and violence; when they curtail or suspend legal rights; when they exclude or deport migrants and refugees; when they mock, attack, and disallow an independent press—these are the times when fascism is rising around us. We use the word "when" to point to fascism as a continuum that can build in stages. On this continuum, those in power mobilize logics of superiority and harness media and technology for the purposes of increasing domination—from oligarchy to authoritarianism to totalitarianism.

Fascist movements feed off populist disaffection with democratic institutions as they are captured by corporate interests that consolidate wealth and power. As Robert O. Paxton explains in "The Five Stages of Fascism," there is "no authentic fascism before the emergence of a massively enfranchised and politically active citizenry. In order to give birth to fascism, a society must have known political liberty."[35] Popular support for fascist regimes is mobilized as the contradictions inherent in a capitalist democracy deepen. For instance, when people are promised agency but time and again experience exploitation, they respond with understandable rage. This rage is aimed against public institutions, which act as a shield for corporate interests. As people lose trust in and recede from the public sphere, corporate power overgrows democracy. We see this happening now all around us.

PARTICIPATION IS OUR POWER

When we experience the vulnerability of a crisis, do we turn against one another and give power to a strong leader, or do we come together to address underlying causes of harm? What makes the difference between these trajectories? As Rebecca Solnit illustrates in *A Paradise Built in Hell*, during disasters we often see people rise to the challenge with collaboration, innovation, and generosity to work together to meet collective needs. These moments provide snapshots of a more participatory way of governing ourselves.

The relationship between participation and power is complicated by this contradiction: *when we participate we build power, and yet we need power to participate.* So the process of growing participation and power is often iterative and incremental. It entails getting a foothold and then using it as a platform to build more democracy and therefore more collective power. We need to build our participation muscle, strengthening our power to participate further. Through repeated participation, we can build distributed, collective power to equalize and include, and use it strategically to chip away at centralized, oligarchic power used to exploit and exclude.

Externally, having power requires audibility (you can be heard), credibility (you are believed), and consequence (you have impact). Internally, power requires confidence and self-love. Internal empowerment and external power are interconnected. Oppression is an external force designed ultimately to have internal consequences, so that a person stops attempting to participate, and thus external suppression is no longer needed to control them. The converse is also true: by building internal power, we build self-confidence to participate in altering the relations of power externally, which helps to reinforce our confidence, bolstering our ability to participate and have impact.

As systems of exploitation seize in contradiction, we can reimagine social systems that distribute power and resources more equitably. Faced with the same contradictions, democratic movements organize people in conversation to analyze the conditions we face. Developing a shared analysis from multiple, local perspectives, we could create a united global front that is urban and rural, multiracial, and represents people of all genders and abilities.[36] Together we can influence the organization of social systems to embrace different premises—cooperation, meeting needs, living in balance with ecological systems, and pursuing joy, pleasure, and freedom. Change is an emergent property of participation that no one person can determine.

When is Participation?

Democracy is the eternal opponent of fascism; our participation is our power. But what do we mean by democracy and participation? We measure democracy by the degree to which people participate in the decisions that affect their lives. We use the word participation when we wish to speak of the degree to which we have:

> access to accurate and relevant information;
>
> power to provide input on decisions that affect us;

the ability to perceive the consequences of our input;

and the opportunity to change our minds and make new inputs.

With this formulation in hand, democracy is the ideal of universal participation of fully actualized beings, not a commodity we have or a victory won. We can assess the degree to which we experience democracy in a given situation or moment by using this list of conditions for participation to analyze our media, governance, education, and cultural systems. We expand on these conditions below.

Access to accurate and relevant information

Information is a central locus of control. Access to accurate information, and the ability to critically analyze that information, are essential conditions for practicing democracy. As media scholar Robert McChesney explains: "Democracy requires a media system that provides people with a wide range of opinion, analysis, and debate on important issues, reflects the diversity of citizens, and promotes public accountability."[37] A democratic media system rejects logics of superiority which dehumanize groups categorically and insists on the participation of all people sharing information from their point of view. Media and storytelling—and how they are created, supported, and distributed—determine the conditions for democracy to flounder or flourish.

Power to provide input on decisions that affect us

Social systems structure power relations, which determine who receives what resources, when, how, and why. Black Lives Matter co-founder Alicia Garza adds a layer of voice and identity to this: "I define power as the ability to make decisions that affect your own life and the lives of others, *and the freedom to shape and determine the story of who we are.*"[38] Democracy is a social system that its members create and maintain to enable participation so that all members can have the agency, connection, and resources to thrive. A democracy relies on and reproduces governance structures and cultures that maximize distribution of power and participation.

Ability to perceive the consequences of our input

Power enables input *and* consequences. Those who benefit from an oppressive system protect it by controlling the visibility of consequences of actions. Does my input have consequences? Can I perceive them? Can others perceive them enough that we can build coalitions? Democratic participation requires all of these.

Opportunity to change our minds and make new inputs

Perceiving the consequences that arise from our participation, we have the chance to learn, hone our analyses and skills, find others working on the same issues, and take additional action with deeper wisdom. We are able to move from the unity of action to the diversity of reflection. Democracy is cultivated through a heuristic process of learning, as the result of many instances of participation on the part of many people, where each of us can perceive and debate the consequences of our participation, and change our minds in a way that guides future inputs.

It Is Time

The problems we face come from every direction and appear to be inevitable and insurmountable. It is through cultivating an analysis of the systems in which we live that we can move away from: "It's big. It's scary. It's hopeless. . . ." to "It's designed, it's vulnerable, and we can change it." Instead of seeing crises as catastrophic, we strive to see them as contested. These designed and vulnerable problems need to be understood in the context of the ever-shifting systems which give rise to them—systems we can intervene in and change.

Capitalism is in fundamental contradiction with democracy, which we need to create a future for ourselves and the planet. To forge democracy we need to continually expand participation. If we elicit full participation, we can create a livable world for future generations. To build a world that works for us all, we need everybody to be formulating their experience, the systems that give rise to it, and the world they long for. These twin labors of formulating both current reality and worlds we long for must be both radically participatory and perpetual.

This book provides tools not only to intervene in the current systems of ever-increasing exploitation of humans and the Earth, but also to generate alternatives, and try them out so they are ready to help us meet our needs in new ways as the old ways collapse around us. Our vision must be big enough and flexible enough to make room for us all.

Isn't it time to assert what we want? To wrest public institutions from corporate control and refuse their logics of superiority? To figure out how to meet the needs of people and the planet unconditionally? To create a united front for clean water and air, healthy food, safe housing, and abundant care? For education that ignites curiosity and work that is meaningful? For freedom of expression, movement, and assembly? And freedom from violence for all? Isn't it time we ask ourselves: what can we do, right here and now, to forge new visions of democracy and build more participation? Can our visions include and sustain their own premises?

This moment invites every family, community, and institution to be bold about the world it dreams of, even as the path from here to there is a work in progress. "What we give our attention to grows,"[39] advises adrienne maree brown. So, what can we give our attention to as we reject the firehose of hate? What world might a firehose of dreams irrigate?

◉

In the words of the poet Paul Celan in 1952,

> it is time they knew!
> It is time the stone made an effort to flower,
> time unrest had a beating heart.
> It is time it were time.
>
> It is time.[40]

FORMULATION

Strategy:
The Spiral of Change

> Many of us have been socialized to understand that constant growth, violent competition, and critical mass are the ways to create change. But emergence [in nature] shows us that adaptation and evolution depend more on critical, deep, and authentic connections, a thread that can be tugged for support and resilience.
>
> —adrienne maree brown, *Emergent Strategy: Shaping Change, Changing Worlds*

While the natural world is currently under attack, it simultaneously provides models we need in our work to make change. Nature shows us the way actions are interrelated and how our seemingly small actions can resonate through a whole system. At a time of crisis, nature adapts and proves resilient, often in unpredictable ways. It models "emergence," which is how we propose to actualize democracy through many acts of participation. As adrienne maree brown teaches in *Emergent Strategy: Shaping Change, Changing Worlds*: when systems fail, and we feel powerless and at a dead-end, we can take inspiration from the nonlinear aspects of natural systems to create recursive strategies for collective action that build over time. If the problems we face are emergent properties of systems, how can we create "emergent strategies," to intervene, wherever we are, moving those systems toward justice and equity, healing and love?

In the first chapter we modeled *analysis*, centering on the fundamental contradiction between capitalism and democracy, the role of logics of superiority in justifying capitalism's exploitation within a democracy, and ways that media and technology can be mobilized for domination or liberation. We argue that it is through growing participation that we can steer away from a rising tide of fascism toward an equitable global society. But how do we do this? How can we empower ourselves and our communities to make lasting social change?

In this chapter, we summarize the Spiral of Change, a step-by-step *strategy* for growing participation and enacting social change on every scale and in every domain. We borrow the spiral as a pattern from the natural world that shows up at a great range of scales: from DNA to chameleon tails to galaxies. Many spirals are fractals where the whole mirrors the different parts, as a metaphor for life where "the health of the cell is the health of the species and the planet."[1] The spiral progresses through circular motion, with iteration, not repetition. We use the spiral as a metaphor for democracy in action, where each of us—from a small group to democratic movements of millions of people—can participate in making change through a process of design, action, and reflection that repeats and grows participation and wisdom. We offer the Spiral of Change as a conceptual tool to play with and improve upon, and not as a dogma to be followed uncritically.

I   Gather People and Stories

We come to voice, and gather to share our stories, weaving connections between our experiences of harm and hope. We build trust across differences and commit to working together on change.

II   Formulate Problems and Systems

The way we formulate a problem determines its set of solutions. Therefore, we analyze the roots of our problems from many angles, taking care to formulate them in language that illuminates a path toward our desires. The problems we face emerge from dynamic social systems that we can describe, perturb, and reimagine.

III   Generate Desires

We generate desires to wrest our imaginations away from the constraints of our problems and establish new realms of possibility where we can design.

IV   Unearth Contradictions

When a problem is unsolvable in the current system, we work to formulate its underlying contradictions, which require a change of system rather than mere reforms within it. Where contradictions become visible, we locate points of leverage where strategic actions can have outsized consequences.

V   Design Interventions

Guided by our desires, we design social interventions at these points of leverage.

VI   Act and Reflect

As soon as we act, we forage for the consequences of our actions, so that we can reflect, change our minds, and grow in coalition. Together we envision new desires and designs. Repeating the steps of the Spiral of Change is how we grow participation and remake democracy. Democracy is the act of collectively designing the society we live in.

Here, we visit each step on the Spiral of Change to explain what it is, why it matters, and how it connects to the other steps. In future chapters, we walk through this process for making change, providing readers with assignments, stories, and interventions. You can start at any point on the Spiral of Change. You might have a deeply felt desire, face an intractable problem, or find yourself joining an action in progress and then reflecting on its consequences. Here, we choose to begin with the experience of harm, where contradictions surface and motivation for change is often born.

Gather People and Stories

Think about a time you have experienced or witnessed harm. When did you first talk about what happened and to whom? How did you describe the problem—and how did this description change in conversation with others? Was there a group already working on the problem, or did you have to create one or forge ahead alone?

The body is often the site of harm's impact—where we experience the contradictions in current social systems as pain, stress, and disease. *Coming to voice* about the harm we have witnessed or experienced is the very first step to healing our body and spirit. Coming to voice is a phrase formulated by bell hooks and other Black feminists to describe the transformation from voiceless object into speaking subject, of moving from "margin to center."[2]

In the process of coming to voice, we work to name the harm for ourselves and others. Gathering together, listening and responding to one another's stories, we share vulnerabilities and build trust. As we tell and retell the story of how we experienced or witnessed harm, first to a compassionate listener and gradually to a wider audience, we become more able to choose our language.

We inspect the language we use, critiquing how the language is "speaking us"[3] as we work to speak the language of the world we want. We must both *weave and unweave* stories in a process of creation and critique. In doing so, we lay groundwork for digging to the roots of problems and seeing how individual experiences of harm are linked and produced within social systems. Generating a sufficient social response to harm is how we prevent harm from becoming trauma.

Formulate Problems and Systems

An essential step between sharing stories about a problem and working together to solve it is *formulation*, which requires attending to language and investigating a problem together with others. When we say "formulating a problem" we are referring to a process of gathering stories from all angles about that problem, unearthing the premises and power relations that underlie each story, and then generating many different formulations of the problem, so that we can choose the language that move us toward our desires. We say "formulate a problem" and not "describe a problem" in recognition that when we formulate, we are not just observing reality—we are also *making* it. Speaking is an *action*.

Having a variety of formulations of a problem helps us build an intersectional analysis and forge coalitions to make additional interventions. As we gather and share stories, we notice similarities and differences, and then ask: *why*? Why did this happen? Of every answer we come up with, we must again ask, *why*? We dig deeper, following the chain of whys and becauses back to root premises, and begin to unearth the systems that produce our problems. This analytical work is essential. If we act only against symptoms and not the underlying disease, we can expend significant energy—even a lifetime—on ameliorating one symptom, only to discover further symptoms.

Herbert Brün spent his life resisting "power over" with countertactics of composition and formulation. He warned us to pay attention to language: "things are what is said about them . . . the language which you don't speak, will speak you."[4] Formulating brings intention and agency to the act of coming to voice. To formulate, we carefully choose language so that it carries our intention. As Susan Parenti puts it: "Formulation is when what I say and how I say it require each other."[5]

Formulation is design in language. Because the way we formulate a problem determines its set of solutions, we must be careful to formulate a problem for solutions we *want*. When we first state a problem, we reach for the available language for it, which ties us to the system that perpetuates the problem. Wrestling with the language of a problem and generating alternative formulations of it are acts of collective resistance and creation.

In the process of reformulating problems and digging to their roots, we uncover whole networks of problems in their complexity. We connect our problems through conversation and projects, and we learn their contours as we work together. Connecting our problems is how we begin to see social systems that are otherwise invisible to us, like interconnected families of roots under the soil.

A system is any set of interconnected parts forming a complex whole in which a change in one part affects the whole. We borrow this definition from cybernetics since it highlights the opportunity to intervene in a system from any position—wherever we are—and have an impact on the system as a whole. To this definition, Herbert and SDaS teacher and cybernetician Steve Sloan added the action of observing, using the phrase "look a system." "I look a system whenever I look at a collection of elements and supply a framework for the relations between the elements that permit me to say that a change in the state of one of the elements is a change in the state of elements as a whole."[6] Steve deliberately omitted the preposition "at" to emphasize the power of the one who looks to constitute, through her language, what is included and excluded from the system.[7]

When we "look a system," we assert that we are *choosing* both a framework and its elements to describe that system. We see problems as emerging from dynamic social systems that we can describe, perturb, and intervene in. We formulate our problems in a way that sees them as connected within a system we can perturb toward our desires. Our processes of choosing to observe and act influences systems and transforms us from object to subject.

Systems oppress by ignoring the perspectives and needs of those they harm. To interrupt oppression, we need the participation of everyone "looking systems" from their point of view. When systems produce repeated tragedies such as violence, discrimination, and poverty, it is time we recognize these so-called "tragedies" as *expected* outcomes of fundamentally undesirable systems. They are functioning correctly, as they were designed to. They are "solving" their (inadequate) formulations of problems, by conveniently excluding the people and perspectives they harm. Understanding the specifics of what we do *not* want can help us get very specific about what we *do* want, serving as a springboard for *generating our desires*—our next step on the Spiral of Change.

Generate Desires

Desire is an antidote to fear. Desiring is a practice that nurtures our beautiful, whole selves. When there appears no way out, our desires create a portal (window, slide, hot-air balloon) to transport us to a world that is full of more alternatives. By articulating desires, we generate friction with current realities. Formulating desires helps to generate alternatives to choose among, while it also supplies criteria (like values) to guide which paths we choose. Having desire statements that we have carefully formulated in our back pockets is an incredibly helpful and grounding tool in making decisions. They help us feel connected to what we want, generate hope for what could be, and gather others around this hope.

We formulate desire statements of what we want that are currently not true and would require a change of system to become true. This is a foundational activity at SDaS, where we use the word "desire" to reclaim it from interpersonal violence and capitalist commodification, and to claim desire for the shameless wanting we have for living in equitable, loving, social relationship. We distinguish a desire from a preference, which is already available in the current system, even if not to us. Without formulating the language of desire, we remain trapped in the language of the problem. So much social control happens in the realm of imagination. When we formulate what we desire, we wrest our imaginations away from propaganda and ruling ideas and open up new fields of possibility in which we can design.

Awash in a sea of "normal" that attempts to justify social violence and oppression, we resist by generating alternative visions for the world we want by formulating desire statements. Desire statements seed new premises and consequences. They are unconstrained by history, tradition, or assertions of impossibility.

We formulate desire statements throughout the Spiral of Change: to guide our formulations of problems, to design our interventions, and to evaluate their results. When we are lost in a problem, our desires become a compass by which to navigate our collective escape.

IV Unearth Contradictions

A contradiction appears as tension between two irreconcilable realities that require a change of system to resolve. This incongruity may show up as two assertions that cannot both be true, such as "all humans are equal" and "these humans must sit at the back of the bus." Contradiction and conflict are not equivalent. Conflict is when we formulate a problem such that it can be solved within the system it lives in. Contradiction is when we formulate a problem such that solving it would require a change of system.[8] Faced with the instability and friction created by contradiction, those who benefit from a system will attempt to "resolve" a contradiction by turning it into a mere conflict. When a contradiction privileges one group over the other and is maintained by force or threat of force, that is *oppression*.

To justify an unjust system, systems' actors use logics of superiority— racism, patriarchy, ableism, and classism—to argue that a contradiction is merely a conflict. For example, in the United States the racialized policy of "separate but equal" was an attempt to turn the contradiction of segregation in a democratic society into a mere conflict—full of friction but tightly controlled. Under policies of "separate but equal," most of white American society attempted to proceed with normalcy, while Black American society continued to experience the deep and painful contradictions inherent in unequal under-resourced schools and neighborhoods and exclusion from the economy and housing. Their experiences and perspectives were in active contradiction to this dominant story.

The work of social justice is to activate the contradictions in oppressive systems. To change an unjust system, one must insist on looking the system from the perspective of the people and stories that are excluded from the story that justifies domination. Movements for liberation mobilize these excluded voices and shine a bright spotlight on the contradiction of inequities within a democracy.

Contradictions reveal points of leverage to move our desires into the world through design and action. Dr. Martin Luther King and his civil rights colleagues designed interventions where contradictions became visible, pressing on these points of leverage where a minority population could influence the majority. They designed actions such as the Montgomery bus boycott to apply pressure on the contradiction between segregation and democracy at a visible, public point of consumption: riding the bus.

Following Dr. King's example, to design interventions, first locate the points of leverage. Points of leverage may often be found at "points of intervention," theorized by the Center for Story-based Strategy as points of production, consumption, and destruction, as well as other areas like decision-making and the challenging of assumptions.[9] The reason to formulate our problems as contradictions is to locate points of leverage for intervention.

To escape the endless wheel of conflict, those who experience or witness contradiction must intervene, surfacing contradictions to challenge and change the premises of these systems. Those who highlight contradictions often face backlash. The good news is that systems of domination—imperialism, capitalism, patriarchy, white supremacy—contain many contradictions that render them vulnerable, offering opportunities to change them. With time and pressure, these contradictions surface as visible cracks where we can seed desirable new systems in the fertile soil of our desires.

V Design Interventions

Guided by our desires, we design social interventions at points of leverage. In the Spiral of Change, design is a creative, iterative process of synthesizing our desires as criteria for choosing what to do. Design is the bridge that takes us from where we are to where we want to go. It is the "aha!" moment when, faced with obstacles, we can nevertheless see how to maneuver to manifest our desires. When we design, we imagine, sketch, constrain, select, avoid, and change our minds. When we design in collaboration with others, we pool our strengths and generate the internal friction necessary to sharpen our ideas.

We use the term "design" in the broadest sense, encompassing every domain—from material, to social, to environmental; at all scales—from family, to region, to international. We can look at any structure and ask: "Who designed this? What were the criteria behind their choices?" A design reveals the desires it is built upon. We are surrounded by so many designs reflecting desires for control, profit, and the concentration of power, that it is difficult to imagine designs based on different desires—for care, freedom, justice, and participation. Part of alienation is the feeling that we have not been consulted in the design of the conditions in which we find ourselves.

In contrast to social engineering, we assert "participatory design," a process which includes those affected by the existing and proposed designs in a heuristic way. We design to increase participation, generating alternatives and decreasing power differences. We design to build confidence and collaboration, to benefit from conflict, and to create the cultural change needed to sustain systemic change.

A design manifests a person's uniqueness through their choices by creating something that, without them, would not exist. Designing society together, we assert the necessity of each person's perspective, that is, their desires for the world they want. Designing is a mode of participation that transforms us from objects into subjects, changing our alienation into agency. Democracy is the act of collectively designing the society in which we live. The scale of change we want will take many iterations of the Spiral of Change, so we design for the long haul.

VI Act and Reflect

Making social change is not just one big, dramatic event, but countless repeated interventions that build momentum toward larger, more visible movements. We tend to focus on the big interventions as "the action," but we invite you to think of these as the few days of the year that an apple tree blossoms. To produce the week of blossoming took the coordinated contributions of seed, soil, sun, water, fungi, and worms. The work is not over. To turn the blossom into fruit will require additional work from those same contributors and the pollinators. For the sapling to become a tree that provides food for many requires ongoing iterations throughout the seasons; so too, for the work of social change. The process repeats, year after year, growing the strength of the tree and our movements.

Taking action at a point of leverage perturbs a system, temporarily increasing its instability and vulnerability to change. Hidden dynamics of systems become exposed. Cracks caused by contradictions widen. Systems' actors rush to smooth these over. This is a moment of opportunity that offers many options; we can observe, regroup, advance, amplify, seed new ideas.

How do we know what the consequences of our actions are? Where do we look? We must *forage* for the consequences of our actions. We use the word "forage" to draw attention to the kind of work it takes to find what is there but may be difficult to perceive. Controlling public perception of the consequences of actions is a primary mechanism of social control. History's victors maintain the status quo by hiding the contradictions, desires, and alternatives exposed by their opponents. Keep consequences visible and your work remains viable.

Often after an intervention comes a backlash, as systems' actors deny, reframe, attack, appease, or delay to stave off crisis and reestablish equilibrium. Backlash presents the opportunity to learn the vulnerabilities of that system, highlight the system's contradictions to an audience, and present alternatives we want. We encourage you to be strategic rather than reactive in this moment—curious rather than merely furious. These are critical moments where hidden parts of the system become visible, opening the possibility of a shift in public perception. You can open up spaces for people who have been silent about a shared experience, where they can speak up and articulate desires, reforming *within* a system to build momentum toward a revolution *of* system, representing a change in fundamental premises.

The oppressive system will respond to interventions by amplifying its own assertions and "flooding the zone" to drown out our work and the alternatives we present. To forage for consequences, we seek out responses that come from the margins—the previously suppressed people and their stories, desires, and visions that become visible in that moment. Foraging for consequences is one way to find allies and overcome disconnection and alienation. Foraging is a way for us to come home to one another, the many who have lived the consequences of social contradictions for so long. This can be a joyous moment amidst the stormy and sometimes dangerous responses of the system.

Reflection is how we better connect our desires to our designs over time. Reflection is the step that makes the Spiral of Change a spiral. As we forage for the consequences of our interventions we reflect on our problems, desires, and designs, and make adjustments to build wisdom and participation.

Remaking Democracy

Practicing the Spiral of Change is how we grow participation everywhere. As a heuristic process, it welcomes more and more participants who shape the analysis and reflection. As the work expands, we negotiate and renegotiate designs with new people and perspectives, improving strategic interventions while increasing participation. Democracy is when people participate in the decisions that affect their lives. Designing social interventions led by our desires is how we grow democracy. Instead of a future owned by a few, growing democracy is how we forge a future shared by all of us.

Practicing a concept—trying more than once—produces a different kind of knowing than talking about it. Through continuously practicing, ideas become embodied and actualized, and we adapt them for our own communities, cultures, and situations. How can the Spiral of Change be useful in addressing your problem? Try it out and see what happens. Here we offer a "playsheet" to try out each step on the spiral.

Writing is an easy medium in which to try things out, but you could choose to make audio or video instead. If you feel stuck, talk out loud with a friend. If you find yourself shut down, take a walk. Ideas often need physical movement or social stimulus to surface. Most importantly: don't skip practicing. You can try these assignments alone, in pairs, or in a small group. With each, share and discuss and reflect afterwards.

Gather People and Stories

Write or speak about a time when you experienced or witnessed a social harm. Describe how witnesses reacted to the harm and what you wish their responses had been.

Visual art variation: Draw the above as a comic strip that shows the harm, the social reaction, and a pivot to your desired reaction.

Formulate Problems and Systems

Write a one-sentence version of a problem you want to work on. Add "why" to the beginning of your problem statement. Answers this new question. Continue until you run out of answers or it feels you have gotten as far as you can to the root of the problem.

Performance variation: Turn this into a dialogue between an elder and child who continues to ask why.

III Generate Desires

Write a list of five to seven desire statements in relation to your problem, phrasing them as if they were true. Consider: what would need to be true such that your problem is adequately responded to or never even arises.

Acoustic variation: Write a love song declaring your desires using a common tune or one you make up. With a partner, make it a duet between desires.

IV Unearth Contradictions

Reformulate your problem as a contradiction between two irreconcilable instructions.

Play variation: While playing with a yo-yo, state one side of the contradiction (the first instruction) as you release the yo-yo to the ground and the other side as you draw the yo-yo back to your hand. Try variations on your formulation of the contradiction.

V Design Interventions

Write about or discuss: where does your contradiction show up or become visible? What is one step or action you could take toward making one or more of your desire statements true in that context?

Rhythmic variation: Try to answer the above in the meter of a waltz (1-2-3, 1-2-3). With a partner, alternate each of your answers in the waltz meter. Now try this again while waltzing with your partner.

VI Act and Reflect

Discuss or write about one time that you had a significant change of mind or when you realized the need for social change. What happened and how did it influence you?

Poetry variation: Write a poem where the first half represents your old frame of mind, there is a line or two in the poem where you changed, and then the second half represents your changed thinking.

CHAPTER 3

INTERVENTION

From Indymedia
to Media Justice

On January 1, 1994, the world woke up to news of an Indigenous-led uprising to regain control over their communally owned lands, culture, and governance in the remote area of Chiapas, Mexico. After decades of peaceful resistance methods, the Zapatistas organized this militant uprising to correspond with the day the North American Free Trade Agreement (NAFTA) was going into effect. NAFTA represented the latest in a series of attempts to strip Indigenous communities of their land and livelihood.

The Zapatistas were among the first to use the internet as a public site of social criticism, to highlight capital's "privatization of everything" and to broadcast a vision of self-governing communities as *un mundo donde quepan muchos mundos* ["a world where many worlds fit"]. Broadcasting regular communiques on the internet, the Zapatistas cultivated a broad international solidarity movement to support their efforts. It was at the 1996 Intercontinental Encounter for Humanity and Against Neo-liberalism that the Zapatistas called for the creation of an international network of independent media to share stories of oppression through the lens of its resistance. They called upon this network to "tell the past and present history of the social struggle in the world . . . to understand it and to derive lessons from it, to learn who we are, what it is we want, who we can be."[1]

What started as this call for an independent media network became the launch of Indymedia during the historic protests that shut down the World Trade Organization (WTO) meeting in Seattle in 1999. Indymedia's success in Seattle inspired the rapid development of an Indymedia network that, at its peak, consisted of 210 centers across six continents.[2] The Indymedia network was built by activists and media makers to amplify the stories of grassroots resistance to the globalization of corporate power. Indymedia organizers were able to connect with others and quickly grow this global network using the open field of the early internet, prior to its hypercommercialization. The Urbana-Champaign Independent Media Center (UC-IMC) was one of the nodes on this network, founded in 2000 by teachers, artists, and organizers, including myself, Danielle. Host to the Indymedia Global Fund, and fiscal sponsor to dozens of media democracy projects worldwide, our UC-IMC is considered a model in using media, art, and technology for democratic social change.[3] UC-IMC's development over the last twenty-five years has helped me conceptualize the Spiral of Change presented in this book. This chapter illustrates the Spiral of Change in action through the story of Indymedia and the founding of UC-IMC.

The Contradiction Within Media Democracy

In 1996, the Clinton administration removed media ownership restrictions, sparking a feeding frenzy where large media corporations gobbled up thousands of diverse outlets, including many Black-owned and college-based radio stations which had played such a pivotal role in the civil rights and social movements of the 1960s and '70s.[4] What remained were six megacorporations with ownership of 90 percent of the nation's media outlets. To cut costs, these media giants shut down investigative and local journalism outlets, spurring massive layoffs. To appease advertisers, they censored criticism, dumbing down public discourse. Media consolidation exacerbated many other problems. For those organizing for democratic change across a host of issues—housing, health care, education, environmental concerns, and human rights—media consolidation deprived our movements of the oxygen of information we needed to make progress. Our work stalled out.

Our democracy was caught in contradiction: *the media tools we needed to see each other, share information and ideas, and participate in decisions, were increasingly controlled by a handful of corporations with financial interests in wars, prisons, and the privatization of the public commons.* Corporate media dehumanized groups of people to maintain systems of superiority required for its profit making. Instead of exploring complex relations, it flattened narratives into simplistic binaries of villains versus victims. It profited off a hopeless drumbeat of problems, overreporting violence and amplifying racialized narratives. We spent more and more time watching tragedy amplified millions of times, in a destructive feedback loop with our emotional systems. Corporations drove up profits by capturing our attention and monetizing it.

Indymedia was created at this point of leverage: while corporations downsized news media outlets, the increasing affordability of media equipment and accessibility to the internet provided opportunities to fill this void. For the first time in modern history, people had access to affordable, mass global communication. In his book *The Organic Internet: Organizing History's Largest Social Movement*, Alfredo Lopez shared his experience of the early use of the internet by democratic movements: "Blocked from virtually every other avenue of mass communications, we found one that didn't and couldn't block us. Rather it allowed us to say everything we wanted to a staggering number of people. We seized it and learned to use it, and we have used it very effectively."[5] The 1990s were an exhilarating time when we felt that we had within reach technology tools to build global solidarity we needed to self-govern, decarbonize our economies, labor less, and meet human needs.

The Battle of Seattle

At the same time civil society was globalizing connection and solidarity, corporations were globalizing profit-making to sustain the growth capitalism requires (see chapter 1). Similar political-economic forces that disenfranchised the Zapatistas were building power through the World Bank, International Monetary Fund and now the WTO, which was charged with removing "barriers to free trade" such as public ownership, labor laws, and environmental regulations. As David Solnit, co-founder of the Direct Action Network (DAN), shared in reflection: "WTO used euphemisms like 'economic globalization' and 'free trade,' but those words disguised the poverty, misery and ecological destruction of the capitalist system."[6] The third meeting of the WTO was scheduled to start on November 30, 1999, in Seattle. In response, a powerful, international confluence of labor and environmental organizations came together, using old-school organizing techniques and new digital communications tools to mobilize a massive number of people to converge on the WTO meeting. In the end, over 60,000 people from 1,449 organizations across eighty-nine countries participated in this historic protest, including members of the School for Designing a Society (SDaS) from Urbana, Illinois.

In the months leading up to our trip, SDaS participants honed our analyses of the problem of corporate-controlled globalization. We formed study groups and hosted a series of public forums, including pro-WTO economists to help us understand their arguments and sharpen ours. That November, eighteen residents from Urbana traveled across the country to join in what was being heralded as a "festival of resistance." Our group prepared street theater performances aimed at teaching the dynamics and impacts of globalized capital. For example, I wrote a skit about the contradiction created by free trade agreements where corporations can migrate and labor can't:

> I'm an American worker, I can't compete with cheap labor. Now my boss is threatening our union—accept his terms or he'll go overseas. Our jobs can go to where labor is cheap. But labor can't go to where jobs pay well. . . . [Laborer smashes against the border wall and falls to the ground.]

As we traveled, I wrote in my diary: *We are going in homemade costumes with post horns and oboes made of straw. We have created acoustic portraits of free trade, flea circuses questioning capitalism, and velvet capes painted with desires.* Sensing what was coming, I added: *At night I dream of hordes of strangers escaping tear gas. I have never feared participating in a demonstration, and I am afraid.*

Once we arrived, we attended a three-day International Forum on Globalization. The event drew several thousand people into conversation with one another and allowed us to hear grassroots organizers from around the world share their stories. Scholar-activist Vandana Shiva talked about how Indian farmers had cultivated seeds over many generations that corporations were now patenting and then making illegal for them to share, causing a spike in farmer suicides.[7] Owens Wiwa spoke of the murder of his brother, Ken Saro-Wiwa, for resisting Shell's pollution of Ogoni land with its oil operations in the Niger Delta.[8] Workers in the North talked about how their jobs were being exported to the Global South, while workers from the Global South shared concerns about the pollution and wage suppression of these new industries. We knit together these different stories into a shared analysis of interconnected problems we faced as capital was globalizing: loss of biodiversity from genetically modified foods, the use of state forces to protect extractive industries, a race to the bottom of wages, the privatization of land and water. We also discussed strategies to resist. Rainforest Action Network organizers described how they pressured Home Depot into ending their sale of old growth wood. Organizers from Sustainable America painted a picture of an economic development model that could feed the world's population.

The forums were followed by colorful street parades where our group engaged other demonstrators and bystanders in conversation through performance. I wore a "desire cape" outlining premises for a new economics, which read:

> I WANT:
>
> To produce what is valuable to us without hurting ourselves or the environment;
>
> Globalization that reduces inequality;
>
> People to participate in the decisions that affect their lives.

The mood was festive. For those first few days, I was able to engage Seattle police officers in lively conversation. But when the WTO meeting was set to begin, police behavior made a dramatic turn toward violence. On those rainy streets in downtown Seattle, we experienced the power of state forces to defend capital.

On November 29, 1999, the International Longshore and Warehouse Union (ILWU) organized a one-day work stoppage, shutting down every West Coast port from Alaska to Los Angeles. Tens of thousands of demonstrators encircled the center of the city, some locking arms and occupying the streets, others dancing and making music. The police, in full riot gear, responded with escalation, beating peaceful demonstrators, who were gassed, encircled, and jailed. At one point, I appealed to an officer as he was about to hit a young woman with a stick as thick as my wrist: "Do you really want to do this? She is not a threat. You can choose not to escalate." Pow! As one of our members tried to escape the mayhem, she was yanked off the top of a bus stop by her hair. I watched in horror as police pulled back the mask of a medic, blasted pepper spray into her eyes, and snapped the mask back, as she gasped to breathe. Police fired rubber bullets indiscriminately into crowds, bloodying protestors and bystanders. I felt powerless anticipating the news stories that would accuse the demonstrators of violence, the firehose of corporate media's spin powerwashing our messages out of view. Instead, I witnessed people-powered media grab the mic.

The Birth of Indymedia

Peter Miller, a radio producer and union organizer in our group, discovered the Seattle Indymedia Center in a makeshift storefront downtown. Peter insisted the rest of us come visit this sweaty beehive of media production, where they were dispatching hundreds of volunteers with audio and video recording devices to report on the protests. Volunteer workers pulled all-nighters to knit together eye-witness accounts to post online. People in turtle costumes talked about how the WTO slashed the Endangered Species Act.

51

French farmers, handing out Roquefort cheese, spoke about how the WTO was wiping out their livelihood. As corporate media spun our protests as violent, Indymedia coverage revealed that police instigated the violence before a single window was broken.

Seattle Indymedia brought together technologist-organizers who created one of the first open publishing systems, enabling thousands of people negatively impacted by the WTO to speak to millions of audience members who visited the website seattle.indymedia.org. Local radio stations and newspapers redistributed the stories. Radio Havana broadcasted daily updates to five million listeners in Cuba. Belgian organizers downloaded the Seattle Indymedia newspaper and printed eight thousand copies to distribute on the streets of Brussels that week.[9] The acronym "WTO" buzzed around dinner tables as people grappled with how their air, water, land, food, and jobs were threatened by this organization they had never heard of.

Large corporate media conglomerates, having downsized their news departments, could not compete with this grassroots effort. By the second day of the WTO meeting, the African delegation, emboldened by the demonstrations and the sudden international attention, refused to sign off on the WTO's agenda. Talks of launching a new round of trade negotiations collapsed. We danced in the streets of Seattle to celebrate. The WTO protests asserted the power of strategic, multi-issue organizing using nonviolent direct action and a nascent Indymedia network amplified this around the world. Reflecting on the making of Indymedia, John Tarleton, editor of the New York-based *Indypendent* newspaper shared, "[We were laying the] infrastructure for a multimedia peoples' newsroom that would enable activists to come together and disseminate their own stories to a global audience without having to go through the corporate filter . . . [it] was an end-run around the information gatekeepers, made possible by the technology of the Internet."[10] Indymedia's "citizen journalists" shared local stories that contradicted the narratives circulated by corporate elites. They showed that Monsanto was not "Feeding the World," they were causing birth defects in children. Shell was not #MakingTheFuture; they were polluting Nigerian land and murdering Indigenous Ogoni organizers.

After Seattle, protests showed up at every major convening of global corporations—such as the WTO, World Bank, International Monetary Fund, and G20. Each time, Indymedia reporters were there to amplify grassroots voices of concern and often left infrastructure in place for a new Indymedia Center to grow. One of the co-founders of NYC Indymedia, Ana Nogueira, shared how Indymedia "connected towns and cities together around a common cause . . . [it] scaled across topics, so that you could see, for example, that there were struggles around housing justice in New York City and see how they were connected to similar struggles in Spain, or in parts of Central

America."[11] Each city had its own Indymedia website that the public could post to and then a collective in that community curated content to a featured panel. These featured stories were aggregated onto a national site, and then the global Indymedia website. These were curated by a collective that linked organizers from around the world.

Gathering the People and Stories

The creation of UC-IMC represented the gathering of many different local groups working toward labor, gender, and environmental justice, alongside artists and media makers, and supported by the wisdom of key movement mentors. Indymedia offered these groups the means to share stories, see the consequences of their work, and connect issues to build broader coalitions.

UC-IMC gathered members of labor from the newly formed Graduate Employees Organization at the University of Illinois and the Socialist Forum, including Sascha Meinrath, Mike Lehman, and Belden Fields. Activists working on gender justice were key to UC-IMC's founding, including members from the 85% Coalition, a direct action group named after the 85 percent of Illinois residents who supported adding sexual orientation and gender identity to the Illinois Human Rights Act. The Coalition was founded by Parkland College professor and feminist activist Mary Lee Sargent and Kimberlie Kranich of Illinois Public Media. For representation of environmental justice issues, UC-IMC gathered members from the Common Ground Food Co-op and those organizing against the threat of genetically modified foods. Three young UC-IMC members—Sehvilla Mann, Molly Stentz, and Pauline Bartolone—led local efforts around food justice and sustainable living and created the IMC radio show "Life in the Bikelane."

From the beginning, UC-IMC members included arts and culture within the scope of independent media, with artist Sarah Kanouse insisting on "arts and narrative" in our mission statement. UC-IMC gathered members of SDaS, which also provided mentorship in composition and performance through Susan Parenti and Mark Enslin. Thanks to the work of anti-Vietnam War era organizers Bill Taylor and Jan Kalmar, Champaign-Urbana was home to WEFT Community Radio, which, since 1981, had trained hundreds of volunteers in radio production. WEFT brought together people to create shows such as *Womyn Making Waves*, *the Illinois World Labor Hour*, *Radio-Girl!*, and *Eclectic Seizure* radio theater. With the launch of publicly available internet, two additional groups formed: the Computer Learning and Mentoring Center (CLAM) which operated a community computer lab and offered free classes in web development and coding. CLAM became a pipeline for employees of a new worker-owned technology business, On the Job Consulting, started by siblings Sigfried Gold and Lori Patterson, whose mission was "high-paying part-time work for artists and activists." These projects and organizations provided a rich, diverse, multi-issue, multi-approach environment in which UC-IMC quickly grew.

Designing Our Indymedia

When our SDaS delegation returned from Seattle, we started dreaming of forming our own Indymedia Center as physical and social infrastructure to share local issues in the context of, and connected to, global efforts. We imagined a commons that could become a resource for many social justice organizing efforts, making space for a diversity of people, analyses, and tactics.

Working within the context of SDaS' invitation to generate desires, founders of the Urbana-Champaign Independent Media Center held months of conversations, taking time to formulate and reformulate our desire statements for this new participatory organization we were dreaming of. Here are several that began as formulations in my notebook and were refined by a group process after the launch of our organization:

> Our IMC amplifies the voices and perspectives of people and ideas underrepresented in the media so that we can build a more equitable society.

> Our IMC provides space, resources, and atmosphere to draw artists and community members together to investigate problems and design solutions.

> Our IMC inspires consumers of media, arts, and narratives, to become producers of these.

> Our IMC creates a "third space" for youth as an alternative to home or school, where they can come to voice and develop their own projects.

> Our IMC provides sustainable infrastructure to proliferate many autonomous, decentralized projects to support long-haul organizing.

What united these desire statements is the vision for an organization that proliferates participation. We wanted to establish a space where people gather to formulate problems, desires and contradictions, design interventions together, forage for consequences, reflect together and begin again.

UC-IMC Structure

After a year of gathering people and formulating our desires, the collective house where I lived hosted the first official meeting of the UC-IMC. We shared our desires for a new organization, then collectivized our media equipment and broke into small groups around different media: radio, print, video, and performance. Working to design our UC-IMC for participation, we borrowed from the nonhierarchical, consensus-based model of the

Indymedia movement. But in recognizing how Indymedia's hyper-focus on nonhierarchical organizing could spawn a kind of libertarian distrust in leadership, structure, and governance, UC-IMC designed important structural components to ensure its sustainability.

The UC-IMC was to be made up of members who paid sliding scale dues and joined "working groups," which were named to emphasize an orientation toward making together. These groups used a form of modified consensus to make decisions. They each designated a spokesperson who would participate in regular steering group meetings to represent the working group in overall UC-IMC decisions. Once a working group was confirmed by the steering group, decisions were to be left to the working groups to determine how they would operate, without interference. There were only a few restrictions: adhere to the mission, keep meetings open to all, no hate speech, avoid putting the UC-IMC commons in legal or financial jeopardy. This decentralized structure supported a core principle that those who are doing the work should be empowered to make the decisions. If a member of a working group fundamentally disagreed with a proposal for that group, they had several options. They could caucus with a small group to draft another way forward; choose to block the decision (with a two-thirds majority able to override the block); or gather others who agreed and propose a different working group. In this way, we avoided the power struggles that derive from a sense of scarcity. UC-IMC founders also felt strongly that our governance structure should be transparent and fit on a few pages to avoid privileging insiders who were well versed on lengthy and obscure bylaws.

This intentional "designing for participation" paid off. We represented the campus and community in this college town. Our youngest media maker was twelve years old and the oldest was ninety. Our members included elected Democrats, Green Party members, socialists, and anarchists; we were teachers, social workers, laborers, artists, business owners, students, and residents experiencing homelessness.

The focus on sustainability also served our desires to proliferate participation. Five years after opening, we purchased our own building. Having seen other organizations fail from too much reliance on one funder or landowner, we firmly intended to own the property where our center was located. This move gave us a full 30,000 square feet to proliferate dozens of community projects: WRFU Radio Free Urbana, the *Public i* newspaper, UC Books to Prisoners, Makerspace Urbana, The Bike Project, Champaign-Urbana Citizens for Peace and Justice, Champaign County Bailout Coalition, Indymedia and Arts Lab, incubating and spinning off dozens of new organizations.

We were the first Indymedia Center to form a nonprofit incorporated as a 501(c)(3) organization, to the consternation of some activists in the broader movement who worried that engagement with the government might compromise our independence. However, forming a nonprofit legal structure positioned us to play a pivotal role in supporting the burgeoning Indymedia movement. UC-IMC fiscally sponsored dozens of projects, including: *The Indypendent* newspaper in NYC, Media Mobilizing Project in Philadelphia, Alive in Baghdad, the Mobile ((i)) reporting van, IndyKids, the Computer Underground that shipped tons of computing equipment to the Global South, and dozens of IMCs. UC-IMC was the host and a key fundraiser for the global Indymedia project, providing fiscal sponsorship for the Growth in Africa project that created a handbook for starting an Indymedia Center. We sponsored microgrants through the Global South Fund. Our members went on delegations to South Africa, Kenya, Thailand, Burma, and elsewhere to provide logistical support for starting IMCs and community radio stations.

UC-IMC Interventions

Throughout its twenty-five-year history, the Urbana-Champaign Independent Media Center has enacted numerous interventions at points of leverage toward democratic change. What follows are several examples of UC-IMC's critical media-making work, often employing do-it-yourself technologies and serving as a community hub in times of crisis. Each example illustrates how UC-IMC members identified a contradiction and worked within it as a point of leverage to design effective interventions.

Exonerating LGBTQ+ activists

Within a few months of our first meeting in 2001, videographers with the UC-IMC traveled with members of the 85% Coalition to the Illinois State Capitol to launch and report on a day of action. The group was working to convince lawmakers to add sexual orientation and gender identity to the Illinois Human Rights Act. The contradiction we used as a point of leverage was: *85 percent of the state's residents supported adding sexual orientation and gender identity to the Illinois Human Rights Act, and yet Illinois representatives had failed to do so.* Every other tactic had been tried over thirty years—letter writing, meetings with legislators, circulation of petitions—to no avail. To shine a bright light on this contradiction and mobilize supporters, 85% Coalition members staged a direct action, unfurling a banner in the state senate and serenading members with their demands. They were arrested and charged with criminal trespass; however, video footage shared by UC-IMC volunteers contradicted the police reports and was used to exonerate them.[12] Continued nonviolent direct action proved essential to finally passing this legislation in 2005.

Building free community wireless

The Urbana-Champaign Independent Media Center was founded at a time when the internet first became more accessible to the general public. UC-IMC founders saw an emerging contradiction between the internet as a digital commons where people can communicate and participate freely and as a digital gated community, controlled and channeled by corporations seeking to manipulate that communication for profit. Our desire was to create free, decentralized, community-owned networks to foster creativity and participation.

What started as a group of nerds tinkering with how to beam wireless internet signals using DIY tools (in this case, potato chip cans) turned into a design for CU Wireless Network (CUWiN). By mounting devices on dozens of rooftops, we were able to connect downtown and local neighbors with the first open-source mesh network wireless system.[13] Funds from the National Science Foundation and Soros Foundation expanded CUWiN's reach to rural America and the Global South, and enabled connection during disasters, most notably in the case of Hurricane Katrina.[14]

Tracking disappeared residents

After the terrorist attacks in the US on September 11, 2001, the Bush administration pushed through the Patriot Act, which allowed the federal government to bring secret evidence against those suspected of terrorism, preventing those accused, their legal counsel, and the public from mounting a defense. The Patriot Act was in clear contradiction with constitutional rights to liberty and due process.

In May 2002, UC-IMC received credible information that Ahmed Bensouda, an Arab activist and former student at University of Illinois, was in the process of being kidnapped from his apartment by secret agents. UC-IMC reporters immediately arrived on the scene as Bensouda, who had been involved in pro-Palestinian organizing on campus, was detained by ICE and the FBI.[15] UC-IMC members quickly designed a rapid response network, and UC-IMC became a 24/7 drop-in center where friends and supporters could walk in, get updates, and organize. Members of the Anti-War, Anti-Racism Effort (AWARE), which met and produced media at the UC-IMC, organized a public pressure campaign, with hundreds showing up at his court appearance in Chicago. Bensouda was ultimately released on bail and the secret charges against him were dropped due to this public pressure.

Reflecting on UC-IMC

It was around 2005 that Indymedia as a global movement started to fracture. UC-IMC began to shift away from some of the premises of Indymedia and migrate toward connections we had developed in the media justice movement. Indymedia had created open, participatory communications platforms that fostered fundamentally decentralized media and storytelling at a time of media consolidation. Looking back, our twenty-five years of ongoing global justice organizing has been instrumental in highlighting the contradiction between the interests of global capital and democratic values, forcing corporate actors to scale back plans for a full takeover of education, health care, public utilities, and local food systems. But capitalism is highly adaptable at co-opting innovations meant for the public good and turning them into profit centers. Tragically, the same free tools that volunteers gave hundreds of thousands of hours to build were absorbed by corporate social media giants, like Twitter, turning our innovations into Frankensteins.[16]

We established the UC-IMC as a new commons in our community, with a supportive infrastructure for community members to plant their ideas and initiatives. The UC-IMC's design allowed projects to adapt as they learned from the consequences of their interventions. UC-IMC's media projects gravitated toward multiracial, multiclass storytelling with documentation and amplification through our independent media channels. Some of this organizing, for example, by the Champaign-Urbana Citizens for Peace and Justice, is described in chapter 21. The core organization focused on being a logistical and financial backbone for a myriad of projects. We understood that effective organizers attend to where energy already exists in a community, offering resources and support to those who are already self-organizing. In this sense, we did not so much lead as follow.

Designed and redesigned through iterative implementation of the Spiral of Change, UC-IMC illustrates a project centered on the power of marginalized voices and stories to surface systemic contradictions, opening up spaces for diverse people to seed a variety of projects for change in fertile soil for their projects, ideas, events, and experiments. Our local Indymedia now has daily gatherings of people—dancing, making, performing, tinkering, reading, roller-skating, clowning, strategizing. There are people trying something out for the first time and others teaching something they are an international expert in. Every corner of the building has been altered by the people who use it. We have a local Black history museum installed by prolific artist and archivist Marilynn Dean Cleveland; a tribute to "Grandpa" Robert Wahlfeldt, who built up the Human Relations Commission to investigate racial discrimination in the sundown town of Danville, Illinois; a spiraling hallway of "Bad Art" that will make you laugh the whole way down; and a wall of finches and other birds lovingly cared for by IMC members, and whose chirps welcome everyone who comes in. Whenever I am in a slump, I go there, as it is a space of loving radical inclusion, where in the walls you can feel the communities of trust and care that have gathered now for twenty-five years. Consider this an invitation to come visit.

I

Gather People
and Stories

CHAPTER 4

FORMULATION

Begin with Telling Untold Stories

Trauma is the experience that calls us to organizing. You decide not to be the misery that loves company and instead choose to accompany people on a path toward defeating misery.

—Gwen Snyder[1]

Our desire to make the world better is often born of the harm we suffer, witness (and inflict), combined with some hope that we may be able to protect those we love and the world from similar harms. Our strategy for remaking democracy, elaborated in the Spiral of Change, starts with story as the basic building block of movements. It is through sharing stories that we pivot from "me" to "we." As Alfredo Lopez put it, "We require connection with other human lives to understand our own. The exchange of our stories is essential to our survival."[2] In telling and retelling our stories, we name ourselves, our problems, and our resources. We orient ourselves in the contexts of histories and cultures. We invite others to see us as we wish to be seen. In listening to each other, we learn we are not alone and find what we have in common. It takes trust, community and time to recognize and begin to heal from the intensity of our lived experiences of problems. In the interchange between tellers and listeners, we weave connections between our different experiences from which emerges a stronger sense of the problems we collectively face. In this way, we begin to recognize and describe the dynamics of the systems in which we live, which would otherwise be invisible to us, like water to fish.

In this chapter we articulate a path from experiencing harm to a world in which such harm is not only healed but prevented. This path leads from a person's story, through language, to community, to the coordination of communities that builds movements for social change. It begins with coming to voice about harm with a compassionate listener, inspecting our language of story to choose how we wish to frame it, and sharing our experience more widely. We work to connect with those who are closest to the problem as they are often best positioned to formulate solutions. We ask, what responses to harm are sufficient to prevent it from becoming trauma? How do we move from the healing process to building communities of care and action to prevent future harm and move us toward change? Movements begin with the telling of these untold stories.[3] This is the transformational change that heals self and society simultaneously.

The Experience of Harm

We all experience harm—whether it's assault, a health diagnosis, eviction, the loss of a loved one, microaggressions, or other adverse experiences. After a harmful experience, we wonder, "How can I get safe? Who can I tell about it? Is anyone going to do something about it?! How can I keep this from happening again?" When the social response to harm is sufficient, we can heal and recover and move on. When the social response to harm is insufficient, a part of us remains stuck at that place, which can manifest in the physical symptoms and psychosocial behaviors we now recognize as trauma responses.[4] An *insufficient* response to harm may look like: being ignored or silenced, blamed, shamed, punished, minimized, gaslit, or having someone take action without our consent. Marc Bregman has an extremely succinct formulation of trauma: "No help came."[5] Trauma is the experience of harm *plus* the insufficient response to it. The insufficient response results in it being ever-present, and we become vigilant and highly reactive to guard against it happening again.

A *sufficient* response to harm involves: having access to a safe space; witnesses hearing and accepting you; space in which to grieve; seeing harm redressed and justice done; regaining personal and collective agency; taking action toward preventing the harm happening again. When the social response to harm is sufficient, we experience healing. Although we can remember it, the experience of harm is not ever-present. This is harm being healed, the experience of hurt that does not metastasize into trauma. Drawing this distinction between harm and trauma helps us link a seemingly private experience of harm to others' experiences, the systems that perpetuate it, and actions to prevent it.

We encourage you to start this practice for healing and change where you have a stake and expertise: with your own experiences. Often, the body is where we experience the contradictions in systems—as distress and disease. The world produces enough food for everyone, yet so many are hungry. Many women hold office, own property, and pursue careers, but more than a third of us will experience sexual violence, and navigate the effects for the rest of our lives. We have won limited access to health care but little access to healing. Our bodies therefore manifest, in our flesh, the contradictions in the systems we move through every day.

Coming to Voice

The social response to harm can be so insufficient that we struggle to acknowledge even to ourselves what we are experiencing. Threats of being hurt or shunned for speaking up are very powerful forces. In an understandable effort to belong in a social environment even though it is hostile to us, we internalize its silencing, gaslighting dismissals. Coming to voice requires at least one compassionate listener. Because listening appears passive, its importance has been too often dismissed. We must deliberately make and hold space for this activity. Too often, we think of responding as fixing or finding a solution. It is harder to bear witness and sit with the complexities of problems together. Acknowledgment of experience—whether our own or another's—needs time to sink in and achieve its potential to allow connection with, and transformation of, the traumatized, stuck part.[6]

When we are unable to find the listener we need, it can be helpful to become that listener for someone else. In his short essay "Listening and Unentitled," Mark Enslin proposes that the starting point for listening is "an awareness of need" and "attention to what is not heard. Suppressed, hidden, distant, ignored, and missing voices, sounds, events, and connections are produced by listening. Listener as producer. There's no non-active listening."[7] The essay ends with the assertion, "Listening isn't for understanding, it's for transformation."[8] The kinds of listening needed for transformation can vary widely. Kinds of listening may include: compassionate silence, echo verbatim, reflect back a summary, ask for clarification, point to the language, listen for what is missing. We can listen to the emotional content. We could listen for the need under anger or sadness. Different degrees of vulnerability require different modes of listening by which we calibrate our responses. We can learn a variety of modes of listening. We can create the context in which it becomes possible for all of us to be heard.

In my work at the public assistance office of Cunningham Township, I, Danielle, observed the need for listening and have been designing a public response. I learned from residents experiencing housing and food insecurity about the dearth of listeners available to those pushed into society's margins. They demonstrated a need for a compassionate listener to hold safe space for them to come to voice. Now, Township staff start their work with each person by developing awareness of need and then connecting them to available offers: for housing, food, transportation, health care, and community events. Many residents have reported that Township staff were the first people ever to listen to their experiences of trauma. This practice has entailed generating new offers, and new programs, to fulfill unmet needs.

In addition to meeting direct material needs, Township has developed community-building and healing events. Trauma expert Meadow Jones brings her trauma-responsive curriculum to creative workshops for Township residents who have experienced violence, homelessness, or disability. Her workshops provide intimate, supported space to pursue healing through writing and sharing. In an interview, Meadow discussed how art practices redress trauma:

> Much of our ideas of how to heal from a trauma have to do with the ability to name it, to tell it into a story. However, trauma itself is disruptive of memory, identity, language, and temporality. Trauma precludes public participation, it erases access to witness and testimony. To engage in art practices is to put feeling and affect into the public discourse. The making of the object may serve as a proxy for speech, speaking when the individual cannot (or is not allowed to), or can only respond in disrupted, nonsequential narratives of experiences.[9]

In Meadow's teaching, she uses artmaking to help reintegrate experiences that feel un-integratable. Art externalizes the fragmenting effects of trauma. She has argued that where language fails, making art steps up. Visual art, music, and dance may say what cannot be said. Poetry and drama have license to break the usual rules that may impede our speaking. These creative approaches also give us permission to try out new ways of listening and responding. When we become compassionate listeners to each other's art, we offer the artist the experience of empathy and connection that begins to constitute a sufficient response to harm. Art can be a medium to bring that which feels shameful or hidden into the light, externalizing it. Our listening to one another, attending to how language is shaping our reality, points us toward generating the language that leads to healing.

Language Shapes Reality

Language is the medium through which we come to voice about the harm we have experienced or witnessed. When someone is harmed, the effects ripple through our community in language. It is the story that hits us, triggers our rage, fears, and tears, and tangles our understanding of the world. Language is how we integrate the not-yet-understandable into what we know. That is why there is such an urge to speak and be heard in these moments, and why stories are a primary contested space of control and denial or liberation and change.

Given that much of coming to voice and the social response to it takes place in language, what language we use matters at many different stages in the process. Many of the assignments in this book come from the teachings of Marianne (Manni) and Herbert Brün and the School for Designing a Society, which emphasize formulation and reformulation of language to explore our choices and desires. It is from Manni and Herbert Brün that we learned three linked dynamics of language.

First, the language available to us carries many unconscious assumptions we would consciously reject. In her essay "Paradigms: The Inertia of Language," Manni Brün warns, "If I fail to notice that I think and speak, under the influence of language, in patterns and constructs accumulated and preserved in the junkyards of long since vanished paradigms, then this shows my lack of consciousness with regard to just that power with which language can quickly make me spokesman for ideologies, in which everybody is almost always 'right' at the 'wrong' time."[10] That is, language is never neutral—it is a reflection of the ideologies and power structures that shape our communications. We should be conscious of how the language we choose supports or resists the invisible consensus embedded in it.

Second, Herbert Brün warns, "The language which you don't speak / will speak you."[11] *The language which you don't speak* is language you speak unconsciously, without a critical ear to its hidden implications. To say that language is "speaking us" is to say that our thoughts are constrained by the language available to us. We may think we choose our language, but when we pause with a critical eye toward what language is available to us, we notice that much of what we say is inherited, and we may not want to reproduce the social reality that it reflects.

Third, in the social world "things are what is said about them," exhorts Herbert Brün, linking communication to social reality.[12] Language is like a camera in this way: what is in the photo appears hard to argue with, but who or what is just outside the frame? If we know that what is going on outside the frame is important, we had better speak up—or widen the frame to show what is missing. When we acquiesce in silence and move on, what was said gets cemented in social reality. In contrast, the act of "going to where the silences are,"[13] as Amy Goodman of *DemocracyNow!* suggests, widens the frame of reality, incorporating more voices. How can we expand our sense of who and what is included in the frame of our concern?

What we say creates temporary social realities, so it is worth our while to be intentional about what reality we want to create. We have noticed that this attention to language has sometimes caused students to feel indecision and anxiety about striving for perfection in a competitive society. We invite you to "play attention to language,"[14] and to have fun experimenting. Let us move away from appraisals of "good" or "bad" language to be curious about what difference a particular choice of language makes.

The Hijacking of Stories

In the tender, tenuous experience of first coming to voice after harm, our stories are vulnerable to hijack. Our vulnerability is easily exploitable by systems of domination and their representatives, who try to increase their influence by linking our story to theirs. When we're down, they offer us a hand in the form of a story that seems to make sense in its conventional structure of blame. In the absence of other hands, we don't pause to notice that this hand may be attached to the armed forces, an isolating religious organization, an abusive partner, or a conspiracy group. We are understandably desperate to make sense of what happened to us. Taking time to reflect on and reject certain stories and choose others can make the difference between eliciting an insufficient social response and a sufficient one—that is, between trauma and healing.

Our stories can also be hijacked by the language of self-blame, victim-blaming, or bigotry. *Self-blame* is the story we tell ourselves in an understandable but hopeless attempt to assert control over harm we cannot control, especially when there is inadequate social response to that harm. When we have no control, we turn our victimization into shame which can become an identity. In the self-blame story, "something bad happened to me" becomes "I did something bad" becomes "I am bad." Like self-blame, a *victim-blaming* story deflects accountability for the harm away from our collective responsibility for each other's well-being and redirects it back onto a single person. This short-circuits the social response and increases the likelihood of trauma. In the story of victim-blaming, "something bad happened to them" becomes "they did something bad" becomes "they are bad and that's why bad things happen to them." When the victim-blaming story is about a whole identity group, it becomes *bigotry*. As we covered in chapter 1's discussion about logics of superiority, the very few who benefit from these logics must convince us all that some of us are expendable. Bigotry is the story used by those who benefit from logics of superiority to deflect responsibility for the harm they cause onto their victims. Self-blame, victim-blaming, and bigotry are chronic story patterns that "justify" harm and prevent social response, proliferating trauma.

Cultural Hegemony

When the hijack of a story gets repeated over and over it becomes cultural hegemony. The reality we live in—the ideas, feelings, and culture—reflects and replicates current power structures. Antonio Gramsci theorized cultural hegemony to explain how a ruling group maintains dominance by shaping culture and defining what is considered normal and possible. Hegemony is the way our desires and imagination are channeled and constrained to preserve existing systems. Whenever we are not conscious of what the language describing a problem is *doing*, we are vulnerable to hijack.

Refusing to let our language be controlled—and choosing it instead—is one liberatory solution for the problem of the logics of superiority, cultural biases and hegemony that are foundational to capitalism and the technologies built in its image. For one instructive example, we offer Mark Enslin's "Black History Minute" (1986), a composition for voice and bass guitar riffing on a formulation provided in Carter G. Woodson's 1933 book, *The Mis-Education of the Negro*—"If you control a person's thinking, you don't have to worry about their actions"[15]—by adding the following lines in a potentially endless loop:

> If you control a person's language, you don't have to worry about their thinking.
>
> If you control a person's income you don't have to worry about their language.
>
> If you control a person's actions, you don't have to worry about their income.
>
> If you control a person's thinking, you don't have to worry about their actions . . .[16]

Woodson was a Black history professor whose work looked critically at the language used to describe and miseducate Black people and which reinforced stereotypes, ignored Black history and contributions, and undermined the self-esteem of Black people. As Mark underscores with his composition: ignoring the stories and experiences of a group of people asserts that they don't matter, creating a feedback loop in which it becomes easier and easier to ignore their experiences.

Choosing Language

Against the dangers of hijack, a person coming to voice must also weigh the dangers of staying silent. In her essay "The Transformation of Silence into Language and Action,"[17] Audre Lorde acknowledges the dangers of coming to voice even as she insists on its necessity:

> I have come to believe over and over again that what is most important to me must be spoken, made verbal and shared, even at the risk of having it bruised or misunderstood. That the speaking profits me, beyond any other effect.... And of course, I am afraid, because the transformation of silence into language and action is an act of self-revelation, and that always seems fraught with danger. But my daughter, when I told her of our topic and my difficulty with it, said, "Tell them about how you're never really a whole person if you remain silent, because there's always that one little piece inside you that wants to be spoken out, and if you keep ignoring it, it gets madder and madder and hotter and hotter, and if you don't speak it out one day it will just up and punch you in the mouth from the inside."

Lorde's conversation with her daughter shows her doing the very thing she reports difficulty with—externalizing the struggle—even as her daughter narrates the dangers of not externalizing it.

In this chapter's section on "Coming to Voice," we learned from Meadow Jones how artmaking can enable expression of what trauma makes "ineffable." Artmaking involves choosing, evaluating, and choosing again: crucial acts of self-interpretation that restore agency and voice to us after experiences of paralysis and silencing. Creative expression, with its license to break rules, eases the process of coming to voice, helping us externalize an experience. bell hooks describes the process thus: "Speaking becomes both a way to engage in active self-transformation and a rite of passage where one moves from being object to being subject. Only as subjects can we speak. As objects, we remain voiceless—our beings defined and interpreted by others."[18]

The healing process of coming to voice, with its "stages of increasing awareness,"[19] can enable us to sense more accurately how it feels or would feel to share our story more widely. In artmaking, we choose what we keep, what we show others, and whether we make more, and expand its variety of ideas. This process allows us to experiment and create—precisely the cognitive capacities that experiences of harm and trauma temporarily shut down.[20] These practices of subjectivity are essential to participation. Writing in the early 1980s from different experiences of racism, the Brüns at SDaS and Audre Lorde in her writings converge in their thinking about the need to choose language. In the process of choosing, a person begins to see what difference their choices make. They see that their choices can have consequences, thus establishing a basic premise of liberation: agency. The externalization of our experience and reestablishment of our agency gradually open up the critical distance that allows us to share our stories more widely.

Power of the Respondent

Our responses to one another have tremendous power in determining the significance of what we can say and do next. This is the "power of the respondent," a phrase coined by Herbert Brün and further theorized by Mark Enslin:

> The respondent to a statement, coming after the statement, determines how the statement is spoken about, determines in which context the statement is placed, and thus what it meant. . . . The respondent has the power to determine how the respondent's listeners label, describe, conceive, remember, judge—the responded-to.[21]

We have learned through the teachings and projects of SDaS: it is critically important to understand language as contested terrain and realize the power we hold as a respondent. Responding to one another is an action that has consequences, so we need to know what we want while also observing the dynamics of conversation. This includes the art of listening for what is missing. Then we can act as respondents—on purpose—in the face of contested social reality. We can make the language carry our intentions. Mark warns, "The power of the respondent is frequently amalgamated with other sources of power: the power of position, the power of authority, the power in numbers, the power of technical reproducibility."[22] With awareness of this problematic tendency, we can use our response to try to reveal these sources of power and redistribute it.

Larry Richards, an invited guest at SDaS since 1992, theorizes conversation through a cybernetic lens. He describes this awareness of power as "a skill of the performer, and therefore of the activist as performer. Skilled performers experience their surroundings in the moment and make instantaneous adjustments, without time delay. The type of thinking that goes into making these adjustments is not one of means-ends rationality; it has to be a different way of thinking that does not require connecting causes to effects."[23] When we practice this dual consciousness of observing group dynamics while holding our intentions for collective healing, we are practicing critical modes of being. This is social care. Awareness and adjustment in our performance of everyday life are what we need to develop a wide variety of modes of listening and response to one another's stories of harm. In this way, we move from coming to voice into conversation, shared analysis, and movement building.

Lois Arkin was an invited speaker at an early SDaS session, where she told a story of the fear and suspicion that followed the Los Angeles Uprising in response to the police beating of Rodney King. Arkin rarely saw neighbors outside and people had stopped speaking to one another. She considered how to rebuild trust among her neighbors, designing an intervention she called "positive gossip" to try to address this problem. She started with the smallest possible action: every time she saw a neighbor, she would wave and say hello. Soon, small conversations began to feel possible again, in which she would add a piece of positive gossip about another neighbor, like: "Did you know so-and-so is . . . really good at chess? . . . makes an incredible jambalaya? . . . has a kid who knows all about cars? . . . helped with my groceries the other day?" She observed that her comments produced positive feelings and over time had a ripple effect among neighbors, making it easier for them to strike up conversations with each other and drawing them back outside to gather. Through observing, holding intention, and using her everyday performance, she exercised her power as a respondent and she helped her neighborhood heal. This experiment was instrumental to her design as co-founder of the Los Angeles Eco-Village in 1993.[24]

Coming to Voice in Community

As a facilitator of mixed groups where participants are often negotiating the complexities of speaking, listening and responding, I, Elizabeth, am always learning about the contingencies that attend these acts of coming to voice in community. The story I share with you here is to help us think through the layers of responses—both immediate and long term—that a community holds.

In April 2005, Danielle wrote a poem for radical feminist writer Andrea Dworkin, a few days after her death. She wrote it while caring for a friend's child, who was napping next to her, comparing their peace with the horror of reading about Dworkin's story of being drugged and raped in a Paris hotel in 1999. This violent act was in retaliation for her feminist work, and contributed to her illness and early death. When asked how she would like to be remembered, Dworkin said, "In a museum, when male supremacy is dead. I'd like my work to be an anthropological artifact from an extinct, primitive society."[25]

When SDaS convened later that spring, Danielle wanted to share the poem with the group but felt too unsettled to read it, so she asked me to do it. The poem I read follows:

Those Who Have Not Been Raped

Those who have not been raped
have a way of sleeping.

Those who have not been raped
float deep inside themselves,
scaling their dreams like athletes,
their heads thrown back, mouths open,
arms flung away from their sides.

(I saw a little boy sleep this way
despite the music of pots and pans.
He slept under the window,
palms up and eyes fluttering,
dreaming of vegan monorails.)

There is a trust on the surface of their skin—
a light dust that can rub off
on another in bed.

My love encircles me—
her body a rib cage,
and I, the frightened,
fluttering heart.

She purrs with sleep.
I am inside her, holding my breath
so the sounds of my own body
do not mask the scratching
of the monster's toenail on the door.

Those who have not been raped—
that tiny self-confident group
who walk like robins,
chest thrown out
down the street,

who sleep anywhere,
any time,
inside,
outside,
under the stars,
among the wolves.

They are golden, blessed children.

And I love them,
those who have not been raped.

This story shows by example how the medium of poetry allows for coming at the experience of harm sideways, obliquely—with the survivor celebrating the person untouched by violence as a way to point to the violence. It shows how poetry can become a collaboration between writer, reader, and listeners. Danielle's asking me to read it aloud to the gathered participants made me simultaneously a performer, a compassionate listener, and a respondent to both her and myself. Reading it aloud to an audience put me in her shoes in a very direct way, and the way the poem points to those who have not been raped made me look at myself through her eyes, creating a magical kind of empathy with her as a subject rather than as an object.

Danielle's poem with the temporary community of participants at SDaS had consequences at different scales over time. Her asking me to read it—and my agreeing to read it—created an experience of trust between us right at the beginning of knowing each other, which would incubate over twelve years, becoming the foundation for our writing this book together.

In the immediate atmosphere of reading the poem at the SDaS session, our shared response created a temporary space of safety, where coming to voice became more possible for more people. After we shared this poem, multiple participants quietly, privately confided their experiences of sexual violence to Danielle, an experience that repeated itself in session after session as she found ways to read her own poetry. That the topic of sexual violence remained in hidden corners of a school dedicated to designing societies in the face of violence revealed the inadequacy of our collective response. Audre Lorde echoes our experience of this process:

> But for every real word spoken, for every attempt I had ever made to speak those truths for which I am still seeking, I had made contact with other women while we examined the words to fit a world in which we all believed, bridging our differences. And it was the concern and caring of all those women which gave me strength and enabled me to scrutinize the essentials of my living.[26]

When I say that our collective response to Danielle and each other was insufficient, I mean that while speaking the unspeakable became more possible, there was still a dearth of trusted listeners. The temporary nature of the community made it possible to share and also made it impossible to heal together over time. Yet, this event had far-reaching consequences that became clearer later on. Danielle's experience of assaults and coming to voice, and of those who confided in her, eventually led directly to her decision to run for Township Supervisor and build safe housing for women, children, and LGBTQ+ residents more than a decade later. (See chapter 15, "Ending Homelessness.")

I have described the social response here as insufficient, yet it was an improvement on some earlier responses to people coming to voice at SDaS in its early years. It is a seeming contradiction that Herbert Brün never spoke at SDaS about his family's murder during the Holocaust, even as he dedicated his life to nonviolent resistance to fascism through experiments in music, language, algorithms, and teaching. Furthermore, when SDaS participants would come to voice about an experience of harm, exposing their vulnerability, Brün responded with cutting critiques of their language and choices, in what appears to us to have been a trauma response. Predictably, this sharp reaction usually had a painful silencing effect on the person detailing their experience and the group. For a person whose conceptual and artistic work conveyed immense sensitivity to language and timing, and who coined the term "power of the respondent," this insensitivity to the timing of critique may be hypocritical, or ironic, but is also perhaps attributable to the insufficiency of his own community's response to the genocide he barely survived. His response, and the tone it set for the group, repeatedly shut down conversations about experiences of harm that students wanted—even needed— to have to be able to participate in either experimental education or artistic collaboration.

Conversation Builds Community

The contradiction inherent in coming to voice is that telling our story empowers us while making us feel more vulnerable to attack. A story can also trigger the defense mechanism of listeners to attack or suppress in others what they fear in themselves. We can feel safe coming to voice when we have people around us who we trust to listen, validate, and protect. We need safe spaces to heal, de-escalate our nervous systems, and be able to work effectively, in community, to strategize and act to interrupt future harm. Conversation is the hinge between coming to voice about harm and making an analysis of it. It is the first level of participation needed to build community. The person who has experienced harm requires a sense of belonging and acceptance that only communities can provide. We need people to know both what has happened to us, and that we are much more than what has happened to us. Additionally, to avoid trauma, we need to situate what has happened to us in the context of what has happened to others, to know about each other—both what we share and what is particular to each. We need a social space in which we can share what is most important to us. To prevent future harm, we need each other's help in organizing against it.

We introduce a cybernetic theorist of conversation, Larry Richards, and a sociologist, C. Wright Mills, to examine the dynamics and importance of this move from the personal domain of coming to voice in community toward the social domain of analysis and movement building to prevent harm. Richards' formulation of conversation is a dynamic in language among people between whom there is difference, but who nevertheless want to keep talking, moving from "asynchronicity toward synchronicity," where asynchronicity refers to "a conflict, disagreement, tension, friction, being on difference planes, being out of sync."[27] If it is too close to the vulnerability of coming to voice, we may be unprepared for too much asynchronicity and need more healing first, but eventually we need to talk to each other through our different perspectives on a problem in order to sharpen our analysis of it. Doing so builds trust in the other and our own sense of agency.

C. Wright Mills describes the "sociological imagination" as the ability to grasp the connection between individual experiences and the larger social structures and historical forces that shape them. It involves recognizing that personal troubles are often linked to public issues and that individuals are not isolated actors, but are influenced by and can influence society. Mills advocated for the importance of gathering with others to develop a shared analysis of one's experience in history: "the individual can understand his own experience and gauge his own fate only by locating himself within his period . . . he can know his own chances in life only by becoming aware of those of all individuals in his circumstances."[28] Community is the pivot point to the rest of the book's discussion about how to convene groups and create projects and spaces for listening and responding to previously untold stories to build movements and to power social change. Individuals need community in order to heal; society needs community to prevent harm from happening.

Building Movements

Community is an emergent property of conversation, and movements are an emergent property of community. Movements begin with story and conversation. The contradiction we face is: *The culture that stymies participation is only changed through participation.* How do we navigate this contradiction and find within it the points of leverage for increasing participation? The kind of large-scale social change we need—where those affected participate in the decisions that shape their lives—is practiced in community, through the collaboration of individuals. This practice of cooperative participation with others is the hard, joyful work that creates the trust, the groups, the movements, and the social shifts we need in order to make greater democracy.

As Dr. Martin Luther King, Jr. put forth, "beloved community" is both an ideal and an achievable vision for global society, where all people share the "wealth of the earth" in a space of social equity, belonging, peace, and freedom from prejudice.[29] In beloved community, we commit to compassion and caring as a means *and* an end, in what King calls "an engine of reconciliation."

In beloved community, we recognize that "we are caught in an inescapable network of mutuality, tied in a single garment of destiny," and that "injustice anywhere is a threat to justice everywhere."[30] We take on the "giant triplets of poverty, racism, and militarism" and work toward the social elimination of poverty, hunger, bigotry, and violence. We are beloved community, who take up the words "dignity, respect, compassion, caring and loving," per David Harvey, "as revolutionary slogans" against alienation.[31] As we move around the Spiral of Change, beloved community is a prerequisite for successful movement building, a standard by which we measure our success and redesign to do better, and the vanishing horizon we long for and strive toward.

In her experience organizing with many local communities, Ella Baker decentralized social change efforts from the 1930s through the 1970s, making them more accessible and human-scaled. She envisioned networks of many beloved communities, where people gather to experience and create the world they want to live in, and where *all* members labor and lead toward collective self-determination in their communities. In counterpoint to the image of the civil rights movement as led by King and (mostly male) church leaders, Baker advocated for "group-centered leadership" where a central role of leaders is to develop the leadership of others. Grace Lee Boggs picked this idea up in *The Next American Revolution* where she argued, borrowing from Margaret Wheatley, that "critical connections" are more essential to movements than "critical mass."[32]

Trusting relationships are the backbone of collaboration. When we don't have trust, even the best proposals and intentions can get mired in suspicion and fear. When we do have trust, we can move together like a flock of birds, each one adjusting to the others' movements to maximize how far we can fly together. Trust provides the basis to be creative, take risks, work through conflict, and resist provocateurs and sabotage. Trust allows love in. In her own work designing and sharing strategies for world changing and worldbuilding, adrienne maree brown calls for us to "move at the speed of trust."[33]

We start with our roots, where we have a stake. Learning together, we can ground ourselves in history as context, as we develop a shared vision and analysis and move from a place of purpose. Continuously showing up for each other means even more when we have built trust in this way about what matters to us. Malkia Devich-Cyril teaches that relationship-based organizing involves sharing our stories and vulnerabilities that help build self-awareness and forge authentic, trusted relationships through which we can organize together. This trust is the home base from which we can take action to shift culture, policy, and institutions toward more equitable outcomes for all.[34] From the basis of trusted relationships, we can commit to working together for change over the long haul.

Sharing stories of our experiences transforms our conceptions of the world and our place in it, so that we can come together to transform the world. As Danielle recounts in chapter 21, at weekly meetings of Champaign-Urbana Citizens for Peace and Justice (CUCPJ), members would ask those impacted by the racist criminal justice system: "Are you ready to organize with us, so that what is happening to you stops and doesn't happen to others?" Through sharing our vulnerabilities, we find our collective strength. The pain of the "I" becomes the relief of the "we." The shameful silence of one is transformed into the liberatory chorus of #MeToo. Movements begin with the telling of untold stories. Sharing our stories brings us together, builds connections, and begins ongoing conversations that can grow into projects, organizations, and movements. This is how we move from harm to healing to building beloved communities together.

CHAPTER 5

ASSIGNMENT

Build Beloved Communities

In our conception of the Spiral of Change, gathering stories and people is a prerequisite for successful movement building. For historical inspiration, we look to organizer Ella Baker, who envisioned networks of *many* beloved communities—where people gather to create the world they want to live in. Her vision of beloved communities braids together personal and social transformation, where individuals "rethink and redefine their most intimate personal relations and their identities" which are "key building blocks for a new, more humane social order and for a successful revolutionary movement."[1] The eight assignments selected for this chapter are to help you learn about yourselves and other members of your group; to encourage your playfulness and creativity; and to develop your awareness of language and capacities for active listening, addressing logics of superiority, treating social wounds, and building beloved community.

Begin by Connecting

This assignment addresses the problem of logics of superiority—e.g., imperialism, racism, patriarchy, ableism, and classism—and their long histories of violence and displacement. It asks us to consider ancestors, but also families of choice and communities of identity. This assignment is inspired by Makani Themba and the Praxis Project, which hosts annual "Roots & Remedies" convenings to create a healing space of connection for organizers and activists working within marginalized communities.[2] We recommend doing this assignment in pairs, in which participants take turns asking the questions and actively listening to the responses.

Roots
Where do you come from? Who are your people?

Rough spots
What are the primary problems or challenges you and your people face in the world?

Routes
Share a story from your life that represents a turning point toward wanting to organize for a better world.

Remedies
What is one change you want to make in the world?

Art Lubes

Art Lubes are quick, fun, and low-stakes assignments intended to help overcome the anxiety of making things in a world that expects perfection. Art Lubes warm you up for creating with others in a participatory space. Select one or two to start with and share your responses. Feel free to make up your own.

Made-up language
In pairs, one person tells and performs a story in a made-up language while the second translates the story into English, repeating the gestures.

Commemorative plaque
Go touch something in the room. What you are touching is now a memorial. Write a plaque to commemorate it.

Doesn't fit
Write a scene of an event where you were a participant or bystander. Now, insert lines that don't fit the scene.

Composition for hands

Introduce yourself with a five-second composition for hands, without words. Then, make a two-second version of the five-second version.

Odd-one-out

Make up a rule that four characters could follow. Take someone's rule and make up a scene for four characters in which three of them obey the rule and one does not. Make another version in which one character obeys the rule and the rest do not.[3]

Interrogative Design

Krzysztof Wodiczko makes art interventions to disrupt the public spaces of everyday life. His "Interrogative Design" practice includes large-scale video projections in public spaces and objects addressing trauma, memory, and communication. In an interview about his practice, he identifies the bandage as a defining metaphor for Interrogative Design, as it both treats and exposes social wounds. Wodiczko shares: "What if that bandage could also be capable of transmitting some truth of the conditions under which the wound occurs, of testifying to the wrong and unacceptable situations and conditions behind this wound? . . . It's amazing how much people could learn if they could see the world from the point of view of the wound."[4]

Invented bandages

Sketch an invented bandage that treats a social wound at the same time as highlights its presence. Discuss the following questions in pairs or as a small group: What do you see? What title would you give this piece? If the wound could speak, what would it say? What could be added to the design that would point to conditions needed to prevent the wound?

Language Shapes Reality

Susan Parenti's "acoustic portraits" are compositions to explore the character of "ordinary" sentences heavy with social and political implications. For example, her piece *No, Honey, I Can Do It!* presents a portrait of the contradictions faced by a female composer caught between caregiving and making art. Susan taught a class with Danielle at the School for Designing a Society (SDaS) based around the desire statement: *Art is a consulted medium in helping to resolve stuck social problems.* The class announcement asks students: "What are the mechanisms through which we can address each other with our proposals, ideas, and concerns? How can we speak in an age of being spoken for, without repeating news media, church sermons, or gossip? By the end of the semester, could you present an acoustic portrait (of 5–15 minutes in length) in a specified context that could trigger a change of mind?"

Haunting sentences
Consider a sentence or phrase that haunts you. Try out ways of expressing it that expose its intent, provide a critical interpretation, or highlight a contradiction.

Playing attention to language
With your problem formulation from the Spiral Playsheet in chapter 2 (or with a new problem), try performing the problem using different types of language. If alone, you can try making objects into puppets that represent characters. If working with a group, assign each person a type of language and improvise for 5–10 minutes, then discuss what you observed. You can select from the following list of examples or formulate some of your own.

> **Emotional:** "I"; uses specific examples, personal appeals, manipulation.
>
> **Evangelical:** Entertaining; uses superlatives, threats, vibrato; treats everyone like children.
>
> **Journalistic:** Objectivity; focuses on violence or sensation; shallow interpretations.
>
> **Rockstar:** Grandstanding from onstage; uses profanity; stilted.
>
> **Sales:** Uses directives, adjectives, comparison; refers to product; courteous; testimonials; jingles.
>
> **Scientific:** Uses statistics; refers to experts; categories; impersonal.

Designing Healing Responses

Trauma results from insufficient responses to harm. Consider a time when you experienced or were witness to a social harm. In discussion or writing, reflect on how these different responses affect harm.

Sufficient response
Describe a time when you shared your story of harm and the way it was responded to made you feel *more* empowered to speak and act to change it.

Insufficient response
Describe a time you shared your story of harm and the way it was responded to made you feel *less* empowered to speak and act to change it.

Internal monologue

When something difficult happens to you, what are some of the sentences you hear internally?

Positive gossip

Try out making positive gossip about someone in the group, school, or neighborhood. Discuss the effects of your experiment.

Art of listening

Describe a time someone shared a story of harm with you. What approach did you choose for listening? What effect did your listening seem to have on the storyteller?

Healing conditions

What were the conditions needed for a healing response to the harm?

Stories of Kindness

Just as sharing stories of harm helps us better understand problems, stories of kindness can help us better understand interventions. In considering what structures create kindness, we begin to design sufficient responses to harm. This assignment was presented by Mark Enslin at the summer 2025 session of SDaS. The assignment is best done in pairs, coming together afterwards to share and reflect as a group.

Unexpected kindness

Share a story of when you experienced unexpected kindness.

Structures of kindness

Share a story of your experience with a structure of kindness.

Archiving the Trauma Diaspora

This assignment is inspired by Meadow Jones' writing workshops, and her forthcoming book on healing trauma through writing, entitled *Archiving the Trauma Diaspora*.[5] At the beginning of her workshops she tells participants: "We are all writers and artists. Everything that makes it to the page is valid. Listening is a moral act. Response is affection. Consent matters." She asks participants to pledge confidentiality, and we suggest developing a similar practice for working in groups as consent and confidentiality are crucial.

Five things

"Five things" comes from a long tradition of researchers including artists and scientists, inviting observation first.[6] Take five minutes to write about five things you experienced today. Consider sight, taste, smells, feelings, thoughts. "Five things" is a foraging practice—we invite you to go into the world and collect experiences to share with others.

Those who have not

Read Danielle's poem, "Those Who Have Not Been Raped," in chapter 4. Then, write about a difficult experience through its negative. For example, you may start with the phrase "Those who have not . . ."

Traits of Beloved Community

Drawing on Dr. Martin Luther King, Jr.'s principles of beloved community,[7] Dr. Arthuree Wright outlines "25 Traits of the Beloved Community," which she describes as an emergent property of relations based on participation and inclusion: "The human community meeting the basic needs of every person *becomes* beloved [our emphasis]." Here, we offer six of Wright's traits of the beloved community and then invite you to share yours: acknowledges conflict or pain in order to work on difficult issues; acts as an inclusive family rather than exclusive club; builds increasing levels of trust and works to avoid fear of difference and others; offers radical hospitality to everyone; provides recognition and affirmation, not eradication, of differences; tolerates ambiguity—realizes that sometimes a clear-cut answer is not readily available.[8]

Becoming beloved community

Write and then discuss in a group, what are some conditions for your desired beloved community that would meet physical, emotional, and spiritual needs. Start by filling in this sentence: My beloved community offers _____.

CHAPTER 6

STORY

As Violence Was
Done to Me

Zora Neale Hurston said: "There is no agony like bearing an untold story inside of you."[1] There is also no freedom quite like sharing it—moving it from inside to outside our bodies. Telling and retelling our stories helps us break through layers of silence to feel seen and heard. Ultimately, coming to voice and sharing stories is how we move our isolated experience into the social domain where we can work together to address it. It is how we begin to heal. It relieves something stuck when we unburden ourselves, naming things we had no name for before. It asserts our experiences in a way that has friction with dominant narratives, opening up spaces for us to act.

As Elizabeth related in her experience of reading my poem to the group assembled at the School for Designing a Society (SDaS) in late spring 2005, we build trust and connection through vulnerability. We heal by sharing stories in the context of healing responses. I am grateful to all of those who have listened well; I have learned to set boundaries with those who don't. What follows is my retelling of a personal story of harm. Note: the story in this section contains information about the sexual assault of a child and suicidal ideation.

I am six. The violence happens in my home, in my bed, while my parents are downstairs, on the day we had anticipated for months, whispering about what presents and treats might arrive on Christmas Day. On this day I learn death is the noose of a hand around my throat. I am made to do things I have no frame of reference for. I am sliced open, body and spirit, a poison seed planted inside my sense of self and safety. Afterwards: Christmas presents, church, singing, and pictures of me and my sister leaning uncomfortably away from our house guests, as they tugged us closer with their vicious arms. Then: fifteen years of silence, decades of panic attacks and mysterious illnesses, and a diagnosis of ovarian cancer in my forties.[2]

I am seven. Breaking free from the church nursery, I find the room my parents are in and slip inside. It is dark. Projected on the wall are children, naked and screaming, their skin ablaze. I see flesh melting off bodies, leaving skeletons. There is a flash in the sky just before every home in sight is flattened. Suddenly, there are bright lights in the room. I am discovered standing in the back of the church's meeting room, shaking, with tears pressing out between my eyelids. I learned: yes, those were real events. Yes, our country dropped the first atomic bomb on a city of innocents. Yes, hundreds of thousands of people, just like you and me, died instantly.[3]

This taught me: *as violence is done to me, so violence is done to others. We appear safe, but we are fundamentally not safe.* This is where my organizing story begins, as a child: seeing my experiences connected to others; noticing the contradictions between the story that is told and the one that is lived; making an early and lifelong commitment to interrupt violence and injustice.

The process of coming to voice about the experience of having guests in our home violate and nearly strangle to death my six-year-old body on Christmas Day in 1978 was both torturous and tortuous. It was both difficult and required a twisted path to healing. Wading through the process of coming to voice helped me see how acknowledgment of a harm is repressed—within me and within the society in which I live—and how art and expression can help us slog through the murky waters toward healing.

My body had immediate responses to the harm I experienced: intense fear of nighttime and the dark, sleepwalking, and nightmares. Emotionally, I tuned into others' needs and developed deep empathy. At eight years old, I committed myself to developing a fluency in braille and American Sign Language (ASL) so I could interpret books and speech to blind and deaf students in my school. I spent countless hours translating books into braille back-wards, punching each dot on a slate and stylus. I had no words for what had happened to me when I was six years old, and I found no space to form it into words. The world around me continued as though it had never happened. So I turned toward connecting others to the voice and light that I too needed—as though my life depended on it. A language was laid over my behavior and my coping mechanisms were praised: "She is a sensitive child, a gifted child." This helped me develop the confidence essential for growth, while also tying my sense of self tightly to external praise.

As a teen, I excelled in and loved school, played varsity soccer, wrote plays, and launched a social justice organization with friends. I also had a period where I was unable to eat solid food, choking on anything that touched my throat. I considered how I might kill myself, and submitted a suicide note in the place of my English paper, receiving a simple "F" in response. One of my childhood best friends (now trauma expert), Meadow Jones, handed me the book *The Courage to Heal*, offering me a frame for my experience that I rejected for years, even as college therapists probed: "Do you remember any incident of early childhood abuse?"

Before I had analytical language, I had an art practice. Making art became a way to move my experience of harm into reality—first onto a page where I could move it around and see what happens. If it had not been for my high school art classes and teacher, Luann Howard, I might not be here now. I drew the female body, soft and lovely and whole, exploring my longstand-ing attraction to girls and women. I instinctively gravitated to what healed me—skipping school, drawing on the beach, journaling, building deep con-nections with people who would become lifelong friends—while Ms. How-ard supported my confidence, overlooked my aberrations, and submitted my artwork for scholarships. Her efforts helped me pay for college.

"We access memories when we can survive them," Meadow offered, after my first experience with sharing my waking vision of specific acts, locations, and perpetrators at age twenty-three. I shared a summary of these visions with the three closest people in my life, and then, I "considered it done." I was well aware of the social problem of rape. I co-founded the Gender Studies Collective at New College and wrote research papers on the motivations of perpetrators—but was also highly invested in my own story that I would not allow violence to affect me: "I am not broken." My body spoke a different story: with panic attacks, nausea, and extreme abdominal pain.

In my twenties, I became known as a local leader, co-founding our Inde-pendent Media Center, getting elected to Urbana's City Council and spear-heading the city's public arts program, police oversight, and solar-powered affordable housing. At the same time, I developed a noticeable tic, where my voice began to crackle and my throat would close in moments of tension. To this day, people still hang up the phone on me, saying "our connection is bad, I can't understand you," and I have to navigate others' misperceptions that I am about to cry or am angry when I speak. Being in public office means you are exposed to whatever people want to say to you or at you. For example, once our mayor's temper tantrum during a council meeting switched my nervous system into "flight mode" and my body jolted out the door before my mind could make the decision to leave. The result was an unfortunate piece in the newspaper that assumed my flight was some kind of admittance of malfeasance. My political mentor unwittingly shut me up for another decade by saying about another powerful woman in town: "Yeah, she is crazy. She was sexually abused as a kid."

Poetry was the first place I could begin to express what happened to me. To speak it directly would provoke a panic attack. I first read my poems in intimate, trusted settings. My boyfriend at the time dismissed this as "sharing my diary," but for others, it drew them to disclose horrific stories in whispers: "me too." I supported a young woman as she relived the experience of her elementary school principal assaulting her in the bathroom. She was not in this world, but fully in that one, howling and fighting off her attacker. I rocked her and grieved for all of us.

When I finally came to voice about my experience, it was then I learned we are not just silent, but there is a silencing of stories that so radically "misfit" with a given reality. I was thirty years old before I shared my story directly. I believed once I had accomplished this difficult feat, it would finally be out in the open, like a fact sitting at the table. It would become something we could talk to and reason with. Instead, the reality of my rape is like a child who is gently, quietly pushed into the corner of the room with a tablecloth thrown over her head. I have to assert it, through stubborn disbelief and forgetting. It is the sign of the deepest of social contradictions, when there is a painful fact that cannot be spoken amongst loved ones.

I have formulated and reformulated the following problems: how would my experience have been different if sexual abuse prevention had been taught in my school or church? If I could have consulted a trauma-informed psychologist when I could not swallow solid food? If we had made space in our high school's social justice organization to share the stories that affected us personally, in addition to our advocacy for the "others" who we saw as less fortunate than us? If my mentors had been able to come out as survivors and I had witnessed the healing that can ensue?

We can come to voice and organize for the changes that would have supported us in healing from harm. In my case, I worked to reestablish sexual abuse prevention classes in our schools in 2018 as a parent and as board member of the Champaign-Urbana Public Health District. When I became

Supervisor of Cunningham Township, our team created transitional housing for homeless families where survivors have access to rape crisis counseling. And eventually, thanks to national figures like Roxane Gay and Tarana Burke, as well as local people like Champaign County board member Tanisha King Taylor, who gave brave testimony of her sexual abuse during our #MeToo rally in 2018, the frozen road before me was plowed by their efforts so I could speak more publicly.[4] We heal ourselves as we heal society. As we heal society, we heal ourselves.

II

Formulate Problems and Systems

CHAPTER 7

FORMULATION

Dig to Your Problem's Roots

Every year from middle school through college, I, Elizabeth, would be crowded into a cafeteria with my female class-mates for a workshop on rape prevention. The educators running these workshops had the best intentions. They were trying to empower us and keep us safe, not blame us, but the available language of our patriarchal society framed the problem in such a way as to erase root causes and place blame on victims. The language framed the problem thus: "One in four women is raped." Using the passive voice, the problem was framed as ours, something that just "happens" to us—with no mention whatsoever of the people doing the raping. The absurdity, futility, and injustice of this frame did not occur to me at the time. I wanted the autonomy of having this threat under my control, so I was eager to learn every rape prevention tip they proffered, year after year, as statistics stubbornly did not change: "Avoid dark alleys"; "Don't dress like you're asking for it"; "Never put your drink down"; "Always carry pepper spray."

Then in 2009, I read a social media post called "Sexual Assault Prevention Tips Guaranteed to Work!" which finally addressed would-be assailants directly:

> When you see someone walking by themselves, leave them alone!
>
> Remember, people go to the laundry room to do their laundry. Do not attempt to molest someone who is alone in a laundry room.
>
> USE THE BUDDY SYSTEM! If you are not able to stop yourself from assaulting people, ask a friend to stay with you while you are in public.
>
> Carry a whistle! If you are worried you might assault someone 'on accident' you can hand it to the person you are with, so they can blow it if you do.[1]

With this post, the author's satire of ubiquitous rape prevention strategies exposes the victim-blaming inherent in the language of the problem. As we see in this example, how we choose to formulate a problem frames our analysis of the problem and what we will do about it. If the formulation of a problem is not an object of consideration, and all the solutions to that problem, when implemented, seem to fail, then one is stuck with essentialism—"it's naturally that way"—or defeatism—"it will never change." Three decades later, after #MeToo centered survivors' stories, we have seen a shift in formulation of the problem from the victim's actions to how our culture produces and protects perpetrators. The formulation of "rape culture" points out how the spectrum of culturally acceptable norms of putting girls and women in their place supports and condones sexual assault.

FORMULATING PROBLEMS

Why Formulate?

Care in formulating the problem is an essential step between sharing stories about our problem and organizing together to address it. As we labor to move our different experiences into a shared description of the problem, we often reach for the available language about the problem, which is likely to lead us to solutions that have already been tried without success. Our brains supply the language the current society has come up with around this problem, which may sound "right" because it fits within the logic of a system that continues to reproduce it. To take on intractable problems requires that we formulate and reformulate them in *many* ways, since each formulation will point to a different set of solutions. Then we can evaluate and choose the one we want *before* we design actions.

In this chapter we show how to generate new language around a problem, connect a variety of formulations of the problem, and build coalitions to address them. We then teach the anatomy of systems, seeking to understand our problems as emergent properties of systems we can influence. Chapter 8 is an assignment chapter with tools you and your group can use to inspect, experiment, and play with problems and systems. Formulating is fun!

Formulating as Social Work

As Susan Parenti presented at SDaS in 2003: "I formulate when I take the time to compose a sentence where the way the thought is worded cannot be ignored. A formulated sentence takes a political stand both in thought and language. It is social *work*. Formulations are short, musical, and memorable."[2] It is social work to argue for formulations of problems that address their premises and point to desirable outcomes. It is social work to call out the language of a problem that points to desirable outcomes. It is social work to call out the language of a problem that points to false solutions—those that maintain the problem and the power of those who benefit from it. This moment of calling out language—not people—is a crucial, delicate distinction that deserves our attention. Susan also discusses the impact of formulation on attention:

> People will feel invited to remember the exact sentence. As notebooks and pens come flying out: "What did you say? Can you repeat that?" Formulations stand on their own. They don't require us to know the background of the speaker or necessarily the context. They resist propaganda and spin. Formulation increases the speaker's alternatives in speaking and writing.[3]

Using Susan's approach to formulating, we provide some analytical tools to help you formulate and evaluate problem statements as part of your project's social work.

Generate a Variety of Formulations

The formulation of a problem determines its set of solutions. The enduring problem of sexual harassment and assault calls for the critical evaluation of current problem-solution pairs, and the generation and evaluation of many alternative ones. Here we inspect a variety of problem-solution pairs regarding sexual assault. We present them not as an argument for one over the other, but to model this process so you can create yours.

> **Problem:** Boys will be boys—they have a natural, uncontrollable sexual energy.
>
> > **Implied solution 1:** Girls need to be separated from and protected from boys.
> >
> > **Implied solution 2:** Girls (and not boys) must be taught to enforce boundaries and always remain hypervigilant.

Problem: Sexual attraction is a game for men to win sex from women where resistance is sexy.

> **Implied solution 1:** Only "yes" means "yes." Everything else—"no," "maybe," "I don't know," or silence—means "no."

> **Implied solution 2:** Women need to learn to stop "playing games" and stop saying no when they mean yes.

Problem: Sexual abuse of children is too common.

> **Implied solution 1:** Adults should never hug or touch children.

> **Implied solution 2:** Children need to be taught about safe and unsafe touching at the earliest of ages and know who to talk to if they feel unsafe.

Notice how each of the problem statements looks at a different angle of the problem and may reflect certain assumptions. Notice how one formulation of the problem can imply many different, even conflicting, solutions. Do you prefer some solutions over others and if so, why? Here we provide some analytical tools to help you formulate and evaluate problem statements.

Distinguish a Problem from a State of Affairs

The most powerful tool for maintaining the status quo is the assertion that "there is no alternative." To which we retort: "Another world is possible. *Sí, se puede!*"[4] When a problem seems intractable, it needs reformulation. We call something a problem only when it is possible to change it and we want to change it. Otherwise, it is merely a "state of affairs"—perhaps regrettable, but unavoidable and unchangeable. For example, death is a state of affairs, but how we die is a problem that elicits our desires and designs.

When a person in power describes your problem as a state of affairs, it's time to insist on *your* formulation of the problem and show the variety of solutions (and hope) that results. When someone describes something as "not *my* problem," they are letting you know they don't want the problem to change and are dismissing it as a state of affairs. Problems are formulated as unsolvable by those who benefit from the perpetuation of the problem. Our antidote to persistent, unsolvable problems is to reformulate them in a way that invites collective design and action toward our desires.

Keep Digging to the Premises

Too often the actions we take address symptoms, and not root causes, because we accept the language of the problem uncritically. Addressing symptoms is like cutting down an invasive plant; it will just grow back from its root. We can spend our whole lives cleaning up the bramble of consequences instead of digging down to the taproot of premises that sprouts similar problems every season.

Merely responding to symptoms leads to burnout. For example, we return to Danielle's cancer. Doctors treat the cancer as the premise, and the treatment as the consequence. But Danielle knew many young women in her community with ovarian cancer, prompting her to see the cancer as a consequence and ask: "Who is the polluter? What are the policies that allow them to pollute? What are the relationships between public officials and the businesses who are polluting? Perhaps the last CEO who questioned the pollution found himself out of a job as shareholders demanded a return on investment?" While a woman is fighting ovarian cancer, her retirement fund may be growing because of the pollution that caused her cancer.

Find Joy in Formulation

Just as our ideas push the language, so does the language we invent push our ideas, widen our vision, and open opportunities. We can try describing a problem in a way that helps us find joy in designing solutions. Problems produce misery; working together to change them can be joyful. Certain formulations of a problem are like vampires, draining us of life and interest in working on them. I, Danielle, used to write campaign messaging filled with words like "fight" and "struggle," until one day I laid my head on the table in exhaustion from these words wrung dry by movement organizing. I pledged to shift from the activist frame of fight to the organizer frame of building. I worked to build leadership, voices, and participation, and watched how this changed my approach to organizing.

Artist Favianna Rodriguez speaks to this dynamic: "Oppressive systems and their resistance often live in the same culture; one creating the other. Just as capitalist industry is based on extraction, its opposition may mirror this, extracting the energies of organizers marched into the battle." She calls for a shift in organizing from an extractive approach to a generative one:

> We need to incorporate pleasure and joy into our movements. We can't always struggle. Oppression makes us feel we don't deserve joy and pleasure. . . . We need to create narratives around the world we wish to see.[5]

When we formulate a problem we can ask: "Does this formulation inspire us to work on the problem?" If not, try another formulation. We encourage you to cultivate curiosity in your problem by discussing the legitimate questions you bring to it. Generating legitimate questions, meaning those with no predetermined answers, fosters a generative process of knowledge creation and the co-invention of the future. We can get stuck in our certainty and repetition of the problem and find ourselves defending a miserable formulation of it. When this happens, it can help to stretch our formulation to the point of absurdity; make art with it; or have it point to an audacious utopian desire. Creating formulations that connect our problems to others helps us cure alienation and build community and coalitions.

Formulate Through Art

In chapter 4, we discussed how art can help us come to voice, regain agency, externalize what has happened to us, and build community and movements. At this more analytical stage of formulating problems, art and play can help us escape the neurological rut of crisis thinking. In crisis thinking, the stakes are always high and we fear making mistakes. Our brains try to help us by shutting down the distractions of creativity and play. But these are exactly the resources we need to imagine what is outside the frame of the crisis, to see the problem in its unlikely connections, and to imagine desirable solutions. In artmaking, we have license to try things out and see what happens.

Susan Parenti is our masterful teacher in this. When she has a problem, she writes a play about it. Her plays invite audience members into conversation about her legitimate questions about a thorny social problem in ways that are absurd, grotesque, and delightful—and make us laugh. For example, Susan wrote *Stop That!* to explore the problem of apathy in the face of catastrophic climate change and *Pester Power* to see how children might play a role. She staged *Unrequited* as a love story between capitalism and socialism to investigate their co-dependence. Her film *Looking for Care in All the Wrong Places* creates a counterpoint between the impersonal bureaucracy of "disease management systems" and the highly personal and vulnerable experience of seeking care for sick bodies. With each, Susan's composition of both the play and its performance context invite audience members to talk with her and each other about these problems. Then, the School for Designing a Society (SDaS) invites audience members to ongoing conversations where they can design their own responses to these and other problems they bring.

LOOKING SYSTEMS

The process of generating multiple formulations of a problem helps inspect root premises, understand underlying power dynamics, and create a set of interconnected descriptions of the problem. As we inspect these interconnections, we name the relationships between them and provide a framework to understand these problems within social systems. We then use these reformulations to build coalitions around the problem and make additional interventions, as we continue through the Spiral of Change.

When systems repeatedly produce a problem, it is time we recognize these systems are not broken; they are functioning normally and correctly, as they were designed to. These problems are *expected* outcomes of systems based on fundamentally undesirable premises. For example, as Elizabeth showed with the pervasive problem of sexual assault, the problem persists in part due to a formulation of it that excludes perpetrators altogether and keeps victims in their place.

We all find ourselves uncomfortably participating in correctly functioning but oppressive systems. We are faced with this painful contradiction: *Within the current system, I can only meet my needs by participating in the exploitation of myself and others. If I find a way to withdraw from the system, I leave the exploitative system intact.* By understanding oppression as the predictable outcome of fundamentally unjust systems, we can take care to design strategic interventions in systems toward a shift in premises. To do so, we must become students of systems and how they function. It is collective work to analyze the dynamics of systems that perpetuate oppression and to challenge their premises and outcomes.

Understand Systems with Cybernetics

Cybernetics provides a conceptual framework to explain the production and maintenance of complex social problems. A cybernetic system is any set of interconnected parts forming a complex whole in which a change in one element changes the whole. This framework suggests ways members can influence the dynamics of systems without centralized control. We use cybernetics to strategize how to generate increased participation for systems change. Through a cybernetic lens, we can understand the problems we face as emergent properties of dynamic systems that we can formulate, perturb and intervene in, and reimagine. adrienne maree brown details principles for emergent strategies to collectively and iteratively intervene in social systems: "I began to realize how important emergent strategy, strategy for building complex patterns and systems of change through relatively small interactions, is to me—the potential scale of transformation that could come from movements intentionally practicing this adaptive, relational way of being, on our own and with others."[6]

Your body is an analog to social systems, both in its complexity and networked processes of self-regulation. Your body is made of elements: skin, organs, muscle, nerves. The relationship between these elements is dynamic as your body constantly changes—its heart rate, digestion process, hormone secretion—to meet needs and address demands. It relies on feedback loops to do this. Too hot? Your body triggers sweat to cool you off. Eating ice cream? It stimulates your pancreas to release insulin which tells cells to absorb glucose and lower your blood sugar. Working in the face of constant changes, your body self-regulates to maintain a stable internal environment—to achieve homeostasis.

Consciousness, thought, and personality are emergent properties of your body. You can't point to any part of your body that contains or produces these alone. Instead, they emerge from the various systems of your body interacting over time. Perturbations are disruptions to your body's functioning—from voluntary choices (like jogging or jumping out of an airplane) or involuntary circumstances (like twisting an ankle or being in a car accident). Whatever the perturbation, your body will work to adapt, seeking a new homeostasis that may involve subtle or dramatic changes in function.

These concepts carry over to the social world. Let's consider the following scenario: a meeting of city council members where they are considering a proposal to cut down a forest to make room for a strip mall, and many residents show up to voice their dissent. Residents, council members, staff members, business leaders all are elements in this system who give feedback, creating a dynamic and unpredictable moment between multiple interests and pressure points. As the city administration attempts to self-regulate in the face of dissent, staff may try to absorb or appease it to minimize the chances of conflict at the time of the vote. Business interests may go on the attack in the press. The day of the vote, residents line up to the microphone to speak. The room becomes electrified as person after person tells their story, offers their point of view, describing the impact cutting down a forest will have on them. People clap; some hold signs and chant. Residents are intervening in a governance system that must grow its economy to be able to afford the inflationary costs of public services.

To perturb a system is to give it an input to which you cannot predict its reaction. The public comments, the demonstration, and the press attacks, are all perturbations that interrupt the homeostasis of the system, pushing it off balance. In a series of feedback loops, council members and staff respond, working toward homeostasis in the face of a flow of communication and power struggle. Council may delay the vote, giving all sides more time to exert pressure. There is a heuristic at play, as council members integrate additional information, altering their actions to cooperate with staff while addressing the concerns of their constituents. In the end, council may vote yes or no, or maybe strike a compromise by amending the proposal—perhaps to locate the strip mall in an area that is already developed.

There are consequences with each of these reactions, and the system has been affected as it adapts to the uncertainties presented. If the protests appear successful, there is often backlash, as those who benefit from a particular relationship between business interests and the city try to re-establish an old order. Quiet meetings are held, obscure rules are changed, public relations campaigns are launched, candidates are selected to run against detractors, until one day a similar proposal comes forward, causing protests once again. Meanwhile, protestors may work to build resilient organizing infrastructure to establish a more democratic order. They connect the issue to others in coalition, teach facilitation and direct action, attend meetings, create their own communication channels. In this way, they maintain pressure to keep the bulldozers out of the forest while fundamentally redistributing power through increasing participation.

Some may enter this story saying, "the decision is already in the bag," but many examples in history show us that when people engage their local government in a moment when leaders find themselves stuck between big business and their residents, participatory democracy can be an emergent property of systems of governance. In fact, many of the green spaces and public commons we take for granted around us were the outcomes of these contested moments.

Consider the Observer

To these cybernetic concepts—self-regulation, feedback loops, homeostasis, heuristics, emergent properties, and perturbations—we add examining the role of the observer in systems. The observer is not separate from but rather influences and is influenced by the system they observe. Including the observer in the description of the observed system represents a critical contribution of Margaret Mead who, in her germinal 1968 piece "Cybernetics of Cybernetics," offers cybernetics "as a way of looking at things and as a language for expressing what one sees."[7] Using this concept, Steve Sloan elaborated "look a system" to name how the observer provides a framework between elements, where their act of looking generates the system observed.[8] Of course the elements exist, but the power of the observer to *choose* their way of looking supplies their relations, which constitute a system and its meaning. There is no system without an observer.

A single perspective looks a system inadequately. When we want to solve a social problem and are researching its root causes, looking a system requires that we learn the stories of all the elements (people and things) we include in that system. Whom and what to include in our description of a system is an essential and *collective* design decision, with consequences. In formulating—or looking—the systems in which we find ourselves, we need each other, and we need difference. To look a system requires reflecting on what's missing, growing participation, and fostering curiosity.

We add to Steve Sloan's contribution, that to look a system is an invitation to do an intersectional analysis. Each of us belongs to many identity groups. An intersectional analysis is one that pays attention to how a particular problem or issue affects different groups and their intersections. It is an analysis of demographics that rejects tokenism, essentialism, and overdeterminism but pays attention to power, history, difference, and the dynamics of participation. It is essential that in looking a system we have collaborators who voice the perspectives of different groups and their experiences of the systems we are analyzing. Only when these various experiences are inputs into our analyses can the design of an intervention adequately respond to a problem.[9]

In looking systems, we are engaged in a power analysis. Power determines who gets access to what resources, tools, or information, and how these decisions are made. We must ask: for whom is this a problem? Who is doing the looking? Who is ignored or suppressed from speaking their version of the problem? Who benefits from the way the problem is formulated and the solutions it points to?[10] Stories are trailheads we can follow in our research. Follow the money and how it incentivizes action. Follow the language and look for what is missing in the descriptions of the problem.

This power analysis in "looking systems" provides an essential link between our local work and the problems that structures of power maintain. With this look, instead of seeing sexism, for example, as a solid, immovable force, we see it as a dynamic network of interactions between people in a system that is in flux, where supremacy and privilege of men is actively maintained through political, social, and cultural structures. These interactions have feedback loops, where the control of women's bodies in the private sphere strengthens political control in the public sphere and vice versa. A single action can affect the dynamics of a system in hidden and conspicuous ways.

To look a system invites a decentering of perspectives of privilege. bell hooks, in *Feminist Theory: From Margin to Center*, posits that for feminism to be truly transformative and address the complexities of women's lives, it must shift its focus solely from the experiences of privileged white women (already at the "center") to prioritize the voices and perspectives of marginalized women, particularly Black women and women of color (moving them from the "margin" to the center). She argues that marginalized groups, due to their direct experience of oppression, see societal power structures in unique ways that are essential to understanding oppressive social systems and building equitable systems.[11]

Move from Problem to Desire

The language we use—to name the system, its elements, their relations, and dynamics—becomes our framework for understanding the results, that is, the consequences of the system's operation. This language framework will attempt to justify the consequences of the system's operation, so that they appear to make sense. We need to understand how undesirable outputs of systems are argued as solutions. Understanding the specifics of what we do *not* want can help us get very specific about what we *do* want, serving as a springboard for formulating our desires, our next step on the Spiral of Change.

We challenge the oppressive consequences of a system by refusing its justification—the "sense" its language makes. The system's language says, in effect, "This is all there is: these elements. This is how they work together: these relations. These dynamics are the results. See? This is reality. There is no alternative." The system maintains itself by hiding possible alternatives and asserting the status quo as the only possible reality. This move is a magic trick that hides the existence of additional elements and relations, and the possibility of alternative relations, dynamics, and consequences.

When we include the people the system excludes, but nevertheless affects, we must then ask each other: what relations between us would be just and sustainable? Which elements are missing and need to be invented? This is a double process of asking not only, "What is?" but also "What do I want there to be instead?" And the recursive process of "What happened?" then "What should have happened?" and "What do I want to happen now?"

Formulate Toward the Future

To find joy in working on our problem, we can frame our language in terms of what we are seeking for the future, rather than using a language that ties us to the inevitability of the past. As we discuss the causes of our problems, beginning answers with "because" orients the conversation toward a determined past. Conversely, answering with "so that" orients the conversation toward the future and our desires. Try a pivot from "because" to "so that."[12] For example, a group may feel motivated to end sexual assault "*because* one in three women is raped in their lifetime." But what if the same group articulates their work "*so that* we can establish loving, equitable relationships free of violence and coercion?" The first formulation is an important fact, but this knowledge has not yet led to sufficient involvement in its change. The second formulation is an inspiring vision to organize people around.

Oppressive forces often hide in the arguments about the past. We can resist these worn-out stories, about who we are or what we should do, by pivoting from a problem to our desired future. In our formulation of the problem, we can choose: "I am doomed to live a story determined by the past" or "I am choosing a future with my story." It's never too late to change the story we tell, but the sooner we realize that we have a choice of story, the more agency we have.

CHAPTER 8

ASSIGNMENT

Develop a Systems Analysis

What is a problem that motivates you to design society? In this chapter, we invite you to work on *that* problem, to formulate and reformulate it so as to grasp it at its roots. You will learn how to look systems to see what is missing, pull apart undesirable relations, and forge new connections.

Before we start, we offer a note on language. The desire to have a voice is powerful in everyone. We all want to speak clearly, eloquently, and to be understood. In formulating problems, teachers at the School for Designing a Society (SDaS) invite students to inspect the language they use carefully. This focus on language can have a double edge, as words and expressions are often felt to mirror our true and authentic selves, and problems may be sourced from personal and painful experiences. We have watched some students blossom into eloquence that comes from serious attempts at constructing their thoughts in language. We have watched others withdraw, react defensively, or be struck silent by the attention to their choice of language.

We ask you to critique what the *language* is doing, while respecting the *people*. We invite you to disentangle your sense of self and identity from oppressive systems through inspection, formulation, and reformulation in language. This is an invitation, not a demand. Consider language as an "it," not a "you" or a "me." Once a person and her language are distinguished, it is easier to play—with formulation, syntax, and sense-making (or nonsense-making). With that said, we encourage groups to watch out for "power-over" dynamics, such as those between: male and female and nonbinary people; white people and people of color; older and younger people; or those who are abled or divergent. Try doing the assignments as puppet characters (any available objects can be made into DIY puppets) or, shuffle the responses of members of the group and have them randomly pick and read anonymous contributions.

Problem Jostle

The "problem jostle" was developed by cybernetician Stafford Beer as a method for cultivating small group discussions around a topic or problem without a predetermined agenda or a leader.[1] They are particularly effective in facilitating open exploration around a question like: "What problems do we want to work on together?" Many SDaS sessions have been designed with students and teachers using the following problem jostle.

Inviting people to your problem

Prepare small tables with 4–5 chairs around each and paper and pens in the center. Invite members of your group to choose a table, and either make a sign to initiate discussion of their problem, or join a discussion around someone else's problem. Ask each table to assign a notetaker (a role that may switch hands as people come and go). Encourage people to move from table to table as they wish. Playing a song can help with transitions.

Formulation and Reformulation

There is often a strong urge to skip the step of formulating a problem. We feel we know the problem so well: "Isn't it obvious! We're not interested in talking about problems, we want solutions!" Insufficient analysis and ill-considered formulation of your problem can lead to false solutions, frustration, and burnout. Give yourself time to think about and formulate the problem with the following considerations.

Problem versus state of affairs

Practice formulating your problem as a state of affairs, making it sound as if change *is not* possible. Then reformulate the problem to indicate that you want it to change and change *is* possible.

Different scales

Formulate your problem on three different scales: that of the personal, communal, and global.

Active voice

Reformulate any problem statements that use passive voice (where the person doing the action is missing), into active voice, where there is a subject, verb, and object. Discuss what changed.

Formulations determine their set of solutions

Write two ways the current system formulates the problem. For both, write two different solutions implied by each formulation. Then write two formulations of the same problem oriented by your desires and try out writing two different solutions implied by each formulation.

Joy in Formulation

When we feel drained by a problem, or get entrenched in our understanding of it, we need to foster curiosity and an approach of "not-knowing" our problem. We can do this by formulating legitimate questions about our problem—ones that do not have predetermined answers, formulating toward audacious desires, or connecting our problems to others to combat alienation and build community.

Legitimate questions

Formulate 1–3 questions that don't have available answers and that ignite your curiosity about your problem.

Formulate toward desire

Practice formulating the problem in a way that points toward a solution you *do not* want. Then formulate your problem in such a way that it points to an audacious, utopian desire.

Unlikely connections

Take two formulations of problems that appear disconnected and connect them in one formulation. Resist sense-making. Notice what happens.

Formulate in Art (Formulart)

We can turn our problem formulations into poems and our poems back into formulations. Making a collage of the premises of our problems, we might discover new logics of cause and effect. Singing our formulations of the problem, we might connect with a listener who has a new perspective to the set of solutions we want.

Silly poetic problems

Choose one of the problem formulations you have generated and write five silly or nonsensical variations on it by substituting words, mad-lib style:

> Take out all the important words and substitute words from some other domain, like cooking, or video games, or some other subculture.
>
> Take out all the unimportant words and substitute other words to make the remaining important words relate differently.
>
> Before or after each important word, insert strings of nonsense syllables starting with the same letter or rhyming.
>
> Take out half the words without worrying about syntax.
>
> Insert three phrases from a favorite song or poem or essay into your formulation without worrying about it making sense.

Finally, decide on an order for these five variations plus your original formulation, and read the poem aloud. Consider reading it again using a different voice for each sentence.

The "What If" Game

We can better recognize our ability to be agents for change when we perceive that we are living in and making history. Articulating how things could have gone differently opens up a crack in the wall of certainty the current system maintains, and shines light on possible actions we can take to make new histories.

Revisions in time

Through research, interviews and discussion, trace the historical lineage of your problem. Make a timeline that starts with the earliest manifestation of the problem and follows it through its twists and turns to present. Find a decision point on the timeline where things could have gone differently. Consider: what if a different decision had been made at that pivot point? Draw a branch off that timeline and imagine different consequences.

A Problem's Many Angles

To get close to a problem, understand its roots, and make effective interventions, we need to look at it from every angle. Herbert Brün presented "six questions to ask a problem" that a group of SDaS students expanded on in 1993.[2] What follows are nine questions to ask a problem to help develop an analysis of power around the problem. Write responses to each using full sentences and then discuss.

Questions to ask a problem

1. What are the components of the problem?

2. For whom is it a problem (and for whom is it not a problem)?

3. In whose interest is it that the problem not be solved?

4. Is there a reformulation of the problem that makes it easier to solve?

5. Is there a problem "behind" this problem? What problem is this problem a symptom of?

6. Why hasn't this problem been solved before now? What is the problem's history?

7. Who should be included in the process of solving the problem?

8. How can I connect my self-interest with the problem I observe? How can I connect the person I want to become to working on this problem?

9. Illustrate the language landscape around the problem. Go to the library, or search online, and find pieces of language the current society uses to describe this problem.

Entailment Maps

Used by Stafford Beer to map organizational problems, Gordon Pask's entailment meshes are graphical representations of a system in its relationships, particularly how one concept entails or is linked to another.[3]

The environment of your problem

On a large piece of paper, sketch out the environment of your problem amidst other problems. Draw problems that create your problem. Draw problems your problem creates. Add problems in the environment and consider how they may be involved. Draw lines between the problems and try writing statements of relationship between these. Notice when there are closed loops.

Your problem as a face

Try to make an entailment map of your problem that looks like a face. Which problem is on the chin? Are there twin problems on the eyes and ears? What problem makes you sneeze—or scream?

Systems Play: Elements and Their Relations

This assignment helps you lay out the elements of your problem, see their relationships, and imagine new relationships.

Relations we have, relations we want

1. Draw three characters involved in your problem in the center of the page.

2. Consider people whom the current system would not include in its description of the problem—perhaps they are neglected, ignored, or denied by the system—but who are nevertheless touched by it. Add one or more of these in the margins. Then add a musician anywhere on the page.

3. From all the characters, choose two and briefly describe their relations in the current system. How do their relations give rise to your problem? Practice this with several pairs or trios.

4. Take the same characters you used above and describe a relationship between these characters that you want.

5. Now add the character in the margin and describe a desirable relationship. What role could the musician play?

Putting Yourself in the System

Making self-descriptions in a system helps us practice putting ourselves in the picture of the system we observe. Steve Sloan created this SDaS assignment as a way to describe the self within a system and invite conversation.[4]

Self-description in a system

Put yourself in the language of the problem and system you have formulated. Write or draw your current "self-description in a system," where you describe yourself, your problem and its premises, the dynamics of the system, and any responses. Try creating a self-description in a system as a poem.

CHAPTER 9

INTERVENTION

Campaign for Prison Phone Justice

Seated in the dark, wood-paneled side room of the US Senate building, nineteen-year-old Wandjell Harvey-Robinson told her story about what it was like to grow up when phone calls were the only link to her parents, both in prison, and how this link was abruptly cut off when she ran out of money.[1] Next to Wandjell sat Jazlin Mendoza, whose voice shook and then steadied as she shared about her father: "I lost the bonding that me and him had as a young girl. . . . He used to take care of me; he used to go out and play over the summers; he used to put out the pool." Jazlin had created radio pieces as a youth producer for Generation Justice in New Mexico, highlighting others' stories. Now she was sharing her own story: her only connection to her father in prison for most of her life had been through a monthly five-minute phone call.

Wandjell and Jazlin were part of a national campaign for Prison Phone Justice that was started in 2000 by family members of those behind bars. The Campaign for Prison

Phone Justice, which continues to this day, has widened the conversation about incarceration to include the stories and perspectives of those affected—those incarcerated, and also, their children, families, communities. In 2015, the Phone Justice campaign won rate caps on phone calls. In this chapter, I, Danielle, offer the campaign as a model for how story-based organizing strategy can shift a public conversation and win a victory for people over profits.

Organizing around the stories of thousands of family members harmed by predatory prison phone rates helped surface a contradiction at a pivotal moment of ballooning incarceration rates in the United States, which impacted nearly every low-income family in the country. Private phone companies were turning huge profits exploiting the loved ones of incarcerated residents by negotiating price-gouging monopoly phone contracts with states and counties. These monopoly contracts allowed the phone companies to charge up to $25 for a fifteen-minute call from prison—while cementing enduring political support for their vampirism by providing financial kickbacks to these public bodies. The average family of an incarcerated loved one paid $250 a month in their struggle to stay connected, while the prison phone industry reaped $1.2 billion per year and the public entities running prisons and jails received $460 million in kickbacks. The result was a massive redistribution of cash from the poorest families in the country to some of the richest companies. For many families, the cost was too much to bear, and connection was lost for years, or forever.

Prison phone contracts first became a profit center in the 1990s when families were hit by shockingly high bills when trying to stay connected to their loved ones behind bars. I first learned of this problem from the experience of my friend Sandra Ahten—who was charged exorbitant rates calling her son in jail as he struggled with substance abuse.

Sandra produced radio pieces and wrote articles on this predatory practice through our new Independent Media Center in Urbana-Champaign, Illinois. The UC-IMC became a gathering place and amplification center for a grassroots campaign, led by parents like Sandra, that eventually forced our county to cancel its jail phone contract and end kickbacks in 2004.[2]

Prison Phone Justice became a national conversation starting in 2000 when Ms. Martha Wright-Reed sued the Corrections Corporation of America for the high cost of phone bills she faced as a grandmother calling her grandson. Her story is particularly poignant because phone calls were the only way she could stay in touch with her beloved grandson who she raised, since, as a blind senior citizen, she could neither write letters nor travel for in-person visits.[3] Around that same time, a young journalist, Sylvia Ryerson, created the radio show "Calls from Home" on the community radio station WWMT, which broadcasts out of Appalshop in Whitesburg, Kentucky and into the eight prisons within their listening area. The show invites family and friends to call in to a recording line to leave messages for their loved ones to receive by radio inside.[4]

Phone Justice is one piece in a national movement to shift the story on incarceration and open the door for policy change with direct impacts: reducing suffering and financial hardship for low-income families. The dominant story justifying soaring incarceration rates has been focused on "criminals" and inflated narratives of "super predators." An incarcerated person's role as a *person in their full humanity*—as a father, provider, brother, son, coach, family man, faith leader, beloved—is kept out of the story.[5] The Campaign for Prison Phone Justice has been a twenty-five-year endeavor spearheaded by impacted residents and supported by organizers, researchers, policy advocates, and faith-based leaders to widen the frame on incarceration to include those intentionally kept out of it: children, families, and whole neighborhoods where many men of color have disappeared.

Our movement saw an opportunity to make policy progress in 2014, when President Obama appointed Mignon Clyburn, the first African American Chair of the Federal Communications Commission (FCC). Under Clyburn's brief term, the FCC said they would finally look at Ms. Martha Wright-Reed's request and consider a cap on prison phone rates. But industry lobbyists and the Sheriff's Association of America were formidable opponents with deep pockets. So, our movement mobilized the power of story—responding to their well-paid industry lobbyists with the hundreds of thousands of voices who were best positioned to humanize their loved ones. These stories spoke in terms of shared values—family, care, and connection. The voices of children of incarcerated parents made visible the predatory horrors and dehumanizing outcomes of capitalism married to state systems of capture and control.

I became Organizing Director in 2014 at Media Justice, working for its founder Malkia Devich-Cyril, whose words had rung in my ears since I heard them speak before the crowd at the National Conference for Media Reform ten years earlier: "*Address material needs. Engage marginalized populations as leaders. Redistribute power.*" Having worked locally with Sandra and others on this issue, I wanted to help advance a victory for Prison Phone Justice during the Obama years. Malkia was candid with me: they had struggled to get elected leaders and funders to see and invest in this issue, even though it was deeply felt by millions of people in every part of the country. But our network of a hundred grassroots organizations continued to assert that capping prison phone rates was a top priority for them. So Malkia scraped together funding from different pots to support our work toward it.

Our campaign strategy centered on the grassroots storytelling that had formed the origins of this movement. Malkia advocated for "culture shift"— using culture to shift politics to change material conditions and law. They suggested the tactic of "story banking": casting a wide and deep net through our network of local organizations to gather stories we could lift up throughout the policy campaign. On Mother's Day in 2015, Media Justice and our Prison Phone Justice partners held dozens of events all over the country to gather stories. Malinda from Oklahoma shared: "I am a mother of three and I can't afford for my kids to even talk to their dad but once every two weeks. He is in a prison six hours away, so we can't visit. If prices for calls were capped my kids would get to know their dad. But we can't at the current rate." On Father's Day, we did another round of events—distributing postcards for families to write on that we would deliver to the FCC. Our partner organization, Color of Change, led the process of gathering twenty thousand stories including this one: "My son is in prison, and I'm disabled, can't travel well even when he was two miles away, and on an extremely fixed income. I just barely pay my bills, let alone send him money or pay the outrageous costs for a phone call. These rates are taking advantage of the family on the outside as well as the inmates. They need to hear their loved ones' voices to keep them encouraged."

Leading up to the critical FCC vote, Media Justice and our partners organized ten weeks of "Right to Connect" events, bringing to Washington, DC several delegations of impacted family members to share their stories. Delegates represented community-based organizations throughout the United States who had been working on the ground for over a decade, gathering those impacted by incarceration to come to voice, share their stories, and grapple with the problems they faced together. Despite finally getting some broad attention from places like *The New York Times*, few officials in the elite circles of Washington paid attention to phone justice.[6] When our delegates started to speak at our final phone justice event, the Senate room was nearly empty. Even though we had called every congressional ally, only our scheduled speaker, Senator Cory Booker, was there—and a handful of congressional aides chewing gum and texting on their phones. We felt deflated. But as the delegates lifted their voices, the room quietly filled. Twelve-year-old Kevin Reeves shared: "My dad has been locked up for twelve years and I have had a total of twelve hours to talk to him in that time." I looked around, startled to see more and more people filing into the hearing. I found myself in a standing-room-only crowd of adults with expensive suits and haircuts, and with tears in their eyes. Puzzled, I cornered a congressional aide: "No one in DC ever sees anything like this," she said. "This is people telling their truths . . . from the heartland . . . with specific, actionable asks." She pointed to her phone: "We told our bosses to get down here," and then lowered her voice, "I have never seen anyone cry in this building." That day, a dozen members of Congress signed our letter urging the FCC to act on regulating rates for prison phone calls.

Our next stop was the FCC building, where we carried bags of petitions and stories through security. Once inside, we spread postcards with handwritten notes out on the huge glass-topped meeting table. Annette Taylor from Champaign, Illinois, wrote: "Please lower the rates so we can talk to our sons." Ms. Taylor had run the Ripple Effect for ten years, gathering family members and allies to write letters of support to incarcerated loved ones. Nazaari, age five, drew a picture of her dad behind bars reaching for the phone, with frowny faces across the page. As we spoke, FCC Chair Clyburn kept looking at the postcards and Vice Chair Jessica Rosenworcel choked up as she responded. Ours was one of many pressure points applied, and in the days that followed, the FCC finally approved capping rates for prison phone calls, cutting the cost of calls by more than three quarters.[7]

The Campaign for Prison Phone Justice has won reform victories within an entrenched carceral system, changing deeply felt conditions of isolation and exploitation for millions of people. The campaign connects the dots between phone call costs (which are the tip of the iceberg) and mass incarceration, driven by the predations of monopoly corporations as they capture and compromise public institutions. In this way, this campaign helps illuminate the collusion of state and corporate power maintained by logics of superiority, justified by media depictions of criminals, and exacerbated by technologies designed to control and profit from communication. Phone contracts captured billions of dollars from low-income workers in a system maintained by providing kickbacks to the government entities providing monopoly access to phone service corporations.

Despite repeated setbacks, the Campaign for Prison Phone Justice has continued to advance. Trump's first administration immediately rolled back progress at the FCC. But many states had already capped their phone costs, affecting the majority of the prison population. Through our Independent Media Center, we ran a story-based, family-powered campaign, championed by State Representative Carol Ammons, that won some of the lowest rates in the US for those incarcerated in Illinois. In Champaign County, costs of calls into our jail inched back up in 2023, and once again, Sandra led a group to pressure the county to provide free daily phone calls and emails to and from jail.

Wandjell Harvey-Robinson went on to found the Freedom Child Foundation, which has worked to maintain and strengthen relationships between children and their incarcerated parents since 2020. As Wandjell told *People* magazine: "This is a population of kids who are not really talked about. . . . I know, for me, trying to hide that my parents were in prison was really keeping me from blossoming. Once I became comfortable with sharing that, so many more people became comfortable with sharing their own stories with me."[8] The Prison Phone Justice *campaign goals* were to end kickbacks and lower phone call rates. But the *movement-building objectives* were to build grassroots power to challenge the premises of incarceration while creating a new paradigm for public safety focused on mutual support and care.

This campaign married the two objectives: meeting an immediate need while challenging logics of superiority used to justify the extraction of profits from misery. Through reforming calls from prison and jail, the campaign also established revolutionary premises. It demanded that families, poor communities, and communities of color be included in our democracy, where a fundamental tension has always been who is in and who is out, who gets to be a full human being in democracy and who is still having to shake off the three-fifth's designation. It showed that the roots of poverty lie not in moral failing or lack of access, but in a lack of power, which ultimately derives from a lack of participation, and that participation can build power. The Campaign for Prison Phone Justice started with story, won through story, and made story and connection more possible.

III

Generate
Desires

CHAPTER 10

Desire as Liberation

I use the word "composition" whenever I wish to speak of the composer's activity and the traces left by it. The composer is motivated by a wish of bringing about that which, without that composer and human intent, would not happen.

—Herbert Brün, *my words and where i want them*

When I, Elizabeth, first applied to the School for Designing a Society (SDaS), I had never encountered an application that didn't require my academic transcript and a lot of essays. The application was a phone call, and the only requirement was a critique of the current society and a desire for a different one. This first interaction with SDaS foreshadowed a profound shift in my orientation toward desire, though I did not yet realize it. When I was told that the first assignment at SDaS would be for everyone to formulate what they wanted, I thought this sounded like a terrible idea! Why would we focus on our selfish and narcissistic wants? The ideology of consumerism—even though I had a critique of it—had so co-opted my understanding of desire, I could not conceive of desire apart from materialism or a commodified sexuality. Living under capitalism had taught me that self and community are in competition, and that desire was necessarily individual and opposed to the common good.

Rarely are we asked what we want—our *social* wants for the society we live in. We are thus not in the habit of even asking, let alone of coming up with answers. As a child I learned in school to develop the muscle of knowing—but not a "big muscle for wanting," as Susan Parenti puts it. A flood of available alternatives *in* the system—which toothpaste to buy, movie to watch, outfit to wear—drowns out the possibility of alternatives *of* system: a world without borders or wage slavery, a culture of mutual aid, a world where violence has been rendered obsolete.

Looking back at the lineage of SDaS, I realize now how much desire is fundamental to this project founded by refugees from fascism. Fascists need our conformity for compliance, while capitalists need our conformity for mass consumption; both would like to erase our uniqueness, which is revealed through our desires. Thus, for participation to be liberatory, it must be based on our desires. Herbert Brün formulated: "Freedom is measured by the number and kind of alternatives we have to choose among."[1] We increase freedom when we generate an abundance of alternatives in response to our problems, guided by our desires. In choosing among the alternatives we have desired and created, we cut through systems-maintaining arguments about what is real and possible. By formulating an abundant variety of desires, we experience our own power and agency and widen the field of possible futures for ourselves and our communities. Desires seed liberation.

Desire Statements

The language of a problem is insufficient for responding to that problem, because it confines what is considered possible and reproduces what already exists. Articulating what we *want* requires our creativity. To access our creativity requires that we, at least temporarily, quiet the fears elicited by the language of the problem. This is a cognitive and neurological imperative.[2] In this "Generating Desires" step on the Spiral of Change, we pivot from formulating problems and systems, where we seek to understand the past and present, to formulating our desires as premises for the future.

Desires open space to consider alternatives, bring people together, guide our designs, and evaluate our actions, which prompts us to reformulate our desires. Desire is how we transport ourselves out of the framework created by the problem to imagine a society based on fundamentally different—and just—premises. Formulating and reformulating our desires in conversation with others brings our language closer to our intentions and increases its impact.

By "desire statement" we mean statements where:

> It is currently not true.
>
> You desire it to be true.
>
> For it to become true requires a change of system.

We take each in turn.

It is currently not true

As you write your statement, ask yourself if it is a currently available option. This question may involve research. We draw a distinction between desire and preference. A preference is an alternative available in the current system. We are not trying to imagine sentences that are true of someone in the current society, even if not available to us, such as: "I have adequate health care." A desire is an alternative that does not exist and could not exist without a change in system. To test a statement for its not-yet-ness, we can ask: are we sure it is not currently true? Am I able to make this statement true, and if not, what stands in the way? Is there somewhere the desire might be true, and if so, what makes it possible there?

You desire it to be true

This is not the time for devil's advocates, or ideas without commitment, or merely parroting someone else's good idea. "What do you want?" is a question worth locking away distractions and sitting in the discomfort of silence for. To elicit vivid images of another reality, we dispense with qualifiers, like "I wish," that tether us to this reality and speak our desires without conditional language. Consider these desire statements from *City Imaginings*, a zine created in Danielle's SDaS class "The City You Live In" in 2001:

> *Cars are mostly unnecessary as urban areas are so well designed, accessible, and aesthetically appealing there are few reasons people would not rather take a solar trolley or walk.*
>
> *Cement is considered a weed. Gardens replace parking lots.*
>
> *Houses are made out of plants that generate light, act as windows, and filter the air.*

We can ask: do we *really* want what we say we want? Is what we want reliant on another desire being met? If so, what is *that* desire?

For it to become true requires a change of system

This means a shift in premises of the system. Often, we desire more of something to be provided for more people, or the end of some harm. For something currently afforded to a few to be afforded to everyone would require a change of system. Similarly, to keep a common harm from ever arising would require a change in premise signaling a change of system. Whether a desire statement requires a change of system is the beginning of interesting conversation that can sharpen our vision of the world we want. Desire statements stand in protest against the current social systems, exposing contradictions inherent in them. Consider this desire statement Mark Enslin shared at SDaS in 2004: *When someone does harm to another, that person is invited to design a society in which they would not have done that harm.* In our current system, the go-to remedy for harm is more harm. In the system this statement lives in, those who have done harm are well positioned to interrupt cycles of harm and design to prevent them. There is a shift of premises from punishment to healing. This third criterion—of system change—is what levers us into the imaginary world of a different society—one that a change of system would produce.

This "Designing Society" assignment has generated many thousands of statements, and subsequent designs, since its first iteration was given to students in 1968. Formulating, experimenting with, and declaring desires in small groups can create a rush of excitement in prefiguring a different, more participatory, and desired reality. Here are a few examples:

> *Permaculturists teach their neighbors to eat their lawns.* —Danielle
>
> *My government uses art to make decisions.* —Elizabeth
>
> *Trees can vote. Those upstream defer to those downstream.* —Mark
>
> *There are three enormous breasts on the wall: one gives water, one milk, and one wine.* —Ginevra Sanguino
>
> *Everyone is my collaborator.* —Al Schneider, Tayloranne Finch, and Ben Usie

We recognize, however, that it is difficult to reproduce in the format of a book the friction and frisson of doing it yourself in a group. Our invitation is that you and your friends create a context in which to try this out for yourselves, and for us.

Every Beloved Thing

Formulating desire statements shifts our mindset from "that's the way things are" to critically thinking "that's the way things have been *designed*, by *someone*, based on *their* desires." If we look at problems through lenses that remind us "someone designed this outcome," there is an opening for the possibility that things could be designed otherwise, and we could be the ones to do it.

This process starts with desire. Every beloved thing we enjoy and benefit from was once a desire statement. The movement for playgrounds was based on the desire statement: *Playgrounds are a necessity for all children as much as schools. . . . The playground system shall represent a plan which will provide a playground within a reasonable walking distance of every child.*[3] Public libraries were organized based on the (at the time radical) statement: *Libraries bring books and information to all people.* We began the project of this book by writing our desire statements for it:

> *This book includes activities in many formats that are delicious to do.*
>
> *Readers of the book are able to have conversations about, and organize around, premises of systems and not just chase consequences and symptoms.*
>
> *Artists and organizers take time together, with this book, to invent the world they want and don't assume they know what that world is and only need to recruit others to it.*
>
> *Teachers, doctors, lawyers, maintenance workers, techies, social workers, and librarians, all have tools to design society together around the contradictions they face.*

Desires in Multiple Domains

Personal, communal, and public domains present different opportunities and restrictions for desiring and designing. The personal domain is a place of familiarity: self, family, or home. For example, we can raise children without violence, make our home energy-efficient, ground family traditions and rituals in our values. In the personal domain, there is comfort, shared understandings, and a few people to coordinate with. The personal domain is a small laboratory to try out establishing desires and designs. The communal domain is one of affiliation: neighborhood, work, school, house of worship, or organization. We can create a neighborhood or church project, organize a union, or create a chorus. In this domain, we have to learn to be brief in our speaking, share space, check our assumptions. The public domain is diverse: city, park, school, public event, newspaper. It has a higher level of chaos, friction, and difference, but also, a higher level of potential and impact. It can be instructive to formulate variations on the same desire in these different domains.

From Desire to Design

Through discussion about these questions, in small groups, we refine our design statements. In the design groups described in the original "Designing

Society" assignment, we find the connection of similarities, the delight of differences between our desires, we help protect each other against misunderstanding, so the desire statement can stand on its own, without explanation. In this process, the group addresses the language of a desire statement, as it is written, rather than politely intuiting what the author may have meant. The group scrutinizes, with the consent of the author, what her *language* appears to be saying. This is a gift. With this feedback, she has the opportunity to bring closer together what her language is saying and what she wants to say, with support from others.

Then, the group works to consolidate the individual desire lists into a group list where the desires toward the top of the list, if satisfied, entail the satisfaction of desires lower down. For example, the desire "*all human needs are met unconditionally*" might be at the top of the list and the desire "*education exists to reduce misery*" might be placed further down. By ordering them in this way, one is arguing that if all needs were met unconditionally, education would necessarily reduce misery.

In this way, the group works to identify which desires are premises and which follow as consequences. The statements that rise to the top allow the group to identify the desires that act as fundamental premises, helping them understand the core criteria and conditions for change. The purpose of this assignment is not to determine which desires are more important or we should start with, but to elicit conversations about how our desires are interrelated and interdependent. The groups move through a series of assignments for making desire statements that are outlined in chapter 11. These desire lists, along with a growing analysis of social problems, become inputs to the design process.

For example, a group of SDaS students created the Urbana Permaculture project. It was a project designed from the group's desire statements, such as this one by Rob Scott: *We design ecosystems which produce the necessities of life, so that people may meet their needs without money-exchange.* From this statement, the group imagined a "five-year plan in reverse," asking: "What would I not regret having done five years from now?" Its founders provided a distinguishing description of the project: "The Urbana Permaculture Project is distinct amongst permaculture projects in having refused to participate in the commerce of food, water, housing, or any other human necessities. The project focuses on social and ecological design, adding alternatives, and educating that practice." Over six years, this group taught residents how to eat their front lawns, build outdoor stoves, introduce passive solar architecture, and pair chickens with the gardens they protect.

Although the design group process can be contentious and circuitous, we persist, so as to model a miniature (and relatively forgiving) society in our group where, to design itself, members must negotiate their different desires. Design groups represent basic building blocks of participation. Lots of groups formulating desires is what participatory democracy looks like. As Steve Sloan articulated in his desire statement from SDaS in fall 2000: *Coordination of the desires is conserved in the network of conversation that comprises society. There exists an opportunity for everyone to participate in conversations that coordinate the desires of everyone in society. Structures for participation are recursively designed as circumstances change.*

Songlines

The Australian Aboriginal creation story describes a primordial Dream Time, when the ancestral animals had emerged and sung the world into being. In the story, people repair and renew the world by following their songlines and singing their songs, which function as maps of the whole continent of Australia. Inspired by this, I, Elizabeth, collaborated with Vita and Ishmael Wallace on the project *Songlines*, as part of their What A Neighborhood! Festival in New York City from 2010 to 2015. Our project was a collaborative public mapping of the Morningside Heights neighborhood through songwriting and parades. At street fairs and public workshops, we invited passersby and friends to write a song about their block, whether its past, present, or desired future. We helped by providing prompting questions and musical notation. We copied the scores onto index cards and convened parades to sing new routes together as they accumulated.

Here are the desire statements that guided our project:

> *We render the neighborhood more beloved, connected, and alive by eliciting the thoughts and amplifying the voices of our neighbors on the subject of the streets we share.*
>
> *More singing in the streets!*
>
> *We give directions through song.*
>
> *Neighbors talk to each other about beloved aspects of, and changes in the neighborhood, and share their wisdom and observations in a memorable form.*

Through eliciting the participation of our neighbors in writing *Songlines*, we collectively mapped over seventy-five Manhattan blocks with just as many songs and performed twenty community parades of different routes. As an example, here is a song composed on the spot by Crucita Matos, whom we encountered on her way to the laundromat on the corner of 123rd Street and Claremont Avenue.

Yo quiero cantar para mi comunidad,

¡Para que todos seamos felices!

La felicidad se construir juntos.

¡Juntos siempre como una gran familia!

The neighbor is not only neighbor!

The neighbor is family!

Vamos a construir uno comunidad de nuevo

¡Para que todos seamos felices!

La-la, la-la, la la la-! La-la, la-la, la la la-!

I want to sing for my community

So that we are all happy!

Happiness is constructed together.

Together always like a big family!

The neighbor is not only neighbor!

The neighbor is family!

We are going to construct a new community

So that we are all happy!

La-la, la-la, la la la-! La-la, la-la, la la la-!

Songline composed and sung by Crucita Matos;
transcribed by Ishmael Wallace on the corner
of 123rd Street and Claremont Avenue, c. 2011.

Many neighbors were surprised and impressed by their own composition skills; they had not expected to see themselves as knowledgeable, creative, and connected to their fellow neighbors. *Songlines* shared local knowledge and re-created a sense of shared place in a neighborhood that has been targeted for gentrification, amplifying the uniqueness of those who live there.

Desire Throughout the Spiral of Change

Having desire statements that we have carefully formulated in our back pockets is an incredibly helpful and grounding tool in making decisions. Desires help us feel connected to what we want, to generate hope for what could be, and to gather others around this hope. Formulating desires generates alternatives to choose among. When faced with a decision, we consult our desires as criteria—as powerful guides toward what we want. Once we have acted on these decisions, we can return to our desires in reflection as measures for evaluating the success of our actions, revising our desires, and designing next steps.

Desire is a fundamental tool for dismantling oppression in a way that liberates both the oppressed and the oppressor. In our struggle to overcome a contradiction, anchoring in our desires helps us create a better world for everyone, even those positioned as our opponents in the current system. Why is that? Desires reject the premises of oppression and not only its symptoms. Desire statements stake out the premises of the world we long for, releasing us from the premises of the systems not of our choosing that set us up as opponents.

Articulating our desires as fully as possible is prerequisite to designing the interventions we want. We need our desires to serve as criteria for making decisions at every step on the Spiral of Change: from evaluating the implications of inherited language around our problem and the language we come up with; to formulating the problem such that it determines the set of solutions we want; to highlighting the contradictions thwarting our desires by emphasizing their contrast; to designing our interventions; to evaluating their consequences; and around the spiral again. With desire, can we make a society that requires all of us to make it, such that no person is dispensable and all are valuable? Acting toward our social desires is how we lead with love.

The following assignment is used by the School for Designing a Society and represents the briefest formulation of our work. Mark Enslin and Steve Sloan formulated it in 1999 to combine the "Right or Wrong, My Desires" assignment from the 1968 Heuristics class with that of the 1981 Designing Society class, both at the University of Illinois. It emphasizes the falseness, or negative dialectics, of desire statements, and moves quickly to group design.[1]

1. Make a list of false statements

Make a list of statements about which you would say they are currently false and you wish they would become true. Take care that the statements are, to the best of your knowledge, false. (Avoid beginning a statement with such phrases as "I wish that . . . ," which would be taken as a true statement.) At this stage in the assignment, the falseness of the statements is to be emphasized.

2. Order the statements

Order the statements in such a way that statements earlier in the list, if they were to become true, might imply that statements later in the list would, as a consequence, also have become true.

3. Form design groups

The design groups are to:

READ members' statements: examine the formulation of the statements;

COMPILE a single list of false statements that all members of your group would like to become true;

SPECULATE on actions, practices, strategies, structures that might create a context in which the false statements would become true;

ASSIGN each other reading, writing, drawing, composition, and research that might follow up on the speculations;

HOST a long-term project that could be a container for the traces of your group's designs (and the work of other groups), for example:

a book
an installation
a video
a circus
a teach-in

CHAPTER 11

ASSIGNMENT

Right or Wrong, My Desires

We invite you to imagine societies in which the kinds of misery we suffer from cannot arise—imagine these societies in full color, with all the details. To do so, we must start with our desires, cultivating our ability to imagine and desire through practice. Through this, we develop stories of where we come from, what we must heal from, and what values we want to uphold. We develop desires to guide our transformation of self, community, and society. These desires become criteria for a new world. They guide our design process.

As a reminder, a desire statement is not currently true; you wish it were true; and for it to become true would require a change of system. In contrast to a desire, a preference is available somewhere in the current system, even if it is not currently available to you. As you begin to generate desire statements, here are some prompts to start. As you write, quiet your inner critic. Be patient and persistent and keep writing.

Problems Sprout Desire

Exploring problems and their interconnectedness within systems provides fertile ground for articulating desires. For these assignments, consult your own responses to the assignments "Questions to Ask a Problem" and "Formulating your Problem as Conflicts and Contradictions" as well as your "Entailment Maps" from chapter 8. Those responses elaborated what you don't want, and they can help you get specific about what you do want.

Desires from problems
Write out at least five desires in relation to your problem. What would need to be true such that your problem did not arise, were eliminated, or shifted toward a better situation?

Desires from systems
Consider the system out of which your problem emerges and write desire statements that point to changes of that system. Consider changes in elements, relations, or dynamics.

Desiring in Many Domains

We encourage you to formulate your desires in many domains on many scales, as change is not one sweeping event but the result of many interventions. To change society, we will need to desire and design across the domains of the personal, communal, and public. For each, discuss:

Desires for work
What do I wish were true about my job—and all jobs?

Desires for family
What do I wish were true about my family—and all families?

Desire buffet
Formulate at least one desire in relation to each of the following: self, relationship, food, justice, conflict, sexuality, gender, race and ethnicity, governance, housing, cities, energy, technology, media, communication, health care, education, transportation, economics, money, business, death, birth, nature . . . adding more categories as you wish.

Desires at different scales
Take your desire statements and reformulate them in the domains of the personal, communal, and public; or make new desires in these domains.

Embodied Desiring

Experiment with the relation between your body and mind to see how one affects the other. Starting to write desire statements feels similar to attempts at meditating, praying, or just relaxing without inputs. At first there is the cacophony of voices and noise. It takes a while to settle and clear out layers of stuckness to get at the sweetness that lies below.

Nature
Go into nature and write desires.

Dancing
Trying dancing and then writing desires.

Balancing
Balance on a ball or tightrope and then write.

Exercise
Weightlift, do jumping jacks, or shadowbox and then write.

Revising Desires

The following four assignments are offered to help you sift through and refine your desires, distilling them into a tightly formulated list that you will consult in your design process. These assignments can be done alone, in pairs, or in a group.

Desire versus preference
Alone or in pairs, review your desires and ask: "Which are already available alternatives in the current system and which do not yet exist?" Reformulate preferences into desires that would require a change of system to be true.

Negative to positive
Negative statements represent the current society rather than envisioning a new one. Look at your desire statements and work to reformulate the negative ones into something you want.

Passive to active voice
Look over your desire statements and identify which are lacking a subject, an agent for change. Who does what to whom to make your desired society work?

Complete sentences
Complete sentences represent complete thoughts. Advertising slogans and marketing memes reduce thinking to phrase-feelings: "Just Do It," "Think Different," "Got Milk?" When formulating, work to have

complete sentences which state a subject, their actions, and the desires motivating their actions.

Clichés I narrowly avoid

To create complete thoughts, look out for and avoid clichés. Circle words or phrases in your desire statements that are the most vulnerable to being turned into an advertisement. Consider a different word or phrase that is less vulnerable. Alternatively, take your desire statements and try to write them into an advertisement for ExxonMobil. Then, rewrite them so that they could not function in an ExxonMobil ad.[1]

Newspoetry

Inspect and survive the language of the news by making poetry out of it. This assignment was borrowed from William Gillespie, editor of the Newspoetry website, who wrote a poem about the news every day for a year.

Swapping metaphors

Take a news piece about an issue you care about and circle every metaphor in the news story, then replace the metaphors with others that point to more desirable solutions.

Subtraction poetry

Subtract words out of a news story until it tells a desirable story.

Neologisms

Our current society lacks the language to articulate and enact the concepts and relationships that would support the society we want. If we only have "male" and "female," all of our experiences won't fit inside these. If we only have "job" and "hobby," how do we describe meaningful life's work outside of these? To imagine new realities, we need new words to express these.[2] This assignment is inspired by Lyx Was and mIEKAL aND, co-founders of Dreamtime Village.

Missing words, real feelings

Make a new word to describe a feeling that lacks one.

Words from the future

Make up a new word that you need to speak about the world you desire.

What is the Language Saying?

The goal of this group inquiry is to refine desire statements with the understanding that they need to stand on their own and be comprehensible to people outside the world of references of the author. In this process, the group addresses the language of a desire as it is written, rather than intuiting the intention of the author.

Five questions

Read a desire statement and have members of a group (or a partner) ask you five questions about it. Afterwards, reformulate your desire statement.

Unlikely Connections

Desires exist in relation to one another, so we must negotiate creating a world in which they connect and emerge together. As Susan Parenti has taught us, by combining our desires in unlikely ways, we can resist old meanings and generate new connections.

Weaving desires

In a group, combine your false statement with another one either from your list or your partner's list into one sentence, using linking words such as "so that," "because," "as a result," or "therefore." Resist having the results make too much sense. Discuss what new connections arise from these combined statements.

Change the Medium

The medium affects the message. To understand your desire statements in a new light, you can change the medium or form. This will allow you to refine your statements and generate more. These are best done in pairs.

Illustrating desires

Taking one desire statement from each person's list, together draw an illustration of those statements coexisting in one world. Discuss and consider reformulations.

Love letters

Write a love letter to another person in which at least two of your desire statements and one of theirs are true.

Premises Versus Consequences

New societies are founded on new premises. From these premises flow many consequences which shift and change over time. Often our first attempts at desire statements are focused on what we can see—the consequences of otherwise hidden premises. In designing to elicit a new society, we need to articulate new premises that could act as its foundation.

Questioning premises

Inspect each of your desire statements and ask: is it premise or a consequence? What would need to happen for your desire statement to become true? Speculate on actions, practices, strategies, structures that might create a context in which the desire statements would become true. Generate new desire statements which are premises for your initial statement.

Removing barriers

Discuss what are the barriers that stand in the way of your desire statement becoming true in the current society. Add desire statements that help remove these barriers—these would become premises of your statements.

New constitutions

Imagine you are writing the constitution for a new nation. Rewrite several of your desire statements as articles in your ideal nation's constitution, from which all laws in that nation will follow.

Coordinating Our Desires

Now that you have stretched and played with your desires, eliciting the input of others, and adding variety, take a moment to silently review what you have and edit it to a "second draft" of five to ten desires. As a group, work toward an aggregate list of everyone's desires statements which will become input into the process of designing a society desirable to the group.

Nesting desires

1. Write or print all your desire statements on 3x5 index cards or separate pieces of paper.

2. In your small group, share your statements by taping them on the wall and reading them out loud, slowly.

3. Together, order the statements in such a way that statements earlier in the list, if they were to become true, might imply that statements later in the list would, as a consequence, also have become true. The premises should be at the top and the consequences below.

4. See if you can order all the statements into one nested list of desires. When you are done, ask if anyone has concerns or edits so those who are quieter members have space to speak up.

Commitment

As we pivot from desire to designing interventions with others, it is worth assessing where we wish to commit to working together. Discuss the following questions as a group.

Five years
Which desire would I spend five years working to make true?

From desire to design
Which desires does your group want to focus on as the basis of its design work?

CHAPTER 12

INTERVENTION

The School for Designing a Society

The School for Designing a Society is a project of teachers, performers, artists, and activists. It is an ongoing experiment in making temporary living environments where the question "What would I consider a desirable society?" is given serious playful thoughtful discussion, and taken as an input to creative projects. Rather than orienting participants to find a comfy spot in the current social system, this School offers tools, time, ambiance, and company in which people can imagine and design a system they would prefer.

—Mark Enslin and Susan Parenti, School for Designing a Society pamphlet (c. 1999)

At the 2005 School for Designing a Society (SDaS), Mark Enslin asked his design group to imagine "impossible instruments," and someone responded, both joking and curious: "A harp made of butter." It was in this design group that I, Elizabeth, met composer-of-the-impossible Jacob Barton, and we bonded over the infinite possibilities of microtones (the notes between the notes) and invented instruments. Against the backdrop of the beautiful Appalachian Mountains of West Virginia, where our host, the Gesundheit! Institute, is located, our design group strung together indi-vidual pieces to play on our impossible, invented instruments. One person composed a protest song in Spanish as a response to the revolution in Ecua-dor at that time. Another parodied an academic presentation on a "Treeolin," an instrument they invented by stringing a fishing line across a hollow tree. I composed an "Aqua Forest Orchestra" of instruments made of water, cans, and leaves and conducted it while wearing a snorkel and flippers.

Jacob and I performed the finale in a pond fed by a waterfall. Jacob had composed this wet duet for recycled beer bottles with their bottoms cut off, played by blowing across their tops. We changed their pitch by dipping the bottoms to different depths in the pond, whose ripples made the pitch waver and wobble. To play, we stood chest-deep in the water, reading from a music stand half-submerged in the shallows, while the audience watched from the shore. At the end of the piece, we swam away across the pond. In the twenty years since then, audience members have recalled to me how otherworldly that performance was.[1]

After a month together spent generating desire statements and design-ing with them, our compositions with impossible instruments made cur-rently impossible premises seem more possible. At SDaS, small design groups are formed for participants to articulate their desires and put them to use, designing in experimental realms such as composition and performance where alternatives could coexist. If we can play across every tone to make music together, can we play across every gender? What happens when we hear musical tones we have never heard before? How does this inquiry affect our sense of possibility of other seemingly impossible things, including ones we may not yet know we desire? Our performances were manifestations of the power of art to bring forth the "not yet" by insisting on, playing with, and making space for currently impossible desires.

Prefiguring the World We Want

Some of our desires can be realized now. When we understand these desires as prefiguring the world we want, that is, as necessary but insufficient to the society we desire, that framing imbues them with more meaning and deep-ens our connection to the desires we have not yet realized. In this spirit, in organizing its sessions, SDaS aims to be inclusive in ways current institutions often are not.

It invites participants of all ages. It draws participants from all over the globe who add crucial perspectives to our collective desiring, and bolster our awareness that "the way things are" is not the only way they could be. It requires no academic credentials, but accepts students based on their inter-est in gathering communally and imagining a society they would prefer. It invites students to teach about their experiences and it invites teachers to learn. Students and teachers introduce themselves not by their titles, resumes, or what they have accomplished, but with the questions they struggle with and their desires for what they feel is missing in current society. Often this orientation attracts people in transition: burnt-out doctors and nurses, retirees, people experiencing homelessness, recent college grads. For those experiencing uncertainty and acknowledging difficulty, the program at SDaS does not have answers, but offers company and things to try, most crucially, asking participants what they actually want, independent of the stipulations of "possibility." It is pay-what-you-can, low administration, and vegetarian, the latter two principles helping to fund the former.

Also in the spirit of prefiguring our desires, many sessions of SDaS are designed to take place in beautiful settings close to nature. Most often, they have been held at the Gesundheit! Institute in rural West Virginia, but also in the gardens and abandoned buildings of Dreamtime Village in West Lima, Wisconsin and the ancient stone houses in the mountain village of Pruno, Italy. Being somewhat isolated from the rest of society helps us commit to being with each other. Being surrounded by trees, waterfalls, and fireflies helps us envision different relationships between humans and the natural world. This context facilitates the project of making community together and encourages us to see the current group as a social microcosm in which individuals have extra agency to propose and experiment with structures, events, customs, and performances in everyday life. It encourages us to make community with storytelling, campfire singalongs, performances, skill sharing, and conversation.

A School of Experimentation

Artists and social change makers have this in common: we imagine something we desire that does not exist and we work to make it exist. For people of all walks of life and skill sets, art is an ideal domain for experimentation. In contrast to other domains like heart surgery, bridge building, or accounting, in art the stakes are low enough we need not fear learning from "mistakes"—there are no right or wrong answers. The questions to ask after an experiment are more capacious than "was it successful or is it a failure?" At SDaS, we invite the audience as collaborators to discuss "what happened" and "what is the effect of what happened" and "what can we try next." We invite performance as a place to experiment with language that is not "me" or "you," but an "it" we can play with together. Through a heuristic iterative process of experimentation and variation, we innovate and learn together. Every iteration calls on our desire first to redesign it, and then, to evaluate it. Every new combination of a slowly rotating group of SDaS organizers asks each other: "What did you like about last time and what do you want now?" Mark Enslin recalls SDaS as "a hub for all sorts of experiments. . . . We tried living labs, urban gardening, collaborative publication, antiwar crosswalk theater, no-failure micro-art, design charrettes, care clubs, citizen journalism, city council poetry, and radio documentaries."[2]

A School to Generate Desires

Each session of SDaS has included some version of the assignment "Right or Wrong, My Desires." In response, our participants often formulated desire statements that they subsequently used to change their lives. One such person is Dario Solina. He came to SDaS having already started a campaign in which he asked friends and strangers to "Change My Life!" after he became disaffected with his life as a successful advertising creative in Milan. Dario took the desire assignment to heart, generating an abundance of desire statements about connection, love, play, vulnerability, and care. He joined Patch Adams on humanitarian clown trips hosted by Gesundheit! where he sang to children in hospitals and danced with men in prisons. Patch explained to the group: "Clowning is a trick to bring love close." After several clown trips, Dario decided not to take off his clown costume. For a while, he continued working at the advertising agency, clowning on his commute and with befuddled corporate clients. Eventually he took the leap of quitting his job and clowning full time. You can watch his TEDx talk, entitled "What's your excuse not to change your life?"[3]

Dario's example is very dramatic. His work went from designing corporate marketing campaigns to looking lovingly into the eyes of psychiatric prisoners, impoverished children, and alienated strangers; his uniform changed from Italian suits to clown clothes. Yet, many other participants who arrived alienated and searching have left SDaS equipped with desire statements that became projects or principles transforming their sense of purpose and connection.

In 1996, SDaS participant Brian Hagy formulated his desire that "everyone has offers." From the context of his work with adults with developmental and intellectual disabilities, Brian created the Prompting Theater, a professional performance group that was led by adults with developmental disabilities in Champaign, Illinois from 1997 to 2020. Prompting Theater members composed new pieces, arranged variations on musicals, and taught performance technique to students in Urbana schools. Prompting Theater was designed to perturb the story of disability, shifting it to one of capability and adaptation.

In 2018, SDaS undertook a "project of focusing" in response to the announcement made by the United Nations that we had twelve years left to limit climate change catastrophe. Susan Parenti responded with her play *Stop That!*—exhorting audiences to stop business as usual and connect their projects to addressing this existential crisis. SDaS hosted the "[Re-Writing, Re-Righting] Cassandra Project," gathering dozens of people from across the world in Urbana, Illinois to commit to "*be* the change needed," and discuss and design manifestations of that commitment. Susan's invitation to the project stated:

> We have 12 years left to limit climate change catastrophe and respond to it. Responses will be seriously playful—no doom and gloom (*but maybe goom and dloom*)—as a strategy to elicit involvement of others, and to elicit focus.
>
> Cassandra was a figure in Greek mythology, a woman cursed to utter prophecies that were true but no one believed. In our project we want to 're-write' (*and 're-right'*) that curse, to find our Cassandras, to listen to them, to understand from them what time it is on the clock—the ticking clock—of the world. We have 12 years left.

Desires generated at SDaS formed the premises for a number of projects like these, including On the Job Consulting, a computer consulting worker-owned business created from Sigfried Gold's desire statement: *Artists and activists have high-paying part-time work.* Urbana's Public Arts program was instigated by Danielle's desire statement: *There is art everywhere.* Desire statements formed the basis of the Urbana-Champaign Independent Media Center (see chapter 3, "From Indymedia to Media Justice") and Health Care Design Intensives, gathering carers to design new premises for systems of care (see chapter 19, "Redesigning the Care in Health Care"). As these show, desire is a mighty engine for the generation of a variety of alternatives, which in turn increases freedom.

A School of Legitimate Questions

In 1968, a group of students at the University of Illinois asked Herbert Brün and Heinz von Foerster to teach a class on heuristics. In an academic context known for its hierarchy, they wanted a class where faculty and students generated and explored legitimate questions; that is, questions they did not have answers for. These shared inquiries gave rise to curiosity, conversation, and collaboration.

SDaS founders designed a whole school around the question: "If a school were designed to address the questions you bring to it, which ones would you bring?" SDaS is a response to desire, and its focus on legitimate questions—as opposed to illegitimate ones where the asker already knows the answer—elicits the desires of its students.

Susan Parenti brought her legitimate question to a 1992 session of the school: "What is wrong with the capitalist system?" To entice the session's students to try out their ideas, she gave the following assignment:

> Imagine a hypothetical dinner with a person (friend, relative, stranger), where just as the dessert arrives, the topic of the economic system comes up and they ask, "What's wrong with capitalism?" Write a description of capitalism that would fit within the amount of time it takes to eat a chocolate mousse.

The responses were turned into three-to-five-minute performances that were later shared in house theaters. Although there are no traces we can find of the ensuing conversations, one can imagine what they might have sounded like, after seeing various experiments in trying to briefly describe the capitalism system:

> "What I saw in your piece is a description of capitalism through its negative. You traced its contours by showing everything that it is not—it presented a delightful image of what could be."

> "Capitalism and socialism are such worn out terms, pulverized by propaganda. I felt the invitation to serious playful engagement with difficult ideas."

> "You ended with a tie to patriarchy, I wonder what it would do if you started your piece with that—as patriarchy predates capitalism—and then returns to it?"

Another legitimate question, "How can children lobby their parents to take action against climate change?" resulted in the performance project "Pester Power," a musical composed by Susan Parenti with input from Rohn Koester and performed by children, for children, in schools and libraries throughout the community. As these examples serve to demonstrate: a project organized around legitimate questions addresses alienation and elicits the uniqueness of its participants.

Eliciting the Uniqueness of Participants

Based on Herbert Brün's formulation of composition, which is motivated by "a wish of bringing about that which without [the composer] and human intent would not happen," SDaS is a composition in the domain of education, one that requires and is made new by the contributions of each participant.[4] Fascism, as Manni and Herbert Brün formulated, is when the survival of the system becomes more important than the survival of its members. Under logics of superiority and mechanisms of control, conformity is praised and uniqueness is a threat. The project of SDaS represents an antithesis to fascism, providing a context for its (inherently worthy) participants to manifest their uniqueness and make meaning together. For so many, it has presented a space of connection, change of mind, and liberation.

As with most sessions, at the beginning of the fall 2000 SDaS session, all participants—those called teachers, students, collaborators, and lurkers—were invited to "design the school" through discussions of legitimate questions and the desires they brought to the table. Student Ben Emerick shared his desire for a "Cybernetics Designing Society Working Lab," then he and Steve Sloan converted a room in the schoolhouse into a space inviting participants' experiments in cybernetic design. For example, one group tried out various systems of coordinating food waste removal and food distribution for school participants and their neighbors. Discussions of desires for the school session led to inventing different shapes for sessions or modes of participation. Students named meetings of the whole group "block parties," one-time presentations "wild cards," and spaces to compose and discuss together "composiums." Sky Hall created visual boards where participants could propose and announce invitations for collaboration; this self-organizing tool became known and used in subsequent sessions as "Sky Boards." Mark Enslin invited participants to name which roles they would like to play in a given project—initiator, contributor, or consultant—nudging those less inclined to initiate to try it out. A variety of formats for participation manifested the variety of desires of the assembled participants.

◎

In 2017, right after she invited Elizabeth to collaborate on this book, Danielle was unable to attend the summer session of SDaS while also caring for her parents, who both had cancer. So Elizabeth wrote her this letter, as a way of sharing her experience of this motley group of people temporarily gathered around one thing they shared: desire for a different society. Working with incarcerated West Virginian teenagers as audience and collaborators, the group formulated desires, conflicts, contradictions, and tried out designs in a performance of care, listening, and collaborating.

August 1, 2017

Dear Danielle,

This year's summer session felt extra special to me. Participants included:

A former public policy worker, who had recently trained as a circus clown while taking time off to care for her own health and her aging parents' health, who wants to bring arts thinking into public policy.

A former engineering student, recovering from homophobia, on his way to med school, interested in psychiatry.

A comedian and healer, recovering from an abusive evangelical family to whom he's still connected, resisting calls for him to get a job.

An absurdist performance practitioner who performs as a Howling Spoon with Dog, a stuffed animal.

A retired Methodist minister, concerned about the coming schism of his Church over LGBTQ+ inclusion, was learning how to hula-hoop.

A teen who said they didn't want to leave themself out met a bear their first day, is interested in urban planning, was upset by overheard racism, offered one-on-one conversations instead of performances.

One person arrived late at night, disappeared in the morning into the woods, wanted to make a movie, was jailed for driving while Black (we provided jail support), and plans to resettle in West Virginia with help from veterans' organizations.

A psychologist and capoeira practitioner from Mexico, working with children, using movement to teach emotional and social intelligence.

A music teacher and agriculturist from Denmark, who amplified the atmosphere of motherly love with her one-year-old child and taught us some singing.

The toggling back and forth between our heads (concepts, seminars), hearts (clowning, Patch's Love Workshops, bonfires), and bodies (movement workshops, babies, dogs) made the learning and bonding deep.

Then clowning for incarcerated teenagers became a shared experience of intersecting problems that we analyzed through Conflict vs. Contradiction.

After our first visit to the detention campus for truant youth, we had a general debrief. The next class period, we all generated desire statements in response to our experiences. Here are some:

> There are no good feelings and bad feelings.
>
> Adults offer deep listening to children.
>
> Children invent and offer each other new media through which to express their discontent and other emotions and experiences.
>
> Collective response to individual suffering is sensitive and nimble, then moves routinely to evaluate formulations as conflict vs. contradiction. The sufferer controls the timing of evaluation and is a primary participant.
>
> Children participate in the decisions that affect their lives.

The next class, we tried out formulating problems (perhaps the one that our desire statement pointed to) both as a conflict and as a contradiction:

> Conflict: Adults need more time with children.
> Contradiction: Unheard adults can't hear children. (Veena)
>
> Conflict: Prisons don't prevent recidivism.
> Contradiction: Prisons benefit from recidivism. (Sleave)
>
> Conflict: Children's hard feelings are not acknowledged in school.
> Contradiction: Detention as a response to truancy generates more problems than it solves. (Dario)
>
> Conflict: If we teach students to respect authority, they will value education and be attentive and present at school.
> Contradiction: Adherence to hierarchy precludes learning and care at all levels. (Al)
>
> Conflict: Bad judges don't listen to children.
> Contradiction: Punishment refuses inclusion and participation and inhibits and postpones learning new ideas and behaviors. (Elizabeth)

> Conflict: Anger is a problem not only for students.
> Contradiction: Anger is the sign of problems and a needed motivation for systems change. (Mark)
>
> Mark then seized on our analyses as impetus and input for composing a performance for the kids at the detention center. So SDaS participants collaboratively made and performed something to address the problems we had experienced together in our previous clowning visit with them. In my estimation this worked so much better than each of us trying to figure out conflict vs. contradiction alone.
>
> Composing and performing to address and involve suffering kids, rather than "only" each other, felt more stressful, more meaningful, and better preparation for our work beyond the school. The performance we made elicited the kids' participation, and we had a weird, radical, and unlikely evening with them. . . . We created a spaceship to imagine their escape from their problems. We asked them what they wanted and amplified their responses as many spoke out of a history of silence. Dario offered a one-minute loving look in the eyes. We ended by singing together.
>
> Love and courage,
>
> Elizabeth

IV

Unearth
Contradictions

CHAPTER 13

FORMULATION

Contradictions Reveal Opportunity

> To turn contradictions into conflicts is the concern of the reformer who criticizes the flaws in a desired system. To turn conflicts into contradictions is the concern of the revolutionary who criticizes the flawlessness of an undesired system.
>
> —Herbert Brün, "Drawing Distinctions Links Contradictions"

Consider a time you received two instructions that collided, such that you could not follow both at the same time. For example, what if your mother says, "I love you. Please always tell me the truth," but when you tell her something she disapproves of such as, "Mom, I think I am gay," she responds, "Don't tell me that!" You are stuck between two statements that cannot both be followed: "I will always love you no matter who you are" and "I do not accept how you identify or who you love." Contradiction often lies in the friction between a stated principle and experienced reality—as a hypocrisy or "double bind." Consider the double bind of a worker: "To live, I need to work two jobs; but to preserve my health, I need to rest." Or a person seeking a job: "You have to have work experience to get work experience." Some of the youth living in detention described in Elizabeth's letter were living in the contradiction of being hurt for being hurt, that is, of having their agency taken by the state of West Virginia as punishment for their responses to having their agency taken due to violence in their home. Perhaps a variety of attempts to change the situation have produced the same stubborn outcome. This is living in contradiction.

Living in contradiction causes pain and emotional anguish. For those impacted by the contradiction, an unaddressed pain festers into trauma. Witnesses of the harm may find themselves part of and privileged by a system they did not choose; their attempts to intervene may be stymied, creating secondary trauma. We can unleash the energy of that anguish toward healing through collective efforts to refuse victim-blaming and insist on systems change.

This chapter is about contradictions—why to formulate them and what they do. A problem can be formulated in many ways, but formulating it as a contradiction can shift it from being fixed and inevitable to being unstable and changeable. A contradiction appears as tension between two irreconcilable realities that require a change of system to resolve. Contradictions lurk, often hidden, at sites of oppression. Oppression is always in contradiction with equity and justice, but it requires a person to name it as such. Systems appear monolithic. Formulating contradictions exposes their instability, where we can locate points of leverage so that small, strategic actions can have large consequences. In this way, formulating contradictions is necessary to making strategic interventions for social change. The work of social justice is to spotlight and activate problems as contradictions in the systems that oppress.

Distinguishing Conflicts from Contradictions

What is the distinction between conflict and contradiction? Both produce tensions, creating pressure for change. Herbert Brün distinguished them in the following way: a conflict is something that can be ironed out within a system and its laws. Like a mistake, it can be settled through correction. A contradiction cannot be resolved in the current system. There must be a change of system for resolution. When a problem is formulated as a conflict, it orients actions toward reform. When a problem is formulated as a contradiction, it orients actions toward revolution, meaning toward a fundamental change in premises of a system.

We invite you to practice formulating and reformulating problems as contradictions as a way to find strategic places to design actions. Let's illustrate the difference between conflict and contradiction with an example. Within the problem of homelessness lies fundamental contradictions in our social and economic systems, requiring intense efforts to maintain the problem as a mere conflict. There are many inherited sentences describing the problem of homelessness from many points of view:

> "I go to work every day to pay my bills; and those people just live off my work."

> "I worked two jobs, and I still couldn't afford the rent."

> "I feel sorry for them but if we build a shelter, people will come from everywhere to fill it."

> "There but for the grace of God go I. Here is a dollar, good luck."

> Add your sentence here: _____.

Let's try out ways of formulating the problem of homelessness: first, as a conflict, then as a contradiction, and then examine which solutions each formulation implies.

The problem of homelessness formulated as a conflict

Let's try formulating the problem of homelessness as a conflict and see what solutions are implied:

> *Millions of people sleep on the streets in America, the land of opportunity. People are homeless because they don't work, are addicted to alcohol and drugs, have mental health issues, or have children they can't support.*

This formulation implies the following solutions:

> *We should invest minimal funding for homeless shelters to warehouse those making poor life choices, keeping them off the street and out of the way of business. Shelters should be uncomfortable enough to encourage people to move on. For the children, we should place them with middle class, heterosexual adoptive households. We should invest the minimum needed to house the few deserving homeless, such as veterans, and pressure the rest to work.*

This is homelessness formulated as a conflict, implying that the problem can be resolved within the current system. The public health emergency of homelessness can then settle into being a fixture of American life. What makes this formulation dominant is the silencing of those experiencing homelessness justified by logics of superiority that assert their unworthiness. Business owners, policymakers, social workers, the public—even some people experiencing homelessness themselves—may all play a role in maintaining the stability of the system producing homelessness. They may assert, in their words and actions, that the conflict formulation of homelessness is the *only* formulation.

Managing Contradictions into Conflicts

As Herbert Brün wrote: "Whenever the maintenance of a system is rated more important than the maintenance of its elements [the people], then the system will solve the problems which assail it and perpetuate the problems which maintain it."[1] Contradictions destabilize a social system; the system's volatility is a sign that it is stressed and vulnerable. Contradictions are like chameleons; when visible, they are vulnerable to being eaten. To preserve and stabilize systems, those who work on their behalf—systems' actors—must disguise the contradictions as conflicts. Their voices tend to be louder and more powerful, backed up by structures that assert their power. Those experiencing the problem may be muted by deprivation, force, or threat of force. They also face the power of cultural hegemony: stories and culture that assert and assume a particular formulation of the problem, often employing logics of superiority internalized as self-blame.

These dynamics are how a boiling contradiction is made into a conflict—like forcing a lid on a steaming pot to keep it contained. But what happens when the steam builds up pressure? What happens when information or stories come to light which don't fit the dominant story? When solutions to a problem perpetuate that problem, and produce new problems, that is an indication that a contradiction may be lurking under the surface of the story. As Mark Enslin writes in "Listening and Unentitled": "It's not eviction that makes someone homeless, it's the whole economic-housing-family legal system of which eviction is one episode."[2]

Experience Unearths Contradictions

To illustrate the process of formulating contradictions, we want to introduce you to the story of Chris.[3] Chris is a forty-year-old African American man who experienced bouts of homelessness on and off for eight years, ever since he lost housing due to an accident at work and went through a divorce. Chris sought shelter with an organization that is designed around an understanding of the problem that people are homeless because they do not work enough, so they require employment. Chris got a job washing dishes at a local restaurant. With a job in hand, Chris was awarded a motel voucher, but he could not move into his own place due to the job's unpredictable hours and low wages.

Adhering to the story that America is "a land of opportunity through education," his case manager at the shelter formulated the problem as: "Chris dropped out of high school." This seemed to be a correct diagnosis, as once

Chris got his GED and retrained, he landed a full-time job. Chris finally had more stable income but could not save enough for the deposit and first month's rent. He found another agency that offered him rental assistance and applied for housing, spending his money for food on application fees. Chris, whose body showed the signs of street life, interviewed but never got a lease offer. Because the rental assistance program required a year-long lease, Chris could only secure a month-to-month efficiency apartment with a notorious slumlord, by donating plasma to raise the deposit. After a heavy rain, Chris' tiny space filled with mold. His asthma caused him to miss so much work that he was laid off. Without an income, he could not get rental assistance. Chris was evicted and this record made it impossible to find any other place.

Frustrated and wary of seeking help, Chris took up residence under a bridge and drank to deal with the frustration and the cold. When we met, he told me: "They say, 'This is the land of opportunity! If you get an education and a job you can have a home!' . . . but I did that and here I am!" Chris received food stamps for groceries, but had nowhere to cook, so he panhandled to buy fast food meals. When he asked for help, he was pelted with accusations, such as: "Why don't you get a job!" and "I don't work so you can lie around!" He felt like a failure and his drinking spun out of control. He was not eligible for the men's shelter as they required sobriety. The tent our office gave him to sleep in was thrown away by the city in an effort to "move them along," as local businesses were complaining.

The problem of homelessness formulated as a contradiction

Observing the impossible situations our society put Chris in, we can reformulate the problem of homelessness in its contradiction:

> Millions of people who sleep on the streets in America—the land of life, liberty, and the pursuit of happiness—are treated as objects, as though their value derives solely from their productive capability, as though their equality is contingent on proving their worthiness. Police and social workers alike use residents' responses to this objectification (such as self-soothing, retreating, or speaking up) to justify denying them necessities, human dignity, and care.

Chris was painfully living the contradiction of the current system. Following all the system's rules was killing him.

Points of Leverage for Change

A system is most vulnerable where and when its contradictions surface and become visible. These vulnerabilities provide strategic points of leverage for making interventions in these systems. Points of leverage are strategic times and spaces where a small intervention can have an outsized impact. Systems of domination—such as imperialism, capitalism, patriarchy, and racism—all contain many contradictions that render them vulnerable, offering multiple points of leverage for change. We formulate the contradiction; we observe to see where or when it becomes visible; this is the point of leverage. There, we design an intervention that amplifies the contradiction enough to give systems' actors pause and invite those affected to act.

Chris' lived experience of the problem contradicts the story that homelessness is a conflict that can be resolved within the existing system by suppressing homeless residents. Chris is well positioned to understand and propose changes to the system that caused the problem of homelessness; but the daily crisis of homelessness, compounded by policies that blame victims and prevent community amongst homeless residents, make it such that we, as a society, will likely not benefit from Chris' expertise on this problem. This is what the contradiction between democracy and capitalism looks like on the scale of one person against the whole system.

We can formulate this contradiction as: *Those who experience the contradictions of the current system are best positioned to critique and redesign that system, yet they are excluded from power and participation to do so.* With this formulation, what points of leverage appear? Can we hire, elect, and gather input from residents with lived experience to provide leadership toward solving root problems? Doing so brings Chris, whose voice and perspective were excluded from social services' look at the problem, into its frame as a subject. Chris benefits from being included, yes, but our society *as a whole* benefits as well, as his perspective is essential to designing responses to homelessness that address root causes. We need Chris' perspective to address the roots of the problem.

At Cunningham Township, we are responding to this formulation of the problem with these design interventions:

We prioritize hiring staff who have lived experience with the contradictions of the current system and the outcomes it creates: homelessness, poverty, discrimination, and violence.

We ensure *all* staff receive support and training to interrupt the ways shame and self-judgment—or blame and bias—can be projected on our program participants.

We invite former participants who have transitioned into more stable housing and health to become paid peer leaders and navigators helping others access support.

We create working conditions that produce high output while providing supportive structures for rest and recuperation: a thirty-five hour weekly schedule; 100 percent health insurance coverage; a wellness fund to incentivize health care that covers all therapy co-pays; ability to flex-work their schedule to care for family and self; training in de-escalation, secondary trauma, and mental health first aid; staff appreciation and celebration.

There have been many Chrises, and their families, friends, and advocates, who have refused objectification and asserted the subjectivity of people experiencing homelessness in all its forms. After decades of interventions, the US Department of Housing and Urban Development (HUD) finally supported a "Housing First" approach that provides shelter unconditionally, without work or sobriety requirements, which has proven successful.

Points of leverage shift as conditions shift—sometimes quite rapidly, because as soon as a vulnerability is exposed, those who benefit from the current system will work to hide it. In our work, we should always be assessing where there are points of leverage and be ready to move as they move. Those who suffer from a system, and their allies, can expose contradictions to challenge and change the premises of these systems. Following this, we show how to design interventions at points of leverage, observe and learn from consequences, and reformulate contradictions.

As we articulate contradictions and intervene at their points of leverage, the system kicks into crisis mode. So, systems' actors will struggle to contain the contradiction by describing it as a mere conflict they can handle. The whole field of public relations has been built around this dynamic. Those who confront contradictions face backlash—as systems' actors deny, reframe, attack, appease, or delay to stave off crisis and reestablish equilibrium. In chapter 22, we discuss how to handle backlash to our designs.

Time for a New System

In witnessing Chris' experience of homelessness (and so many like his), I have to reject the original formulation of the problem as a conflict: one where he chooses unemployment and alcohol in a land of opportunity. I am prompted to dig down to a formulation of homelessness as a contradiction—continuing to ask the question, "Why?" After discussing this conflict with my economist colleagues, they schooled me on the relationship between unemployment and inflation in the design of the US economy—a lightly state-managed capitalism. In essence, what they shared is that if too many people are employed, inflation skyrockets, pushing up the cost of everything, and the US economy stagnates or declines. Unemployment is the predictable outcome of the capitalist system that requires growth. So, the state regulates interest rates to maintain a certain level of unemployment to stabilize the economy. Some people must be unemployed in this economic system.

Guided by this discussion and understanding, here is the problem of homelessness formulated as a contradiction: *Millions of people sleep on the streets of one of the richest countries in the world. Americans are proud of their democracy, but are sustained by an economy that requires unemployment and ensuing deprivation, which a robust democracy would refuse. Homelessness is an emergent property of the system of capitalism, which manufactures scarcity amidst abundance, and only meets those needs that are profitable. Homelessness would not exist in a democracy premised on full participation.*

I shared this contradiction with Chris. He responded: "So if we all get jobs, the economy fails? How does 'you all just need to work' solve the problem then?!" We both nodded: "Yeah. Time for a new system."

CHAPTER 14

ASSIGNMENT

Find Leverage for Change

Formulating contradictions is a lifelong project, with each revision reflecting a deepening understanding of the problem and its connections to other problems. The work of formulation and reformulation is often collective, incremental, and can feel joyful as we get closer to root issues. It is essential to developing wisdom and making change.

In this chapter, we practice formulating contradictions and then using these to identify points of leverage for change. We start by modeling the process of inspecting a problem as a conflict, seeing whether the solutions implied solve the problem, and engaging in exploration of contractions. Here we use the example of the Build Programs Not Jails Campaign in Champaign County, Illinois, that effectively held off efforts to invest in jail building from 2012 until 2022. It illustrates a continuum of formulations from prison reform to abolition.

From Conflicts to Contradictions;
From Reform to Abolition

Problem as conflict: Prison reformers assert the problem of incarceration as a number of conflicts. *The problem is formulated around* **how** *humans are locked in cages, not the caging itself: Incarceration is too dirty, too racist and sexist, and too profit-making.*

Solutions implied: If we see the problem as the way we incarcerate, we may generate solutions such as: we should reform prison conditions and ban privately owned prisons.

Reflect: If we can incarcerate people in more humane conditions in publicly owned prisons and jails—then is the problem solved—and if so for whom? Illinois banned private prisons. Champaign County invested in a $20 million jail building project that promised to address mental health needs and privacy for women and LGBTQ+ identified residents. Meanwhile, the number of residents sleeping outside doubled. We reflect on such solutions as a kind of "carewashing" of incarceration to justify investment in confinement over supportive services.[1]

Reformulate the problem: *More public money is spent on jailing residents than housing them. There are so few mental health options for the poor that the only way to access mental health support is in jail.*[2]

Solutions implied: Invest in housing and health care by reallocating resources from incarceration.

Points of leverage: Shift the narrative around public safety from policing and jails to housing and health care. Pressure counties and cities to divert resources from policing and jails to rental assistance and emergency medical funds.

Observe and learn: Efforts to divest in policing and jail building come up against powerful interests. The Fraternal Order of Police (FOP) negotiated contracts that mandate staffing ratios guaranteeing an outsized take of city budgets. People of the middle class of all ethnicities are mobilized against the poor by narratives that create a false contest between safety and civil rights.

Contradiction: *Overwhelmingly, those who are incarcerated are poor and have committed crimes of poverty; incarceration exacerbates their poverty. Friends and families of the incarcerated spend $2.9 billion a year just on commissary accounts and phone calls, not counting court costs and restitution fees.*

Solutions implied: Repeal laws that criminalize poverty such as those against panhandling, prostitution, public camping, vagrancy, and drug use. Address the cascading economic effects of confinement: loss of employment, income, housing, and community support.

Points of leverage: Start emptying the jails. A strategic point of leverage to do this is to end cash bail, as around 70 percent of those confined in local jails remain there because they cannot afford bail.[3] Illinois was the first state to end cash bail: a judge decides whether a resident should be jailed before trial based on risk factors rather than setting a price for their freedom.

Observe and learn: By chipping away at the population in jails and prisons, we can demonstrate the need for less investment in them, divert resources from jailing to services, and show how structures of support and care prevent harm.

Reformulate the problem: *The prison abolition movement rejects the premise that prison solves social problems, and formulates incarceration as a contradiction: As a response to each act of violence, prison exacerbates and proliferates that violence, increasing, rather than decreasing, the need for prison, in a snowball effect.*

Solutions implied: To solve the problem of crime, we must end all forms of violence: poverty, housing insecurity, lack of health care, discrimination, isolation, misogyny, and racism. In the words of Angela Davis, we must "make prison obsolete."[4]

Points of leverage: Ultimately, we need a shift to housing and health care as human rights and all humans treated as equals. The first challenges capitalism as an economic system that generates scarcity amongst life-saving necessities to produce profit. The second takes on superiority as a logic of oppression.

Now that we have illustrated the the process of formulating from conflict to contradiction, we invite you to try with yours. Consider using the problem you worked on in chapter 7 and walk through these seven steps to practice:

1. Formulate the problem as a conflict

A conflict is something that can be ironed out within a system and its laws. Like a mistake, it can be settled through correction.

Variations on a conflict
Write out your formulation of the problem as a conflict in three different ways where it appears there is an available solution in the current system.

Consider implied solutions
Write out the solutions implied by each conflict statement.

2. Consider whether the problem is sufficiently addressed by these solutions

Consider a framework based on these questions to screen for whether and when to seek reform for your problem.

Does your problem require a change of system?
Not all do. If not, seeking reform alone may solve your problem.

Does your problem generate crises for impacted people?
This can make it harder for impacted people to participate in systems change. We must work to reduce the harm of existing systems with actions that meet current needs and enable participation while organizing for systems change.

Do you understand the roots of your problem? Can you describe the system in which the problem exists?
Pursuing reforms may help you better understand the problem and needs and avoid chasing false solutions or amplifying harm. Reform can help you trace the contours of the system and learn its shape, which can be helpful for guiding criteria and dynamics.

Do you have a base of support to make progress on systems change?
If you are alone or your group is small, homogeneous, or lacks cohesion or a shared analysis of the problem, it may be best to focus on building and educating your base. You can do this by moving on a reformist solution, winning, and then celebrating while also showing the insufficiency of the win and mobilizing toward the next goal.

3. Formulate the problem as a contradiction

Double bind
Formulate your problem as two instructions where each makes the other impossible.

Hypocrisy
Write about a time when what someone *said* painfully conflicted with what someone *did*, or where the social story about something differed from the social reality. Formulate this hypocrisy as a contradiction.

Gaslighting
Write about a painful situation or experience that keeps happening where you are told it is not happening or it is your fault; formulate this gaslighting as a contradiction.

4. Consider solutions implied by this formulation

Dance solutions
Consider the formulation of your problem as a contradiction, then write about what solutions are implied by that formulation. Play with the dance between these by altering your contradiction formulation and writing updated solutions based on those changes.

5. Locate points of leverage

Just like the ecologist who cultivates her ability to see and distinguish varieties of plant life in a sea of green, so too must those working for social change be able to hone our ability to see contradictions in our daily lives. We must seek out these ever-shifting and often obscured places and times that are ripe points of leverage for intervention.

Moments of visibility
Write 2–3 paragraphs about a time when the problem you are working on became visible to you. What was changing in its environment, or in you, such that it became visible to you? Make a list of spaces and times that the problem is emerging right now.

Reactions to visibility
Write about the various reactions (negative, positive, and in-between) that people had to its visibility.

Historical research
Research and write a short description of an earlier time in history when your problem became visible. What happened? How did

it disappear? What happened between then and now, when it is reappearing?

Illustrating emergence

Draw some concrete with plants growing up through the cracks. Write your contradiction on the concrete. Name the plants that are forcing visibility of the problem now.

6. Locate points of intervention

To identify points of leverage for change we can go to where the action is and formulate the way the contradiction is surfacing there. The Center for Story-based Strategy has a great method for locating "points of intervention"[5] for organizers to consider in crafting actions.

Story-based strategy points of intervention

Where is there a **point of production**, where things are made?

Where is there a **point of consumption**, where things are used?

Where is there a **point of destruction**, where violence, waste, or brokenness becomes visible?

Where is there a **point of decision**, such as the meeting of a city council or corporate board?

Where is there a **point of assumption**, where underlying beliefs and mythologies control the issue?

7. Choose points of leverage ripe for intervention

With practice, you will find that contradictions show up in many places. Not all places where contradictions become visible are ripe for your interventions. It is worth screening for which points of leverage are best for you and your particular group to push on.

Strategy screen

Consider where and when a contradiction you are working with becomes visible and then screen it for action by asking these questions:

Is selecting this site guided by your desires? Is it within your ethical framework? (If not, then discard.)

Does it use skills your group has on hand? Do you have the capacity to intervene here? (If not, consider adding collaborators.)

Is it possible to win some level of victory soon? Scaffolding progress toward desires through incremental steps of winnable victories can help you build a base of support and momentum toward larger-scale change.

CHAPTER 15

INTERVENTION

Ending Homelessness

In May 2017, on my first day as the elected Supervisor of Cunningham Township in Urbana, Illinois, I, Danielle walked into this public aid office with one staff member remaining (the other three had quit the Friday before) and surveyed the scene. It was a throwback to the 1980s: cubicles, typewriters, adding machines, and signs everywhere barking orders and threats. The phones began to ring, so I answered them. Nearly every caller was seeking something we did not offer: housing help.

I grew up close to issues of homelessness and housing. I come from a family of helpers. My parents were core volunteers at the Catholic Worker House of Gainesville, Florida, waking before dawn to make breakfast for migrant workers starting shifts before daybreak. My family housed a refugee family fleeing Laos, a Tanzanian Catholic nun, a Haitian student seeking asylum, a large American family whose house was foreclosed upon, and many others. From these experiences, I learned how to help, but not how to analyze root causes. It was through my organizing work that I discovered how essential it is to practice formulating contradictions to make repeated interventions in systems, with the goal of influencing systems-wide change. This story illustrates that process in my current work.

Township is the oldest form of colonial settler government in the United States, formed prior to cities, counties, and the republic itself. The function of townships in Illinois has shrunk over time to fill the gaps not filled by other forms of government, with a legal mandate to provide assistance to those out of work due to a disability. Township offers a form of hyper-local public aid, where elected supervisors like myself have broad discretion to create needed programs for the community, including rent and utility assistance, senior centers, youth scholarships, food pantries, and more. Our Township provides general assistance to residents out of work or with a new disability as a bridge until they are employed or approved for social security benefits, a process that could take years.

When I ran for the position, I knew from public reports that Cunningham Township was sitting on a significant fortune amassed by denying help to these residents. My predecessor had pushed so many people off assistance during her four-year tenure that our township went from supporting 192 residents to supporting only twenty-six by my first day on the job. One more year, and she would have achieved what appeared to be her goal of zero clients. This was during a time when poverty was on the rise in Urbana, but there was not a single news story published from the perspective of clients. Instead, only a single story in the student newspaper reported: "Michelle Mayol, the Cunningham Township supervisor . . . explained at the meeting that many Urbana citizens had attempted to defraud the system by claiming false social security need" so she "went through each file and asked suspicious clients to prove their need."[1]

In my first months as Supervisor, time and again a visitor would poke their head in the front door reluctantly, fear on their face. We would smile and welcome our visitors. It was then that they started to share what their experiences had been. One woman said, "I used to dread coming here. I would pray for strength before I came. I would walk out in tears." An older man summed up their approach: "You got nothing and then they make you feel like nothing." Another gave his assessment: "This office was a disaster, they treated you like scum of the earth." Urbana is a progressive, Midwest college town, home to the first rape crisis hotline and one of the first domestic violence shelters. The Urbana City Council passed an ordinance against discrimination based on sexual orientation and gender identity in the 1970s, before San Francisco. We have declared ourselves a sanctuary city. I asked myself: *How in this town can abuse of the poor like this happen unnoticed?* There is a perverse incentive amongst social service providers who lack adequate oversight: there is less work to do if you serve fewer people. Terminating support services is unfortunately too easy: make the systems of service too cumbersome or too toxic, and then blame the poor for their failings, a narrative justified by decades of propaganda from the Reagan era through the Clinton era to now. The role that race plays in the problem cannot be stated enough: Black residents make up the majority of Township participants in a city that has been one of the most segregated in the state.

It had been three years since Governor Rauner had been elected with the Koch brothers' money to "starve the beast" by cutting state support for social programs, making the support of local government even more essential. Our shelter system had collapsed just as the effects of climate change came rolling in. When the arctic blast of 2016 pushed Urbana into subzero temperatures, I called the mayor at home to ask her to open City Hall as a warming center, as there were no overnight warming centers in our town. She gave me a number for the local emergency management service, insisting they had a plan and could direct me. I called the number only to receive a recorded message that did not allow me to leave a message. So, I called the mayor back to let her know that the emergency number was a number to nowhere and to ask again to open City Hall, but she routed my call to voicemail.

If a person dies in the cold and no one reports on it, did it really happen? Elected officials were betting on "no." From this and other experiences, my immediate plan as Supervisor was to address our community's dearth of shelter and support for residents experiencing homelessness, along with reviving the General Assistance program. With neighbors calling for housing help every day, I quickly launched a rental assistance program to prevent homelessness and started to assess the gaps in the homeless services in Champaign County.

When I started at Township, I wrote this contradiction statement in my notebook: *Hundreds of people sleep on the street in Champaign-Urbana, a town that has no year-round shelter, but has invested hundreds of millions of dollars in other public spaces (such as renovating the courthouse to be palatial, or raising the roof of the basketball arena to improve the acoustics of games). We have enough collective resources to provide housing for every one of them, but lack political will.* With this formulation in my pocket, I worked with interns from the university on a series of interventions for collecting stories and creating and analyzing local datasets to paint an accurate picture of homelessness and housing insecurity in our community. We showed data on rising poverty, with and without students included, to overcome the long-standing story that our community's poverty statistics were inflated by residents in school. The mayor responded to our public presentation with blushing honesty: "Urbana doesn't feel like it's a poor community."[2]

We analyzed the data behind homeless women, families, and LGBTQ+ residents and noted that what support services we did have were primarily for single homeless men. I asked: "Where do LGBTQ+ residents experiencing homelessness go?" I learned that we did not track such data and, worse, that residents identifying as transgender were not welcome in the men's shelter operated by a Christian organization (in violation of the state law many of us worked to pass). I asked, "Where are the women?" and was told by several homeless providers, "There are just not that many homeless women." Digging deeper, I discovered that the federal definition of homelessness, which guides the vast majority of federal and state funding allocations, excludes the situation of many mothers with children who are moving from house to house— sometimes two weeks with an aunt in subsidized housing, or children staying with family and the mother with a boyfriend, or the whole family staying at a house where drugs are sold. I learned there was a policy fight to expand the definition of homelessness that had been repeatedly struck down by Congress.

In early 2018, Cunningham Township piloted a program to give families with children short-term hotel stays. When some of the women we worked with struggled to move into housing, I was told by social work colleagues: "They don't want to be housed." I asked them: "Why would a mother with children who are in such an extreme situation as homelessness not be motivated to take the steps offered toward housing?" Their response: "They must not really be homeless." I talked with homeless mothers, and with consent, looked into their histories. I looked at the data. I discovered one in ten of the sixty-two mothers in our pilot shelter had been coerced to conceive their first child when they were under the age of sixteen, compared to less than 0.1 percent of live births in the county.

Let's return to the problem of homelessness formulated as a conflict from chapter 13: *Millions of people sleep on the streets in America, the land of opportunity. People are homeless because they don't work, are addicted to alcohol and drugs, have mental health issues, or have children they can't support.* The official story that homeless residents are unhoused because they engage in negative behavior is troubled by the fact that over half of all homeless women are escaping from physical or sexual violence, and that 92 percent of all homeless women will experience sexual violence in their lifetime.[3]

In November 2018, I was invited to speak at the local Rotary Club, where a group of municipal leaders—among them the heads of the city, schools, library, and parks—were assembled. I decided to bring these contradictions I was observing to them to see if they had insights, as I felt stymied. I opened the talk: "I had a presentation prepared for today. I was going to provide charts and graphs of all the data on homelessness our office has gathered. I decided to scrap it and instead spend time with you, the leadership of Urbana, brainstorming solutions to a specific case. . . . You, more than most people, operate and are aware of the services in town."

With their rapt attention, I continued: "Let's walk through a real-world situation that is surprisingly common in my office. A woman with two children—ages three and eight—walks into my office. They are homeless. They were staying with their aunt, their only family member in town, who cannot have guests longer than two weeks without losing her voucher. So after a month, worried about her own housing, the aunt had to ask them to leave. For the past three nights they have been sleeping in their car, moving around to find corners of parks and quiet streets where they will not be bothered—and it is getting cold. We all can see that this is a medical and education emergency. Where can I direct them?" Multiple leaders (Rotarians) spoke up confidently in response.

> Rotarians: "*They can go to the Courage Connection!*"
>
> Danielle: "No, they have to be actively fleeing domestic violence within the last thirty days with a perpetrator who is local and an imminent threat to enter the domestic violence shelter."
>
> Rotarians: "*They can stay at Crisis Nursery!*"
>
> Danielle: "No, they only take care of children six years and under. Mom and the eight year old would have to sleep in the car in their parking lot."
>
> Rotarians: "*There is a new Emergency Family Shelter, right?*"
>
> Danielle: "Yes, and it is full, with a wait time of up to 150 days. To be eligible, this family must remain continuously unsheltered in this cold weather until they get in. They may freeze before then."
>
> Rotarians: "*Isn't there something at CU at Home?*" [Their voices were squeaking by now.]
>
> Danielle: "No, they only take single adults."
>
> Rotarians: "*How about the Salvation Army?!*" [Their desperation was palpable.]
>
> Danielle: "You have to be making at least $600 a month to be in their hotel shelter—this mother does not have childcare to be able to get a job."

Before me were the decision-makers who had the budgets and power to ameliorate this situation. I ended with a formulation of the contradiction meant for this audience: "*In our politically progressive community, with its Research 1 university and large body of politically liberal professionals, how is it that we have families with children living in cars?*" I paused, having learned that moments pregnant with contradictions call for silence that can prompt think-ing. I finally broke the silence with an invitation: "There is no local solution . . . I am asking for your help to make one." There is a power to asking people to think through a problem they assume there is an off-the-shelf solution for, so they trace the steps from conflict to contradiction.

The consequences of this talk unfolded in various ways over the next two years. The local library opened access to library resources for homeless residents and ended all library fines. The police and park district call us when they locate homeless residents and we are now working to formalize an alter-native crisis response system. The school district refers any family with hous-ing precarity to us to prevent homelessness. These are all consequences of contradictions made more visible by a strategic intervention of formulation. It did not alter power relations or represent a change of system, but it reduced daily harm while pushing toward a system based on different premises: a system where no resident is disposable and everyone is seen as equally wor-thy in their dignity and offerings. We set a new mission that reads as a desire statement: *Cunningham Township works to end homelessness and hunger in Urbana by centering on care, solidarity, and love for one another as neighbors.* It was one trip through the Spiral of Change; there would be many more.

It is instructive to try out different formulations of the contradiction to see which interventions they imply. I tried out formulating the problem in a moralistic way: *The Bible commanded, 'You shall open wide your hand to your brother, to the needy and to the poor, in your land' and yet the 70,000 Chris-tians of Champaign County allow brothers and sisters to sleep outside with no shelter, while the county has over 200 Christian churches that sit empty every night.*[4] In fact, the moral weight of this formulation of the contradiction has led members of the faith-based community to cobble together shelters to fill the gaps caused by the sudden closure of all the local shelters for men and youth. These shelters were admirable—also stressed from lack of resources, while refusing public funding—and run by friendly volunteers, who were, at times, discriminatory against transgender and queer residents.

I tried out formulating the problem in economic terms, so that it points to lack of investment in public housing: *Over 500 bookings in the jail, or 4.5 percent, are for residents without addresses. Jail is the new public housing—and it comes at the public price tag of $110 per night stay.* This formulation points to redirecting funds from jail expansion and criminal justice reform to hous-ing. As you will see in chapter 21, this is a strategy Champaign-Urbana Cit-izens for Peace and Justice pursued, but in the end a $20 million dollar jail project was voted in.

Finally, while piloting family hotel stays at Township in 2019, I chose this formulation of contradiction focused on the physical safety of children:

Local girls are raped as children, and then again as teens, and forced—by policy and culture—to bear children without the resources either to care for themselves or their children, or to heal from the trauma they have endured. To house their children, they may be subjected to additional predation and abuse, finding themselves in cycles of violent or unhealthy relationships. Their children may be taken from them by the state, which deepens the trauma they and their children experience, causing mental health issues that expose them to further housing instability and harm. Looking back, this formulation names a root cause of women's homelessness as lack of safety, physical and sexual assault, and trauma; it struck close to home for me as a survivor.

With this formulation in hand, I started to work on addressing the cycle of violence and trauma that is produced and reproduced for children experiencing homelessness. I wanted to create safe housing to keep families together and support them in finding permanent housing. At Township, we worked to locate a partner and funding to expand emergency family housing. At one point we had a nonprofit lined up to run it and all the necessary funding, when a change in leadership at that organization unraveled everything. When the COVID-19 pandemic hit in 2020, we realized we were out of time to find another organization to operate a family shelter. I decided to open a temporary family shelter through Township. We made a call to the community for private donations and received over $100,000 in the first year. We located a hotel that was emptied by the pandemic and, with Jazmine Hernandez, an intern graduating with her Master of Social Work, launched a small shelter. With friends at the Unitarian Church, we organized a volunteer "Bucket Brigade" to deliver food, toiletries, and safety supplies to residents shut in due to the virus. With Urbana Park District and Sola Gratia Farm, we launched Solidarity Gardens to ensure those buckets were filled with fresh vegetables grown by neighbors with spare land, or time, or both.

Able to prove our successes, we went to the voters to ask for a tax increase to make the family shelter sustainable in the long term. In the worst economic downtown in almost a century, nearly two-thirds of Urbana voters said yes to increasing our tax levy by 40 percent. The power of taxes is that by every household giving an additional $3 per month, we were able to raise $600,000 more annually. With this guarantee, we purchased two apartment buildings in downtown Urbana to shelter homeless families with children in what became our Bridge to Home program. We put out a call for furniture and received more than we needed. We put out a call for volunteers to clean and prepare the apartments, and they were set up in one weekend, with children of the volunteers picking out gift baskets for the children moving in. We worked with the Housing Authority of Champaign County to have vouchers assigned for our homeless families and get rapid rehousing support to help families bypass shelter altogether. We help over fifty homeless families with children annually move into more stable housing and help dozens of residents with disabilities do the same. This is what community looks like.

The formulation of sexual violence as a root cause of homelessness helps us craft the program design, but it misses economic factors. The larger economic realities remain: two-thirds of renters in Urbana are rent burdened, spending more than a third of their income on rent. We reformulate: *Wages have not kept up with the cost of housing, such that half of all renters nationally and two thirds of all renters locally are rent burdened. This means many families are one or two emergencies away from losing their homes.* This formulation points to the need for an increase in wages—the majority of states have set their own minimum wage in the face of federal inaction on this—and more power for labor to set their price and working conditions.

The above formulation misses an analysis of the intersection of capitalism and misogyny and how women's lives are devalued and the abuse of their bodies "justified." In reflecting on this, I reformulated: *Women and families face increasing housing insecurity due to the convergence of late-stage capitalism, where housing scarcity is used to drive market growth, and racialized patriarchy, which positions women, especially women of color, on the frontlines of dislocation, discrimination, and violence in the pursuit of endless growth.*

How we formulate contradictions opens up different ways of seeing and using points of leverage to make interventions for systems change. As we see, there are multiple roots and therefore multiple contradictions embedded in problems, and these contradictions will shift as systems adapt. The objective is not to find, and then fight over, the one *best* contradiction or *best* answer, but to continue to explore, understand, and then make progress in intervening in systems. Often, different organizations will work on different aspects of a problem. They align their formulations with the audiences they are designing interventions for. Understanding the plurality of contradiction presents an opportunity to build coalitions between organizations rather than fight over the right approach. A variety of formulations point to a variety of ways to intervene.

V

Design
Interventions

CHAPTER 16

STORY

Designing Care for a Loved One

When I, Elizabeth, was twenty-three, a horse accidentally kicked my mother in the head, resulting in a brain injury. She had to relearn how to walk, while her boss demoted her from being the director of class action litigation to doing case law. She had spent decades making systemic change: forcing all polling places in New York City to be wheelchair accessible before the ADA, suing slumlords on behalf of all their tenants, securing social security disability benefits for green card holders, to name a few. Now suddenly, Connie Carden found herself working case-by-case to get children into the right classroom. She wanted to change this system too, to render her job unnecessary, but she was stuck.

Feeling frustrated, she relearned not only to walk, but to run, and to run marathons. Starting at the age of sixty, she completed the New York City Marathon three years in a row, with finish times of 4:44, 4:34, and 4:14. Five days after her third marathon, she suffered a heart attack, resulting in a second, more severe brain injury that robbed her of most of her memory.

While design concepts could not lessen the pain of what had happened to her, they were immensely helpful to me in figuring out what to do next. A doctor friend drove seven hours to tell me that medical science couldn't offer us much, and that I was the expert on what her life should be like. A nursing home was her most likely future, but these institutions would threaten her autonomy and fail to pay her attention personal enough to stimulate her adequately, which would lead to depression and health problems. I knew that frequent visits from friends and family would be the linchpin of her wellbeing, and that convenience and conviviality in her situation would attract the most visitors.

I had Danielle's formulation of democracy as "*the degree to which people participate in the decisions that affect their lives*" ringing in my ears, so I asked my mother what she wanted. She said: "A sense of purpose."

I arranged for her to work at a soup kitchen, continue attending her women's discussion group and choral rehearsals, and organized piano lessons and Pilates classes. Because her cognitive disabilities prevent her from coming up with her own sources of stimulation, I try to see to it that her activities are abundant and varied. She likes reading, doing jigsaw puzzles, playing cards, and going to the park. At night, my partner reads novels with her and plays the piano, connecting his needs to prepare for class and relax with her needs for external narrative and musical company. She's an invariably rapt audience member. In the park, she applauds when the players make a basket and reaches from her wheelchair to smell the roses. Even though she can't recall events or hold up her end of a conversation very well, her sunny energy, interest in people, and her determination to participate win her friends and admirers wherever she goes. This reciprocity of good feeling is made possible by her being well cared for by people who appreciate and engage her.

As I write this, my mom, my partner, our five-year-old daughter, our new baby—born the day we signed a contract for this book—and I live together in Crown Heights, Brooklyn, supported by friends, family, neighbors, teachers, and caregivers. I come to this formulation through caring for my mother: *Care is the work of meeting human needs in the context of human complexity for the purpose of eliciting connection, uniqueness, and growth.* Designing her care has informed my politicization over the past twenty years, and my visions for the society I desire, where care even better than hers is available to all. Claiming my mother as a radical mentor for designing care has deepened my connection to my work, my neighborhood, and the movements I participate in.

CHAPTER 17

PRAXIS

Where to Begin

The society I want needs every person
everywhere to design it.

—Marianne Brün, *Designing Society*

Design is when we make that which, without us, would
not exist.[1] Design is when we put our desires into action
and manifest our uniqueness through our choices. We
design toward our own liberation and the liberation of
others, to make room for possibility, generate ideas, and
therefore increase freedom. We are all designers. We all
have desires, intentions, and criteria, and we use them to
make choices. Claiming a place for all of us as designers
and initiators challenges long-entrenched stories about
who designs, and who serves coffee to those who design.
Despite our culture's ubiquitous individualism, we nearly
always design in collaboration. And collaborating can be
a joy. We invite you, dear readers, to be designers—with
or without training, with or without sufficient confidence.
The only requirement is that you want to make a change
and are willing to do something about it.

In the last section, Unearth Contradictions, you identified sites of contradiction as points of leverage for systems

change. In this section, we invite you to experiment with designing interventions at these points of leverage, guided by your desire statements. This is where you move from strategy to generating tactics through design. Your design can be an experiment to learn something; a provocation to unstick a problem; or an intervention toward a desired goal. Your design may be a single intervention or a series of interventions. It may have many parts or phases. Although your design may have stated goals, rarely can you predict outcomes. But you can design heuristic iteration, where you observe outcomes and make decisions about your next design based on your observations.

Just as we began this book asking you to formulate your desires, so too we begin this section on design by inviting you to design interventions. So far, the sections have been structured to teach formulation, practice with assignments, and then reflect on those concepts in action with a story of an intervention. In this section on design, we change this pattern. These next two chapters interleave our formulations and assignments as praxis. Here, you will start designing with three basic tools—selecting criteria, generating constraints, and drawing distinctions—to generate material to work with as you study design principles and tools. (Just as in a pottery class, you need clay to practice technique.) This is followed by another playsheet that can help you turn design sketches into a project. The next chapter provides principles you can bring to bear on your nascent designs. We illustrate with an intervention in health-care design; and finally, we offer design tools borrowed from different domains: group process, cybernetics, permaculture, and performance.

Select and Reject Criteria

Criteria are statements you consult to make decisions. We generate significance by intentionally choosing the criteria we use to make decisions. We invite you to carefully select (and actively discard) criteria to guide design decisions. It helps to generate some criteria up front before you design and allow other criteria to surface as needed during the design process.

Following Herbert Brün, we measure freedom by the number and quality of alternatives one has in making a choice.[2] We distinguish choice as "the act of choosing" and "alternatives" as the objects to be chosen among. When there is only one option, there are no alternatives, therefore, no choice and no freedom. If there are many alternatives to choose among, there is more freedom. The process of design involves the generation of many alternatives (consider a group brainstorming dozens of options for what to do).

Once you have a lot of alternatives, how do you go about making a choice, turning your freedom into action? To make a choice you consult criteria: desires, values, feelings, and past decisions. There are any number of criteria that *could* inform a single choice; take care to select and reject them as you see fit. Ideology often operates through inherited criteria we are not aware of. Some of these criteria we would reject if they were brought to our attention. Others we listen to or amend. These can show up as the voices of a parent, grandparent, boss, teacher, or person of authority. Herbert Brün called these voices one's "inner committee of criteria" who show up whenever one is confronted with a decision. Composer and SDaS co-founder Rick Burkhardt animated this concept with a "criteria sombrero" he fashioned with holes in the brim for a performance at SDaS in 2008. When confronted with a decision, up through the holes popped different puppets as criteria, competing to advise, admonish, or encourage his character.

Some criteria you may want to appoint to the committee, so to speak, and others you fire from it. For example, I, Elizabeth, choose care as a primary criterion in my designs, along with abundance and redundancy to support care. I describe the process of codesigning care with my mother in chapter 16. I use the word "care" when I wish to speak of the work of meeting human needs in the context of human complexity for the purpose of eliciting connection, uniqueness, and growth. I would argue that each of us needs food, water, daylight, shelter, physical and emotional safety, bidirectional love and care, education, belonging, other people to connect to, a sense of purpose, art, physical activity, and the ability to participate in the decisions that affect our lives. At the same time, each of us has a set of needs particular to us, which may fluctuate, such as: an allergen-free environment; a particular ratio of time with others to time alone; access to particular foods, medicines, or activities needed for our well-being. When I design with care as a core criterion, I take all these needs into account. Through meeting their needs, care actively elicits the cared-for person's uniqueness.

Care meets needs. Care is not only a criterion for design, but it helps us all be designers. When needs are met, we are able to take the risks and contribute our uniqueness without fear of punishment. In this way, we add meaning, specificity, and connection to the world we're building. Care nurtures participation. What are the emergent properties of care? Imagination, kindness, and the unexpected.

Decision reflection

Take a moment to consider a decision you made recently. How did you approach it? What sentences or arguments went through your mind? Try writing a few down and giving them names.

Criteria skit

Write a short skit for you and a handful of puppets where you are considering what to do about a problem and the puppets, representing different criteria, attempt to persuade your decision. Name the criteria and give them voices. They could be roles (mother, teacher, pastor, artist); principles (like compassion, determination, responsibility, curiosity); or desires. Consider where they came from; for example, did you inherit or invent them?

Choosing criteria

Revise the skit, in which you are now: hiring some criteria, firing others, and creating ones that are missing. In a group, this can be a fun improv game where audience members tag criteria in and out of the scene.

Use Desires as Criteria for Design

Your desire statements are criteria for designing. In chapter 10, we introduced the concept of desires as orientation for design and in chapter 11, we practiced making desire statements. Return to these statements and make new ones if you wish.

Choosing desires

Which desire statements do you wish to use as guiding criteria for your design?

Generating desires

What are additional desire statements you can generate around this project? You can think of these as intentions or guides for your design.

Set Constraints

Constraint spurs creativity. We have come to recognize this is a fundamental paradox of art-making: our brains seem to light up when they have a puzzle to solve. Bringing this orientation when we find ourselves navigating the constraints of oppressive systems, we can sometimes approach them as design constraints to maneuver around.

Inherent constraints

Constraints already inherent in a situation may not initially seem generative, in fact they may bring along feelings of frustration, but they can be turned into design challenges. Name the existing constraints of your design. For example: "I will write short stories that fit in the time frame of my baby's nap."

Connecting needs and offers

List needs and offers and use these as constraints to design connections. For example: As I am recovering from surgery, I will write letters to prisoners to address our experiences of confinement.

Desire as constraint

Select a desire or set of desires to constrain your design. For example: Architect Friedensreich Hundertwasser desired that trees pay rent through shade, oxygen, air filtration, dampening noise, and bird habitat. He designed buildings where trees inhabited units, growing out and up the sides of buildings.

Bad design as constraint

Think of a bad design. Articulate the missing criteria as constraints you wish the designers had used. For example: Can openers . . . "must not spray the food on the user." The economic system . . . "must not chew through human lives."

Experimental constraints

Experiment with different constraints to see what happens. For example: Rachel Prizant Kotok compiled a book of palindromic poetry—*Morpho Didius: Palindromic Poetry*—where every poem reads the same forwards and backwards. She uses this experimental constraint, the palindromic form, for writing the process of healing from trauma.[3]

Imagining future constraints

What will participants in your project wish your design constraints had been?

Design to Avoid

Even designs with the best intentions can have unintended and undesirable consequences. Consider Quaker-led prison reform. Their intention was to provide space to allow a person to reflect on their actions "alone with their God," but this resulted in the traumatic design of solitary confinement.[4] When designing, stipulate that which you want to avoid as part of your design.

Design against misunderstanding

What are the worst-case scenarios of your design? Where is your design vulnerable to misunderstanding? Imagine different intended audiences and how they could mistake your intentions. Consider changes to your design that stay true to your intentions but avoid these misunderstandings.

Negative desire statements

Formulate desires statements for your design written in the negative: *I do not need to work two jobs to afford life.*

Make Distinguishing Descriptions

A distinguishing description of your project sets it apart from what has come before and highlights its unique offerings. Formulating these helps to sharpen your thinking and your project design. The best distinguishing description is brief. It is strong on nouns and verbs rather than loading up unnecessary adjectives and adverbs to distinguish your project. It avoids clichés, buzzwords, and overused idioms.

Self-description

Write a distinguishing description of yourself, meaning a description that is not used to describe any other person.

Love letters

Write a distinguishing description of someone you care about such that it captures the uniqueness of that person. Give it to them. Prepare for a surprised and loving response.

Draw Distinctions

The signal that you need to draw a distinction is when you notice that a concept holds too many ideas. When you find you are stuck or confused, check if it's time to draw a distinction. When you turn one concept into two, you open up more alternatives. For example, drawing a distinction between a job (for survival) and work (your purposeful project) opens up the alternative to hold a job while pursuing and identifying with one's work. Or, drawing the distinction between sex (biology) and gender (identity) has opened the possibility that these two might not match, which opened the possibility of being transgender, which opened the possibility of being nonbinary, which opened more space inside the binary for all of us to occupy with our gender performances and the feelings of freedom of expression we experience or long for.

Consider this desire statement by Danielle, which draws a distinction between biology and behavior, opening up space for many more people to be mothers: *A mother is someone who provides care for someone else who is challenged to meet their own needs. Most people are mothers for some period of time in their lives. Mothering is an activity supported in every institution and aspect of social life.*

Draw a distinction in your problem

Examine your formulation of the problem and look for the words that carry the most meaning or do the most work to carry your intention. Try to draw a distinction between what you do and do not mean by these words. Reformulate the problem accordingly.

Draw a distinction in a desire statement

Repeat this process with three desire statements. Look for clichés and words that would benefit from more specificity.

We offer this playsheet as a tool to design a new project or further develop a design in progress. These are the foundational questions we ask ourselves when beginning to design an intervention.

What is your project? Provide a current formulation—the one you use in conversation.

What **problem** is the design addressing?

Formulate the problem as a **contradiction**, such that it cannot be resolved in the current system.

What are the **desire statements** that guide the design? Write at least five.

State your **intention** for the design? Finish the sentence, "I want this project so that _____."

What are the **criteria** that you want to help guide your design?

What are the **criteria** that you want to reject in designing your project?

List things you want to **avoid** with your design.

What are some **distinctions** you want to make in your design?

What **distinguishes** your design from similar projects that already exist?

Provide a **distinguishing description** that could not be used for other projects.

How does your design **generate alternatives**?

How does your design **decrease differences in power**?

How does your design **increase participation**?

CHAPTER 18

Principles to Guide Your Design

> We believe that everyone is an expert based on their own lived experience, and that we all have unique and brilliant contributions to bring to a design process.
>
> —Design Justice Network,
> "Design Justice Network Principles"

Design is a way to manifest our desires in the world in which we live. We use the word design when we want to connect *creativity* (the act of making) to *impact* (the act of moving something forward to make progress). Design implies care, intention, and strategy. It invites experimentation and revision. Democracy is an emergent property of collectively designing our society.

Design has many meanings in the world of business, engineering, and technology which emphasize the technical aspect of the term. We use the word design in the context of intervening in dynamic social systems, where design can open up fields of potential rather than determining specific outcomes. We do not use design to mean "social engineering," that is, the use of centralized planning to manage social change and regulate the future development and behavior of a society. We advocate for "participatory design," where those impacted by designs participate in their making, so that we shift culture and structure toward a more equitable society. We imagine a world where the joy of creative agency and manifesting one's uniqueness is freely available to everyone—to quote the Zapatistas: "a world where many worlds fit."

Here we present some design principles that address the who, how, and when of participatory design. We start with designing for participation to help you increase the inclusivity of designs. In designing for systemic change, we offer design criteria toward equity. Finally, in designing for the long haul, we recommend processes by which to reflect and learn. Throughout this praxis chapter, we offer invitations for consideration and practice, as well as questions for you to reflect on in relation to the intervention you are designing.

DESIGN FOR PARTICIPATION

When the leadership and participation of those impacted by decisions is a premise from the start, equity becomes an emergent property of the design. Equitable design supports the participation of those experiencing the pain of the problem, whose legitimate questions it centers.

Consider this desire statement: *Everyone participates in the decisions which affect their lives such that society meets all human needs unconditionally.* How can we design to increase participation such that this audacious desire becomes our shared reality? This book in its entirety is a guidebook for participation. Here we provide some questions to consider so as to build participation into the foundations of your design in these areas: collaboration, confidence, intersectionality, and coordinating a variety of tactics.

Participation questions

How can you design your project to increase participation?

How can you design your project so that increased participation results in better decision-making for all those impacted?

Design for Collaboration

As Herbert Brün's assignment "Floating Hierarchies" makes apparent (see p. 202), chamber musicians are experts in small-group decision-making processes and nuanced coordination. They have honed their skills in tracking dynamics and roles. But how many of them do you think recognize their skill set as necessary for the future survival of humanity?

There are many ways we already engage in collaboration. In designing for collaboration, we must attend to and grow the collaborations we are already engaged in. For example, "Wow, my reading group turned into a full-hour discussion on how to prepare for climate change in our neighborhood." This new attention entails noticing dynamics and structures in our groups, reflecting on them, and bringing them to the group for discussion. In designing interventions, taking time to formulate *the structures of collaboration* we want will generate compounding benefits. We can reshape our experiences of collaboration with our collective gratitude, critique, and curiosity. That said, there is so little foundation in our culture and social structures for collective decision-making, it is important to name this and hold a long vision for this transformation. This is our desire statement about participation: *Greater participation results in better decision-making*. It is not always true, but we commit to designing a society in which it is.

Collaboration questions

Where are the stuck places in your design where collaboration would enrich it?

Who are all the people impacted by the problem you are working on?

Who is already working on a similar problem? Where is there wisdom in this work?

Can you invite them to a discussion and potentially co-design?

Who are unlikely collaborators who could bring in an important point of view? (For example, consider inviting an artist to a design session composed of engineers or an engineer to a design session with artists.)

What pitfalls of collaboration have you experienced and how can you design to avoid them?

Design for Confidence

Designing for confidence entails identifying and avoiding the mechanisms, both blatant and subtle, by which those in power have excluded many from collaboration and decision-making. Additionally, it involves learning what mechanisms and cues, both blatant and subtle, send the opposite message to encourage the participation of the habitually excluded.

Like the financial economy, there is also an economy of attention, and the two are linked and feed into one another. In the economy of attention, some people have their stories heard and attended to, and others have their stories interrupted or silenced. Some stories are believed outright; others are subject to dismissal or gaslighting. Over time, those dismissed stop talking, participating, or even believing their own stories. Theirs is a kind of emotional and mental occupation. Repeated experiences like this ossify into different levels of confidence, which create different "classes" in the economy of attention. To expand participation, we attend to the economy of attention and grow the confidence of those at its margins.

Participation is often misunderstood as speaking but it is equally about listening attentively, reflecting, and learning. An engaging lecture might have a high level of participation as students take notes, compare the words to their assumptions and experiences, and ask questions. A roundtable discussion where everyone is checking their cell phones might look like a participatory space but is less so than the lecture described above. An event with great turnout where half the attendees (let's say the women and people of color) are shut down, fearful, and unable to speak their thoughts is a failure in participation. The group has been robbed of their perspectives. To design for confidence, we need to build our own and develop the confidence of others. One of the first steps to increasing participation is self-reflection about your own experiences. We invite you to try out the following assignments.

Confidence assignments

Discuss or write about spaces and projects where you felt confident, seen and heard. Remember what it felt like. List the conditions and circumstances that led to that.

Discuss or write about spaces and projects where you felt shut out or shut down. List the conditions and circumstances that led to that.

In the next gathering of people you attend, become an investigator of attention and confidence. Draw a picture that represents the flows of attention. Note who appears to participate confidently and who does not. How do you know? Try playing, lovingly, with ways to shift these flows—with body position, eye contact, speaking in a way that implicitly acknowledges speakers who seem to have been ignored or call on those who are quiet to speak.

Discuss or write about how your design can include and build the confidence of participants and make use of multiple ways of knowing.

Design for Intersectionality

Designing for inclusion requires you to develop an intersectional analysis—one that recognizes that a social problem affects different groups in different ways, and that each of us belongs to multiple groups. "The qualities and skills that matter most for intersectional leadership are curiosity, listening, openness and creativity," said Rinku Sen. "By asking questions, we can look at a problem not just through the lens of our own experience, but also those of others whose identities might make them vulnerable to harm. . . . The standard isn't how intersectional is your identity, but how intersectional is your analysis? Regardless of identity, the analytic tools are always available to help us solve problems for everyone."[1] Intersectionality is not layers of identities; it is an *analysis*, a way of connecting the experiences of living with different identities. If we start with intersectional analysis, we can avoid reproducing designs which fall short or do harm. Bringing an intersectional analysis helps us understand oppression and its interconnections by designing solutions that work for a wide body of people and forging coalitions that can build power to create equitable social systems.

Intersectionality assignment

Borrowing from Sen's analytical method, take the following steps: find out who else might be experiencing the problem you're solving, seek them out (or respond when they seek you out), listen to them deeply, share your truth, and apply that new understanding to your strategy.

Coordinate a Variety of Tactics

We can be so much more effective if we ask ourselves how very different tactics can work together to perturb systems toward a shared vision. Every time you hear someone arguing against one tactic in favor of another (this often happens with the valence of radical versus liberal) let a little bell ring in your head and ask yourself: could both tactics be pursued simultaneously in such a way as to increase your chances of success? In Chapter 1, we discussed a good example of a successful coordination of a diversity of tactics in the New York State rent laws overhaul—in which electoral politics, policy advocacy, autonomous- and non-profit-led canvassing and organizing, and direct action came together to create an unstoppable force.

Coordinating tactics assignment

Discuss how you can coordinate multiple tactics from the following list of tactics.

> **Direct service** reduces the harms of the current system while building solidarity and community. The taxing impacts of problems can exhaust the capacity of those affected to analyze root causes or organize toward systemic solutions. Meeting direct needs is absolutely necessary to enable the participation of the people most affected by any social problem.

> **Education**, including research and advocacy, both influences policy and changes culture. It is how we build shared analysis and a base of support.

> **Creative work** is not only in the service of these other tactics but stands on its own. It can ask big questions, help reframe problems, shake up understanding, or make unusual connections.

> **Legal work** can institutionalize and enforce ethical standards of human conduct, defend the rights of the marginalized, and shake up entrenched practices of oppression.

Policy advocacy presents specific changes to law and procedure that create frameworks for what we want.

Electing candidates who are accountable to their communities is key and the ballot is one of the few places where we assert equality with "one person, one vote." Organizing against voter suppression and felony disenfranchisement is core to any project requiring policy change.

Direct action, including civil disobedience, resists oppression and makes hidden contradictions visible, while manifesting the world we want to live in.

When we coordinate a variety of tactics, we are designing for intersectionality and building networks of solidarity. The *variety* means we must design many entrances into our project and many roles for different interests and identities. These approaches foster a culture of participation in which we look to see what we can do, who else we can include, what each person brings, and how our positions and contributions can fit together for the benefit of all.

DESIGN FOR SYSTEMIC CHANGE

Fear, scarcity, and violence generate more fear, scarcity, and violence. Designing a world of love, abundance, and peace requires generating alternatives to break these destructive, reflexive patterns, and developing a different momentum of safety and well-being. Abundance entails not only more than enough of what is needed, but more than enough of a variety of alternatives for meeting human needs. If freedom is measured by the number of alternatives I have to choose among when making a choice, a large variety of alternatives increases my freedom so long as these alternatives are practically available to me.[2] Using Herbert's formulation of freedom, we see that abundance can be generated by increasing alternatives. A primary effect of neoliberal privatization has been to increase the number of alternatives available to the wealthy by stripping alternatives from the public. This is the mechanism by which poverty oppresses: in the decisions that affect our lives, poverty drastically reduces the number of alternatives we can choose among.

Increasing Alternatives

Over the past twenty years, what has become more expensive are essentials to material well-being: health care, college, childcare, housing, and food.[3] What has become more affordable are material amenities: furnishings, clothing, cell phones, toys, TVs. Freedom means not being forced to choose between food, rent, medicine, and a phone call to a loved one in prison. We are free when we have time to be with our families, and give attention to the health, happiness, and growth of ourselves and our communities. We are free when we can choose education and work that fulfills us.

People who can make choices have power. Power accrues through alternatives. We must work to increase alternatives and choices to generate abundance for everyone. We encourage you to try following the steps in the assignment provided below.

Increasing alternatives assignment

Write about a painful time when you did not have enough alternatives to choose among.

List alternatives you wish were available to you now that are not.

List alternatives you wish were available to everyone.

What alternatives will your design add?

What conditions are necessary for people to be able to choose from these alternatives?

Decreasing Power Differences

Increasing the number of alternatives available *to everyone* will necessarily entail decreasing differences in power. According to Herbert Brün, this is what distinguishes ethical behavior.

It is myopic to conceive of democracy as only by the ballot, when in our workplaces and political bodies, we silently acquiesce to oligarchy, ceding ever more power to ever fewer people. Decreasing power differences means sharing decision-making power and holding decision makers accountable to those affected by the decision. How do we design structures that decrease power differences?

At the beginning of "Undoing Racism" workshops run by the People's Institute for Survival and Beyond, facilitators ask for a show of hands of who considers themselves a "gatekeeper," meaning someone who controls access to some resource or decision-making authority. Usually, a few people raise their hands, but not many. At the end of the training, the facilitators ask the same question. One of their goals is to have everyone identify as a gatekeeper. They guide everyone in the training in looking at their own lives to consider: first, what resources and decision-making power they have access to; and second, how they might share those resources and power to undermine racial hierarchy.

Decreasing power differences questions

What power differences manifest at the site of your project?

How can your design lessen or eliminate those differences?

Making Parallel Institutions

One contradiction in our current society is that to meet our needs we must participate in the systems that maintain oppression and ecological destruction. Every time we pump gas into our car to pick up our kids we are contributing to climate catastrophe, and the political lobby denying it, that jeopardizes their future. Every time we buy groceries to go home and cook, we are adding to the mound of plastics growing so quickly that its volume will soon surpass the volume of fish in the ocean. Labor abuses fund the affordability of cheap goods, and yet, often we lack alternatives. How do we withdraw our support from these systems while also meeting our needs?

Parallel institutions build infrastructure and knowledge to be ready to replace undesirable systems when they fail. The collapse of old systems generates fear and power vacuums; in these contexts, self-interested strongmen can grow their followings, shrinking spaces for experimentation and imagination. Building parallel institutions is an anti-authoritarian move that prefigures the society we want by "building a new world in the shell of the old."[4] By creating parallel systems now, we smooth the transition from undesirable systems premised on control and profit to desirable systems premised on cooperation and equity. For example, ecovillages are communities dedicated to developing and modeling parallel ways of meeting needs that greatly reduce or eliminate the use of fossil fuels. At the Earthaven Ecovillage in Asheville, North Carolina, residents live in passive solar homes with power from micro-hydro power systems and have built experiments where bicycles power their washing machines.[5]

Parallel institutions assignment

Select a human need related to your problem.

Imagine two different ways to meet that need.

Add two more audacious ways to meet that need that leapfrog possibility.

Imagine an institution built around those ways of meeting needs.

Write a short story that includes one from each of the above.

Designing for Reform to Revolution

We began with gathering stories and people to puzzle over different formulations of the problem. We reformulated our problems as both conflicts and contradictions, pointing toward reforms and revolutions. In doing so we face another contradiction: *To build a foundation of support for working toward a more desirable society, based on different premises, we need to win victories here and now, but most winnable victories are reforms within current systems.* Working to change these systems we can unwittingly reinforce their premises, thwarting our long-term goals. We refer to these as "false solutions." To avoid false solutions, we work on reforms guided by our desires. In this way, we map the contours of the system, providing invaluable feedback while building a base of support. The sweet spot in organizing for systemic change is to design a staircase where every step leads toward our desired society, even though some steps are placed within this one. We can build toward revolution through reforms, whereby changes *in* system lay the groundwork for changes *of* system. Winning these victories now reduces harm, helps us educate ourselves, and builds broader support for bigger victories later.

Reform to revolution questions

What are some false solutions in the work we are doing?

What are reforms we can win now that would lead us to the systems change we want?

DESIGN FOR THE LONG HAUL

There is a seduction in a plan, in a concrete design. In a goal-oriented schema, progress is measured in relation to the design. Such a rigid structure cannot embody the heuristic process needed for designing a non-oppressive society. In a goal-oriented process, you decide in advance what result will constitute having accomplished it. You implement the process and see what happens at the end. A heuristic process, in contrast, involves observing, learning, and adjusting to new information at every step of the process. A goal-oriented process happens once. A heuristic process happens continually, allowing your interventions to be agile and giving you opportunities to change your mind.

Social systems are complex and in flux, so changing them requires this kind of flexibility. We recommend that your design includes its own mechanisms for change, by building into your project design many occasions to reflect, learn, and reevaluate the next move you've planned. Your formulations of your problem and your desires function as your lodestars, yet they too may be re-examined and adjusted as new information and circumstances present themselves.

Heuristic design assignment

Pencil in a timeline for your project and insert into the timeline occasions of reflection, assessment, and redesign. Use an eraser liberally.

Treating Conflicts as Teachable Moments

As a heuristic process, designing a society must include more and more participants. As it does, designs must be negotiated and renegotiated—a process that inevitably involves disagreement. Conflicts can be teachable moments and facilitated conflict can improve a design. Mary Parker Follett, a nineteenth-century organizational theorist who promoted noncoercive power-sharing and reciprocity in approaches to management, wrote: "Our 'opponents' are our co-creators, for they have something to give which we have not. The basis of all cooperative activity is integrated diversity. . . . It is possible to conceive conflict as not necessarily a wasteful outbreak of incompatibilities, but a normal process by which socially valuable differences register themselves for the enrichment of all concerned."[6]

When designing a project with others, moments of conflict are often ripe with ideas but we tend to steer away from them. Often, we are worried about hurt feelings and relationships or want to avoid the influence of ego and socially produced hierarchies in our projects. We suggest explicitly welcoming conflict and friction into the design process, while making some agreements for navigating these, such as: slow down; ask questions; articulate the position of your opponent; check for understanding. Facilitated conflict can improve a design.

Conflict as teachable moments assignment

Think about a conflict you participated in or witnessed and rescript yourself finding ways to be curious and de-escalate.

Write three questions you wish you had asked (legitimate, not rhetorical questions).

Designing Against Compromise and for Consensus

There is a commonly held belief that when there is a conflict or tension, the best solution is to find a compromise that represents a "middle ground" between the two. Certainly, this may be true when negotiating with a child who wants to go to the pool while you need to run another errand. But when it comes to issues of health, housing, food and safety, do you really want a compromise? Consider these compromises: ketchup counted as a vegetable in school lunches; slavery ended except for those incarcerated; sexual assault on university campuses handled internally by the school's administrators instead of by the courts. Compromise is a design failure. At its worst, it's a kind of nihilistic justification for giving up in the face of intractable power.

To design against compromise, we invite you to experiment in the domain of consensus. Consensus is when a group creates the best available outcome for a decision through the full participation of its members. Consensus is designed to harness conflict and tension as beneficial to better decision-making. As Food Not Bombs co-founder C.T. Lawrence Butler taught the teachers of SDaS: "The consensus process requires a commitment to active cooperation, disciplined speaking and listening, and respect for the contributions of every member. Likewise, every person has the responsibility to actively participate as a creative individual within the structure."[7] Where a compromise involves each party giving up something, consensus is a process to design another pathway to address the concerns of those involved.

Design against compromise assignment

Consider the opposition to the systemic change that would solve your problem.

Anticipate what compromises they will tempt you with and write a manifesto of your refusal.

Consider the points of opposition to your idea that seem reasonable or "legitimate" but that you don't know how to solve. Brainstorm possible ways forward that take them into account.

Designing Against Decay of Information

When are we in the presence of a new idea? How do we know? In our consumerist society, especially in advertising and political discourse, the messages of marketing are designed to be already understood, thus foreclosing the act of thinking. Politicians are exhorted by their aides to "stay on message." We often treat messages that are insufficiently communicative, in this strict sense, as problematic.

Our gripe with communication as a criterion for guiding our formulation is that when something is too easily understood, it is too easily forgotten, signaling that it has failed to stake out new ground. It is too obviously part and parcel of our current society. It does not elicit our engagement. It is boring to our brains. If we are trying to bring into being a world that does not yet exist, we must resist the gratification of what is too easily understood in this world. Instead, our formulations must arrest the attention and engage the interest of our audience. We want our formulations not to be immediately understood but to elicit unprecedented thinking. Anticommunication interrupts the conformist consumerist haze.[8]

Design against decay assignment

Write down any clichés that relate to your project.

Try replacing words so that slightly confusing formulations are the result.

Try them out and note the reactions and conversations they elicit.

CHAPTER 19

INTERVENTION

Redesigning the Care in Health Care

Everyone gives and everyone receives care. Everyone wants and everyone needs care. Care is an arena fertile for articulating desires, designing interventions at every scale, and learning to generate structural solutions. We started this section, Design Interventions, with a story about designing care for a loved one, and we return here with a story about redesigning the care in health care systems. These stories take place at two equally valid scales of design that can teach each other: the personal and the structural.

From 2005 to 2009, the Gesundheit! Institute and the School for Designing a Society (SDaS) hosted over a dozen Health Care Design Intensives.[1] They convened hopeful medical students and burnt-out medical professionals who had entered health care with a commitment to care but found themselves in the misery of the modern health care system. The sacred profession of healer had become a leading profit center in an economic system forever looking to grow.

The industrial logic of the assembly line had been applied to the human sphere of health care. Managed care had shrunk the time of a doctor's visit to a handful of minutes, while doctors were expected to carry a load of more than a thousand patients. Despite cutbacks on time with doctors, health care costs were surging. And tens of millions of residents—one in every six— lacked access.[2] If they were lucky to have access, patients and their families were subjected to impersonal, hurried, detached care in a technology and pharmaceutical centered system of disease management during some of the most vulnerable times in their lives. It was in this context that Susan Parenti and Dr. Patch Adams gathered an unlikely combination of medical professionals, artist-facilitators, and clowns to empathetically, curiously, playfully desire and design health care systems we would prefer.

Patch had been working for decades to establish a free hospital based on fundamentally different premises of care on land owned by the Gesundheit! Institute in West Virginia. SDaS had made Gesundheit! its primary location for its summer sessions for more than a decade. It was at my first session of SDaS in 1993 that I, Danielle, had shared with Patch the mysterious, seizing abdominal pains that I was experiencing. These had resulted in a dead-end surgery for endometriosis. Through hours of careful listening, Patch was able to identify the problem as irritable bowel syndrome (IBS) and offer suggestions across a range of complementary care strategies that helped me end years of pain. Through the attention of a person trained in understanding the complex interconnectedness of bodily systems, I experienced firsthand how powerful the relationship of the caregiver and care-receiver can be.

I was one of the facilitators in this series of Health Care Design Intensives held across the country. Our 2006 Intensive was held at the American Visionary Art Museum in Baltimore. Artwork by wildly creative people diagnosed with profound mental health issues (and often marginalized or incarcerated) was the backdrop for our creative intervention to heal the healer and the health-care system. As I convened our design group for the first time, a nurse hobbled into our circle, gasping in pain as she shrugged: "I just have nurses' knees." A medical student said in our initial go-around that she was seeking to regain empathy: "The way medical education is designed is that it creates so much stress that the student reverts to self-preservation." A confident surgeon bellowed his introduction: "Well, to be honest, I am here because I am ready to quit." The emotions were so tight we could not start until we did a round of the "Hokey Pokey" to shake off despair. As a teaching collective, we carefully designed these Health Care Design Intensives to unwind despair and juice up creativity with these strategies: formulations of new premises; presentations of a variety of models of care; working in design groups; and clowning.

New Premises of Care

At each Health Care Design Intensive, Patch offered the fundamental premises of the Gesundheit! Institute: care is free; initial interviews are four hours; the health of the caregiver is as important as the health of the care-receiver; and patients are treated as friends.

These formulations transported participants out of the premises of their current workplaces and stuck places to begin to articulate what they want in care. Among this audience, used to providing care through an expensive and complicated maze of technology and depersonalized processes, Susan focused on what she called the "indispensable minimum need for care: a healer, a patient, some tools, and ample time. That's it." She invited participants to see the patient, doctor, and support staff as actors on the stage of the clinic and participants to consider "*re*-designing the character of the care-actor."[3] That is, to redesign their own performances of the roles they were used to inhabiting in the health-care system and to protect the core aspect of health care: the caring, trusted relationship between healer and patient. She argued that although we may not control the systems we operate in, we control our own performance in that system; as an element in a system, our actions influence the whole.

What Erving Goffman called the "presentation of self in everyday life," Susan took further as an invitation to design that could be iterated or collaborated on with others. "The way a person decides to present herself—her language, her gestures, her dress, her behaviors—is a form of design," Susan said. "By that we mean that this person's performance of herself can generate a temporary reality—intended by her—in which other participants can live and benefit. . . . Care-actors can use their presentation of self to establish solidarity with themselves and their patients, indicating an alliance with the patient, not with the system." Susan argued that as care-actors, "we need to restore trust in the healing relation and distinguish the caring relation from the uncaring system" that forms itself around it.[4]

Varieties of Care

The Health Care Design Intensives featured presentations of a variety of international experiments in designing health care—including American providers who designed around or opted out of insurance and hospital networks. "We need hundreds of models of innovation. That's how change happens," said Susan to the group.

Practitioners in Venezuela's Barrio Adentro [In the Neighborhood] system showed health care integrated with social services and community participation at public rituals and events. For example: high school students were paid to do blood-pressure screenings; residents could get vaccinated while attending a festival.

B.K. Bevill presented on Second Wind Dreams, a project designed to overcome the severe isolation of nursing home residents by connecting them to those in the community who could benefit from their wisdom. Her presentation started with a silent, one-woman performance of the experience of Alzheimer's and aging, ending with her peaceful passage. She then described the Second Wind Dreams model and invited us to consider creating our own. Their nonprofit invited local groups across the country to adopt a local nursing home and interview residents about their desires. Bevill detailed that some seniors would ask for modest things, such as a cup holder for their wheelchair, while others asked for larger things, like the opportunity to go horseback riding. A retired teacher asked to teach a class again. A woman wanted to be able to see her great grandchildren overseas but had never used the internet. The community group then organized to fulfill the senior's dreams, developing friendship and connection as they did so. Second Wind Dreams was an intervention intended to create a cultural shift in the way communities view elders: away from being disposable and sidelined toward being indispensable and central.

Design Groups

In groups formed by a mixture of patients, doctors, nurses, and other health-care workers, artist-facilitators began the design process of articulating our desires and planning what interventions we might make in the care situations we find ourselves in. Our group's desire statements included:

> *Hospitals and care facilities are designed to teach you about your body.*
>
> *Sickness is an opportunity to care for myself and self-regulate my body.*
>
> *Nursing homes are the places where children from elementary school are introduced by their teachers to learn about the ancient times and listen to stories.*
>
> *Health-care training environments nourish the care-actors so that by being whole and happy, they can continue to care and heal lovingly.*

We used writing, drawing, and skits to generate and try out ideas. I remember several of the prompts for care-actors to reimagine their roles: "Perform patient in a way that teaches empathy to a cold and unlistening doctor"; "Perform doctor without centering on diagnosis."

Clowning as Trick to Bring Love Close

Every Health Care Design Intensive involved clowning by invitation at the local nursing home, jail, children's home, or cancer ward. Clowning was thrilling for many participants who reported that they found little chance for creativity or whimsy in their daily lives. It was a way to reconnect medical professionals with their longing to heal their caring relation with patients. The playful attentiveness of the clown unleashes the power of direct human relationships to heal. "Clowning is a trick to bring love close," explained Patch as participants pulled costumes and silly hats out of painted suitcases to assemble their clown characters. As we piled into a van to drive to the nursing home, Susan explained, "The clown, like the doctor and nurse, walks toward suffering." When our clown crew batted balloons, residents came alive as they reached for the balloons to hug them or keep them afloat. I remember the bed-bound veteran who, after several lines of "You Are My Sunshine" on the ukulele, fluttered his eyes open and reached for my hand to hold it as I hummed with him for half an hour. After clowning, we returned to reflect. Often there were tears as participants moved out of their defended, professional character into their open, feeling clown character. Kate Deccicio, an artist who worked with lifetime patients in a mental hospital reflected on our experience: "Clowns see and interact with the healthy part of a person; doctors see and interact with the sick part." Susan reflected on the role of the clown in her essay "Re-Designing the Character of the Care-Actor":

> On our clown trips, the clown walks into a room and faces the same group as the health-care provider does: very sick people, chronically ill people, poor people, dying people, people locked in or locked out, the families of these people, the staff, the nurses and the floor cleaners. . . .
>
> But here the clown, unlike the doctor, has no higher rank than the patient. (On the contrary, people tend to feel a bit superior to the clown, the fool, greeting with a grin the clowns' ambling up to their bedside.) Here, the clown can't "hide" behind technology or tests, is not busy doing "medical procedures," as the health-care professional is. Here the clown doesn't assuage suffering with drugs; there is no pharmapursuing of care . . . while the clown is there—the overriding attempt—is to make human connection.[5]

Dr. John Glick, a founding member of the Gesundheit! Institute, said about clowning:

> I've learned much about the incredible power of playful attentiveness, how a clown can calm an agitated fearful person, how a person's

physiology changes from stress-based anxiety and arousal to relaxation and fun, and how shared play and laughter decreases suffering, how easily clowning creates a framework for friendship. . . . Smiles, touch, eye contact, music, these are crucial elements of the healing interaction throughout all cultures and all times.

After the Beslan tragedy, where 300 children were murdered at school by terrorists, many survivors received medical and psychiatric care in Moscow. Four clowns visited a unit where six young children were housed, and when we began, the children were aggressive, frightened, and agitated. Across their faces played a complex series of expressions signifying echoes of a horrible experience: anguish, anger, fear, confusion, cruelty. Finally, we were sitting at a table, eating cake, when we began a spontaneous game, whereby the boys made ugly faces and sounds at the girls, who made ugly faces and sounds at the boys. Taking turns, we each expressed our maximum silly gross stupid behavior toward the other side and laughed at and with each other. After this game we were all friends, and the children were relaxed, sitting on our laps, cuddling. We had inadvertently found the path to intimacy and play and trust.[6]

As we finish this chapter, access to health insurance subsidized by the Affordable Care Act is threatened, even as evidence of a multiplicity of experiments in redesigning care into the health care system surround us. My child's pediatrician models consent before touching, after we are ushered into an exam room from the sunny waiting room full of plants and toys at the public school's health clinic. Clowning has been incorporated into medicine across the world—such as J'ai Mal Partout – CiRCO iNFiNiTO [I Hurt Everywhere – Infinite Circus], Le Rire Médecin [The Laughter Doctor], Clowns Without Borders, and the Medical Clown Project. These prefigure desirable premises for care that we want to be able to point to, as we continue to perturb the contradictions of the "disease management systems" designed to boost profits (and costs) to obscene levels. In both prefiguring what we want and exposing the premises we do not want, it helps to insist on Elizabeth's formulation of care: *Care is the work of meeting human needs in the context of human complexity for the purpose of eliciting connection, uniqueness, and growth.*

CHAPTER 20

PRAXIS

Cybernetics, Permaculture, and Performance

In 2008, a student came to the School for Designing a Society (SDaS) with the beginnings of a design for a housing community for homeless veterans like himself. He had formulated desire statements in the form of a mission and vision. He laid out before us sketches of the land and its buildings that would be built by participants. He even had a financial plan. What was missing was the group who would build the project—and how *their* participation in designing the project would be invited in the design. This student was enthusiastic, and also shy, prone to self-criticism, and had been living in the woods with little contact with other people. In his abundance of time alone, he had created elaborate designs that were so complete, there was no room for what he longed for most: connection and collaboration with others.

Teaching at SDaS has provided us with many experiences of, lessons from, tools and techniques for working in groups. In this chapter, we equip you for design projects with a toolbox of some tactics taught at SDaS that were borrowed and adapted from domains that concern themselves with systems design. First, we suggest attention to your structure as a group, its facilitation and design-making structures.[1] Then we offer tools from cybernetics,[2] permaculture,[3] and performance, with short examples, and discussion questions and assignments to try out for applying these to your domain. In our experience, some of the most interesting and effective designs come from applying concepts across domains.

The format of this chapter is to provide patterns for design, inspired by three books we love and return to again and again: *A Pattern Language: Towns, Buildings, Construction*, by Christopher Alexander, Sara Ishikawa, and Murray Silverstein; *Beautiful Trouble: A Toolbox for the Revolution*, by Andrew Boyd; and *Beautiful Solutions: A Toolbox for Liberation* by Elandria Williams, Rachel Plattus, Eli Feghali, and Nathan Schneider. We recommend these to you as foundational texts in the study of design of social change and human thriving.

Group Decision-Making

Design nearly always happens in groups, but rarely is the process of the group explicitly designed. We encourage you to gather a design group of people who are aligned with the basic values of the project, add skills and contacts, and offer necessary friction and challenges to sharpen ideas.

Decide on how to decide as a group. Build decision-making structures so you can design well and experience the pleasure of working together. Without such a provisional structure, the instigator of a project will often take the lead by default, and others may flounder to find their place and/or disappear—while the instigator complains they are doing all the work. Or, a small group of friends will start something and then invite needed others, who may harbor lingering feelings of being outsiders rather than joining as early collaborators.

We suggest bringing together a diverse set of collaborators to discuss the legitimate questions participants bring, and to not just organize around one person's answers. Design activities to develop relationships, with enough time to "move at the speed of trust," as adrienne maree brown advises in her teaching of facilitation.[4] Build evaluation and reflection into every meeting or gathering so there is space to talk about process and not just product. When group dynamics get rough, slow down and name them. Listen. Attempt de-escalation. Maintain connection. Reaffirm purpose and intention.

Determine decision-making

Who are we? How do we define the "we" of our group?

What are we trying to do?

How do we make decisions?

What are our roles?

How do we handle conflict?

The more homogeneous the group, the more likely the participants will rely on shared culture and assumptions to answer these questions. But beware: the more homogeneous the group, the less likely the project will be informed from multiple perspectives, or have ideas challenged to grow outside of their comfortable boundaries. Discover what *distinguishes* group members from each other, not only what you have in common. Consider adding structure within a group to help you navigate difference.

Facilitation

Structure starts with good facilitation. Facilitation is the art of attending to the structure and dynamics of participants of a gathering to help it reach its goals. It is the group who leads and decides the group's goals, not the facilitator. While individuals are responsible for expressing their own concerns and thoughts, facilitators are responsible for tracking the sense of the group and helping articulate it.

Facilitation is more delicate than marching a group through an agenda on a time clock; it is more like navigating a complex structure through unknown terrain. The facilitator (or facilitation team) acts as a guide to clarify the process, keep to the agenda, manage time, and model democratic values (such as honesty, cooperation, egalitarianism, and responsibility). A facilitator pays attention to the energy in the room—both what is visible (people, agenda, structure) and what is not visible (emotion, stories, hidden agendas). They help participants feel part of the collective work and participate fully in decisions. Like domestic and other forms of care work, these activities are often overlooked and often done by women and femmes. Facilitation and decision-making structures are the invisible glue that holds projects together. Cultivate facilitation as a valued practice among your members.

Practice holding evaluations

At the end of each meeting, go around the group and have each person briefly answer, without interruption, defense, or discussion:

How did this conversation go for you?

What suggestions do you have to improve our process?

Use this output as input for facilitating future meetings.

TOOLS FROM CYBERNETICS

We have discussed how and why cybernetics informs our analysis of systems and our strategies for perturbing them in our project to remake democracy. Here, we introduce three tools from cybernetic theory for you to consider and use in your design projects: (1) floating hierarchies, (2) perturbation (of nontrivial systems), and (3) causality.

Floating Hierarchies

The intransigence of inequalities in our society shows up in the stability of unchosen hierarchies. When a hierarchy is challenged, it is often only nom-inally—by either a change of personnel within the same structure or the replacement of one hierarchy with another. Power concentrates when a hierarchy becomes too stable, too permanent, and loses accountability to the groups affected by the decisions. There are many situations in which no hierarchy is necessary, though it's important to be on the lookout for the "tyr-anny of structurelessness," in which—usually under the cover of a declared horizontality—unspoken leaders exert power no one agreed to.[5] Not every situation needs to be governed by the decisions of a general assembly.

"Floating hierarchies" is an approach offered by Herbert Brün to answer the design question of when is hierarchy helpful and when is it a hindrance.[6] He composed this approach into a piece of experimental chamber music with a graphic score, which asks the four performers to also become composers and interpreters of the score in such a way that decision-making power is both multiple and rotated among the players. The stability of the hierarchy, and thus its threat, has been removed by design. In the case your project requires a "helpful hierarchy," how can you design its instability, imperma-nence, and accountability to the group its decisions affect?

Brün's experimental approach to composition has analogs in social organizing, for example, Barbara Ransby's assertion that, contrary to main-stream narratives about Black Lives Matter being a leaderless movement, it is leader-*full*.[7] That means it is full of what Charles M. Payne calls "group-centered leadership."[8] In her article, "Ella Taught Me: Shattering the Myth of the Leaderless Movement," Ransby positions group-centered leaders "at the center of many concentric circles. They strengthen the group, forge consen-sus, and negotiate a way forward."[9] They are like Brün's "floating hierarchies," accountable within and across the groups they belong to. In the Garden Per-formance Project—a 2006 precursor to *Songlines*, discussed in chapter 10—preschoolers invented instruments from recycling, created an orchestra, and then took turns performing and conducting.

Floating hierarchies questions

When is hierarchy helpful and when is it not?

How do we design a hierarchy resistant to its own stability and permanence, and that continually renews its accountability to the group its decisions affect?

Perturbation of Nontrivial Systems

Systems may appear pervasive or monolithic, but cybernetics offers the concepts of trivial and nontrivial systems as a means of disturbing business as usual.[10] Most machines are trivial systems that when given input A will give output B, predictably. Living systems are nontrivial: given input A, they may give any number of outputs. A good car is a reliably trivial system. A good life partner is trivial enough that you know how to connect with them in the routine intimacies of everyday life, but nontrivial enough to keep your relationship engaging.

One commonality among oppressive systems is their tendency to treat human beings, who are by definition nontrivial, as if we are trivial. Systems in which triviality and nontriviality are thrust together can be especially tricky to navigate, so we must take care to design in a liberatory way that points toward alternatives rather than illusory control over specific outcomes.

The social systems we live, act, and design inside of are nontrivial, unpredictable in their interdependence. We cannot determine outcomes—and that indeterminacy is to our benefit as designers if we keep it in mind as a constraint. Instead, we can perturb and observe. To perturb a system is to give it an input to which you cannot predict its reaction. Rick Burkhardt once described perturbation as feeding the system some intervention that would give it a "bellyache." Such a move can be the deliberate purpose of our designs—such as a street performance, a protest, a public artwork, or a random act of kindness. For example, in 2004, the Yes Men put up a fake website for Dow Chemical in advance of the twentieth anniversary of the Bhopal chemical disaster that had killed thousands of people. The BBC contacted them for a statement, and they did an interview where they impersonated a Dow spokesperson, officially apologizing and pledging to disburse $12 billion for compensation and a clean-up fund that would be financed by liquidating Union Carbide. The story, even after its debunking, was at the top of Google News for a day, and CNN reported a Dow stock loss of $2 billion on the Frankfurt Stock Exchange. Though the hoax was debunked after two hours, it brought extra attention to Dow's continuing refusal of justice and showed the BBC to be sympathetic, as they invited the Yes Men back for a second interview to draw even more attention to the issue.[11]

Perturb nontrivial systems

In designing your project, practice perturbation. Remember and discuss perturbations you have witnessed: when an unusual input was given to a system, how the system reacted to try to regain its equilibrium, and what can be learned about the system from its reaction. Consider what you don't yet know about your system that you need to know. Brainstorm what perturbations you could instigate to elicit an information-rich reaction from the system.

Cybernetic Causality

Cybernetic causality is an alternative to goal-oriented design, which can compromise human freedom. Rather than design social systems for a specified outcome, cybernetic causality suggests designing for fields of potential. Cybernetic causality also asks us to consider the past through the lens of what didn't happen and ask, "*What if?*" For example, the Afrofuturist work of Stacey Robinson's collages reveal "decolonized Black futures" in ways that prompt us to ask why we would have it any other way than full Black liberation, full equality.[12] We recommend trying the following assignment.

Design for fields of potential
Look at your desire statements and formulate strategies for generating a variety of outcomes aimed toward your desires and discuss: how is creating a field of potential different from setting a goal? Why didn't previous attempts to address the problem result in desirable outcomes? Consider times when history could have produced more democracy and equity. Discuss what could have happened, what didn't happen, and why?

TOOLS FROM PERMACULTURE

Permaculture is a system of "permanent" agriculture designed to create abundant food and habitat for all species.[13] It uses the word permanent in its name to distinguish its commitment as aiming beyond "sustainability" toward closed systems, requiring no inputs from outside sources beyond sun, rain, and wind. It is based on emulating the stability, interconnection, and cyclic functioning of resilient ecosystems found in the natural world. Through observation, and respect for the constraints of climate and resource availability, the concept posits design principles for human designers to use in their designs of ecosystems. "Connecting needs and offers," "edges," and "polyfunctionality" are design concepts that easily translate from the domain of permaculture to other domains of social change.

Needs and Offers

A permaculture designer begins by observing the changes and stabilities in light, temperature, moisture, and wind in her site over time. These are her constraints. She then assesses the needs and offers of the organisms she wants to feed and shelter, such as her chickens and her children. The designer goes about connecting these: the humans produce kitchen scraps for the chickens' food; the chickens' manure replaces nitrogen in soil depleted by a nonlegume crop.

Every human has needs, both universal and individual. The businessman making a seven-figure salary needs authentic connection with others. The doctor working overtime in the hospital needs fresh air and exercise. The school principal needs the perspective of the student to build a successful school. Even the controlling partner needs to feel safe. Concomitantly, every person has offers. The child with Down's Syndrome might be a master cuddler. The chronically homeless person knows every square inch of town and might be an expert at directing people to places and services. The elder might have spare time, the wisdom of years, listening skills, and a lap to offer. The teenager might be a Jedi master of technology. Designing in such a way that needs and offers are connected makes every person indispensable and establishes resilient, self-reliant communities that are resistant to dominating forces. For example: Urbana's (former) public nursing home was designed with a child daycare center located inside. Elders could watch the children play, or they could read and draw with them, dispelling the chronic boredom and depression of a nursing facility. Children received one-on-one attention and care that is often impossible because of high staffing costs.

Connect needs and offers
List the elements of the system in which you want to design. List needs and offers for each element. Imagine and articulate designs that connect needs and offers.[14]

Polyfunctionality

In permaculture, polyfunctional design places elements so they can perform multiple functions, increasing the efficiency and resiliency of the design. A chicken coop may be located next to the home with a run around the garden, so that the chickens provide morning eggs within reach of the kitchen while offering bug control and fertilizer as they roam. A work meeting combines decision-making and the labor of carrying out the decisions, often resulting in a shared feeling of productivity and connection among attendees.

Design for polyfunctionality
Which functions in your system could be polyfunctional?

Which functions would benefit by being paired with each other?

Which functions require the most resilience?

Which functions are the most trivial and which are the most nontrivial?

Edges

In observing ecosystems, those practicing permaculture have noticed that the edges between domains often support an extra abundance and variety of plants and animals, food and habitat, distinct from those native to either domain. At edges, there is heightened productivity amongst mutually beneficial organisms. This is true of the edges between forests and meadows, between land and water, between saltwater and freshwater. A person practicing permaculture with mutually beneficial crops will intermingle them, or create a wavy border that maximizes their contact, rather than growing them merely adjacent in concentrated blocks like conventional agriculture. It's also true of social environments—think of how the porch, or lunchroom, serve as places of high levels of information and potential. Those edges may be physical spaces, but they may also be embodied in people, like an intergenerational household or a person in a multiracial family living at the edge where multiple cultures touch. When the Urbana-Champaign Independent Media Center bought the downtown post office to turn it into a center for media, arts, and organizing, we applied the idea from permaculture of maximizing edges between different projects and events to foster serendipitous interaction and cross pollination. Try the following assignment for playing with edges.

Play with edges

In choosing the site of your design, think about domains and their edges, whether they are physical, social, or more abstract. To brainstorm more domains, consult your desire statements. What domains does your design touch on, and could you incorporate any others?

TOOLS FROM PERFORMANCE

The framework of performance offers many tools and strategies to those who want to make social change possible. In essence, it allows us to separate intention (desire) from performance (design) in the social world. Implicit in the practice of performers is the fact that after the song, string quartet, play, or dance has been written, performance choices abound in the rehearsal process. These choices make profound differences in the effects the piece has on an audience. With the concept of rehearsal and choices in mind, a performer may *maintain* their intention, while experimenting with different performances of that intention to see which performance results in consequences they desire.

Amidst the general alienation of our society, as we each strive for a sense of belonging and a requisite forum and medium of self-expression, the decoupling of intention from performance is a liberatory idea with deeply humane implications. Distinguishing intention from performance invites variety and experiment in performance to produce an effect that satisfies the criteria of the intention. Additionally, it enables us as audience members to offer each other the benefit of the doubt: "Your performance had this effect on me. Was that your intention?"

Performance (in Everyday Life)

At every moment, you hold the tools of language and performance to manifest your desires in the world. "Performance in Everyday Life" brings the framework of performance to quotidian interactions. Susan Parenti describes "three basic steps involved in performance: (1) having an intention, (2) choosing amongst alternative ways of showing that intention, and (3) paying attention to the consequences of the chosen way of showing one's intention."[15] Following her prompt, we can approach our performance of self, including the daily, seemingly ordinary ones, as changeable objects of composition and social intervention. We can use performance as a medium to try out ideas with an audience, who can be invited to offer feedback. This dialog allows us to create dynamics with effects that can be watched, altered, and watched again. Preserving our intention while trying out a variety of performances can loosen us from the trap of self and identity we have created. It is an incredible relief when the weighty myth of "authentic selves" dissolves into a playfulness around roles in performance. Performance lends itself to "laboratories" of society.

Performance helps us hone our "public" skills. We want to revive interest in the social and public realms, in opposition to the shrinking of our commons. Public spaces, public toilets, public forums, and public ways of speaking are neglected. Part of developing these skills is distinguishing between private, communal, and public realms in our performance of self. We desire that everyone has a voice as a premise of democracy. Yet when we do not know how to speak publicly, we suffer through our attempts at democracy. For example, a father comes to city council to ask for more after-school programming, but speaks quietly, as if he were at a dinner table; we cannot hear or benefit from his proposal. An academic comes to warn against the use of surveillance technology, but their performance mirrors a class lecture and the urgency of the warning is lost. Studying performance addresses how to fulfill participants' lifelong desires to be heard and to speak with presence in any context.

The first time I, Elizabeth, met Susan Parenti was at a concert in 2004 during the Iraq War. She was wearing clothes that made her look friendly, and shoes painted with the words "Visualize Impeachment." With the following assignments formulated from this encounter, we offer some tactics for performing desires and exploring our desires as intentions.

Perform your desires

Select a desire statement you would like to project into the world and design an outfit that conveys it in some way or starts a conversation about it. Wear the outfit for a day and note and reflect on people's reactions. Change one aspect of it tomorrow and compare people's reactions. Which do you prefer?

Perform your intentions

Try out three different ways of performing each of these essential social labors: kindness, curiosity, setting boundaries.

Compose introductions

Write three brief introductions of yourself and your project: one to a potential partner or advisor you have not yet met; one to a house party of friends; one to a public meeting. After you have written the words, invent marks to indicate tone of voice and gesture. Hand to another person to perform as a score. Discuss: what were the intentions (desires) of the character introducing themselves? Did these match their author's? Suggest a change in performance that further explores the author's intentions.

Power of the Respondent

In chapter 4, we discussed the "power of the respondent" in the context of healing from trauma, but its utility extends into any social interaction. The question is: what can I say in this moment to move this conversation toward the desirable? You are using your power as a respondent when you choose, for example, to refute what has just been said, add a distinction, reframe the situation, or make a new connection. Observing the speaker is a practice of listening and developing strategy in performance. You observe the people and their dynamics as a way to develop a plan to intervene—the speaker, their respondents, contradictions between intention and language, your own intentions. For example, in 1998, a group of CIA recruiters were speaking on campus and I, Danielle, was part of a group that one by one donned Groucho Marx glasses and sat in aisle seats, provoking critique and tittering with our silent responses.

Respond to injustice

Write a short skit or puppet show about a time you witnessed an injustice. In it, show three different responses that could be tried. Discuss as a group what each response solicited or provoked.

Invite audience members to suggest other responses to try out. Try stipulating a particular gesture or facial expression with each response.

Performers' Workshops

Prior to creating SDaS, a number of its founders created the Performers' Workshop Ensemble (PWE) in 1980, which sought to replace the stasis of critique with the dynamism of experimentation and iteration. They held "Performers' Workshops" wherein a performer presented a work-in-progress to an audience that would respond by giving the performer instructions to try out. The instructions were not to be argued for or against. Instead, the performer re-presented the piece while adopting the instructions and adapting the performance. Participants then discussed what they saw and what the piece did, following up with suggestions of new instructions to try out. If we see ourselves as performers, and every situation as a stage, we can use this approach in planning for, holding, or debriefing about an event or presentation.

Perform a presentation

Consider an upcoming presentation your group plans to make. Have the presenters rehearse their presentation as they would for an external audience. Ask the audience to respond *only* with suggestions of things to try out. The performers then adapt the presentation with these suggestions, on the spot. Note changes in effect but postpone discussion about which performance was most effective until *after* you have tried at least five variations.

VI

Act and Reflect

CHAPTER 21

INTERVENTION

Local Organizing
Against Police Violence

Champaign-Urbana Citizens for Peace and Justice (CUCPJ) was a Black-led, multiracial group that organized from 2004 to 2017 to expose and remedy racial and class inequities in Champaign-Urbana, Illinois.[1] In this chapter, I, Danielle, demonstrate how CUCPJ dramatically shifted both narrative and policy: blowing the whistle on police brutality, winning the right to videotape police, building civilian oversight of police, instigating criminal record sealing and expungement, creating a community court watch group, diversifying juries, and blocking a jail-building referendum. With CUCPJ, we built social and political power. Electing co-founder Carol Ammons as the first African American State Representative in 2014 opened the door for prison phone justice reform and ending cash bail in Illinois—two areas where Illinois has led in the nation.

Champaign-Urbana Citizens for Peace and Justice models an approach to organizing that is transformative of history and the souls that create it. The story of CUCPJ illuminates how a group diverse in race, class, and gender made numerous interventions in a racialized system of criminal justice using strategies and tactics that later helped me formulate the Spiral of Change. Seeded nine years before #Black-LivesMatter spurred a national conversation, CUCPJ exemplifies how local, largely volunteer-run organizations in the United States were responding to police violence, laying the groundwork for an international movement for change in the early twenty-first century. The progress we made as CUCPJ was not always clear in every moment (it sometimes felt we were going backwards), but its impact emerged over many iterations of design, action, and reflection. Its story is one of progress forged over time, with quiet periods followed by periods of great momentum, backlash, and then the slow institutionalization of reforms.

To begin this story, we start at the point of crisis, after years of the festering problems of police misconduct and violence, and with a multitude of cautionary voices raised and ignored. We start, at the point of crisis, with the police killing of a child. Say his name: Kiwane Carrington.[2]

In honor of CUCPJ leader Dr. Reverend Evelyn Underwood, we open with this prayer: *The humble seeds of powerful change are inside and all around us. May we see and nurture them, learning from and building on the work of our predecessors. May Kiwane, those who love him, and those impacted by his death, gain the peace that comes from justice; and may this story be part of that process.*

Police Killing of a Child

On the rainy afternoon of October 9, 2009, police shot and killed Kiwane Carrington, an unarmed fifteen-year-old African American student, outside his home in Champaign, Illinois. The entire event—from the chief of police arriving, with his gun drawn and shouting, "Stop or I will shoot!" to a bullet going through Kiwane's heart at close range—happened in a matter of minutes.

As soon as Kiwane took his last breath, the fight over reality commenced in a war of words and perception. Police and Champaign's local newspaper, *The News-Gazette*, collaborated to assert one version of the story: Kiwane was part of a group of truant Black youth who were burglarizing a house. CUCPJ members quickly uncovered another story: school was out, and Kiwane was with his best friend on the back steps of the home where he had stayed and eaten breakfast that morning, trying to find refuge from the rain. A photo of Kiwane quickly circulated: a five-foot-tall child with a sweet face. These were parallel narratives: supported by centuries of white supremacist dystopian fantasy, one story presented the youth as dangerous and presumed guilty by their skin color; the other was the story of a son, student, and friend who was recovering from the death of his mother and unjustly killed by police. These stories represented nonintersecting realities in our college town community, notorious for being one of the most racially segregated communities in Illinois.[3]

When police killed Kiwane, the system of racialized policing was caught in the contradiction between "police are here to serve and protect" and "police kill Black children." The police moved to turn this contradiction into a one-time conflict, or a mistake. The only independent witness to the event, Kiwane's friend, testified that the shooter was Champaign Police Chief Robert T. Finney. Chief Finney was never put on administrative leave and was allowed to edit his own testimony to state police. His story—backed by the city's leadership—was that the gun of the second officer to arrive on the scene accidentally discharged, killing Kiwane. Over the next few years, we would watch the accused officer collect over $500,000 in pay and quietly disappear. It would take two years of intense organizing before Chief Finney was quietly transitioned out of employment—after which he started a consulting company training police departments across the country.[4]

As of today, there has been no justice for Kiwane, just as there has not been justice for thousands of victims of police killings across the country in the years since his death. Looking back now, we can see that 2009 was the beginning of a dramatic increase in fatal police shootings of civilians, with police killing Black residents at a rate three times higher than white residents.[5] Only with the largest protests in US history occurring after the police murder of George Floyd in 2020, would the nation learn that 99 percent of police killings result in no charges. Public employees regularly killing Black citizens is a manifestation of America's deeply rooted racism—and the process of digging at these roots and pulling them out is essential to realizing the vision of a true, multiracial democracy. Where do we begin this work? We start in our own communities.

Three days after police killed Kiwane, his family held a People's Press Conference at our Independent Media Center—to share their own stories in response to news stories that attacked and maligned Kiwane's character. A group of Kiwane's friends, heartbroken and nervous, jostled as one stepped up to the mic:

> All the police are real slick with their badges. . . . You don't see how they come harass us every day on the block. It's to the point that I get harassed by my first name. I come outside, they follow me to the gas station. That's not cool for anybody to live their life. Every boy behind me has been harassed by 'Champaign's finest.'[6]

A few days later, youth led hundreds in protest, filing into a local church calling for affected residents to turn out at the next Champaign City Council meeting. They packed the city council's chambers, with residents sharing over four hours of public testimony about decades of abuse at the hands of local law enforcement. Black residents recounted many times when they called police for safety and support, only to find themselves harassed, detained, and even brutalized. One resident, now a teacher and coach, shared:

> I had an incident with the [Champaign] cops when I was sixteen. I was in front of my house when I called the police because somebody around the neighborhood had a gun. They told me I was trespassing while I was in my own house . . . the first thing they did was restrain me . . . with their arm around my neck. I couldn't breathe. I have asthma. They said I was resisting arrest. The first thing that happened when I hit the ground, the cop kneed me on the head, I went unconscious. I still have the marks on my arms when they put me in shackles and threw me in the back of the truck.

Through dozens of stories, connections were forged and systems of state violence were named. It was not one officer, but many generations of officers. It was not a one-time occurrence, but a long, traumatic history of policing in Champaign. These actions are human rights abuses. This moment, where the people spoke to a dumbfounded city council, represented a tipping point after years of many family members speaking up on their own without being heard.

CUCPJ: Modeling How to Make Change in Systems

In 2004, five years before police shot young Kiwane, Champaign-Urbana Citizens for Peace and Justice (CUCPJ) had formed at our local Independent Media Center, the nest we had created for making media, art, and organizing in the long haul for social justice. CUCPJ was instigated by Carol and Aaron Ammons, an African American couple who studied nonviolent direct action organizing and atonement from the direct lineage of the historic civil rights movement. Their civil rights mentors taught them foundations of successful organizing—including healing from shame and self-forgiveness, lifting up social contradictions, and organizing in coalition—led by a vision of beloved community. Carol and Aaron called a small group of organizers together for a planning meeting over a pancake breakfast where we took turns describing our desires for a multiracial, multi-issue group committed to taking on the myriad problems we saw in the criminal justice system.

We held weekly meetings every Saturday, which functioned as two-hour mini-workshops on how to make systems change. These were face-to-face meetings at the same time and place, with facilitation, where every voice was heard. The first half of the meeting was a process of putting everything we had on the table: *what* is happening? We always started with any newcomers, inviting them to share stories about being harassed and brutalized by police, falsely accused, overcharged, or abused in jail. We invited visitors who talked about lacking effective legal counsel and being locked up for many years, unable to communicate in prison, lacking housing to parole to, unable to get their children back, and facing ongoing discrimination due to their felony conviction. Chris Evans, an artist and member of CUCPJ, would diagram the discussions to visually track and integrate ideas, connecting many ways of learning. Then, the facilitators would switch to: *why* is this happening? We would wrestle with this question, knitting together our different experiences, arguing over what a root problem was and what was a symptom of a deeper problem. Then we would pivot toward commitment by asking: "Are you ready to organize so that what is happening to you stops for everyone?"

Only after we had worked on an analysis of the problem, and surveyed the group's commitment to changing it, would we focus on designing our action: *how* are we going to change it? We worked strategically to build winnable campaigns around the problems that we discussed, hearing from many perspectives as we worked to formulate and analyze the problems. We designed interventions, making plans for educational events, court watching, letter writing, meetings with decision makers, media, art and poetry making, and direct actions. This process greatly benefited from the generative friction of a multiracial space. We built our base of support through small, incremental victories amplified by our independent media outlets, and the mainstream media who would follow suit. Once our campaign achieved momentum, we could take bigger, bolder actions. In this way, we moved out of the silence and isolation of individual experiences and into connection with each other. Impacted residents took notice and joined our efforts. This is how we built power.

It is one thing to build a group of committed volunteers to make change. It is another thing to keep them together. A firm commitment to meet regularly and build trusted relationships by leaning into friction and difference would become the backbone of our work, led by principles of relationship-based organizing. The commitment to meeting weekly was key for letting us weather the storms of difference. CUCPJ member Martel Miller challenged us in one meeting: "This is not a Black problem. This is a white problem. What can you do as white people to get other white people to stop?" The white members of CUCPJ came to see how our experiences were not universal, and to engage our white peers in addressing the white supremacy we grew up in. Thanks to those deep organizing friendships, I was able to chip away at my internalized racism in a way that years of scholarship in critical theory and Black history never could.

We had to speak our flawed understandings out loud and wrestle with them together. Black members had a sit-down conversation with a Black pastor who had been organizing with us while preaching homophobia from the pulpit. White members engaged white feminist friends in racialized history when discussing the case of a Black man falsely accused of groping a white woman. Members voiced their biases: "Kids these days need to pull up their pants and learn respect." "Immigrants are taking jobs from us Black folks." "The Black Agenda has been hijacked by the Gay Agenda." A one-time visitor might hear this and never return, determining that CUCPJ is "anti-immigrant" or "anti-gay." But our commitment to show up week after week to make our conflicts generative, created a space of listening, learning, and respect as well as action.

Looking back on this time from the current era of bot-fueled social media flame wars, it is hard to imagine such conversations happening without the whole organization imploding with conflict. We started as very different individuals organizing together around a common concern. Over time and conversation, we developed a shared analysis, deeply loving, life-long friendships, and many projects for liberation. In a book documenting her experiences coalition-building for Black Lives Matter, Alicia Garza, sums up well "how we come together when we fall apart":

> We need movements that can hold complexity so that we can learn how to reach for one another, even when reaching for one another makes us uncomfortable. We need movements inside of which millions of people can grow and learn, movements where people can come as they are, as long as they are willing to be transformed in the service of our full and complete liberation.[7]

Carol and Aaron Ammons, who provided clear and consistent leadership in the group, centered attention on building an inclusive organization of shared power where a mother who worked three jobs could speak alongside a university professor. We were building an organization of committed people who could respond to many issues, rather than a series of reactive campaigns that rise and disappear in response to specific crises. We were building a "we" not just a "me"; we focused on the work of changing systems for everyone, not building personal profiles. The importance of this kind of continuous movement building and leadership development cannot be overstated.

Digging to the Roots of Problems

In our first year, success came swiftly. We joined a coalitional effort and successfully halted Champaign police from acquiring taser stun guns. This work was followed by a campaign to assert the public's right to videotape police that eventually led to a change in Illinois law to allow residents to record police officers in public.[8] Looking back from #BlackLivesMatter protests, it is hard to remember a time when it was illegal for ordinary residents to document human rights abuses by law enforcement.

These quick and promising victories in 2004 did not prepare us for what was to come after. Victory opened a door through which a torrent of stories of police harassment and brutality flowed. From 2004–2009, we took on case after case of police violence reported to us, documenting the harms, and fighting for justice and systemic change.

For example, in 2006, our work contributed to a jail sergeant being charged with a felony for repeated abuse of inmates with a taser. The same year, an Urbana police officer was accused of using the 911 system to find and rape a resident. In part due to CUCPJ's exposure of the story, the City of Urbana paid her $100,000 and the officer was terminated. In 2007, when four Champaign police officers stopped and assaulted a seventeen-year-old resident and then charged him with obstruction, officers admitted during his trial that they were carrying out the instruction to stop people and collect their information, as part of an effort to "proactively police" the predominantly Black neighborhood. Later the same year, the police shot their guns through and ransacked the house of an uninvolved African American resident and her grandchildren when an armed suspect fled through her house in an attempt to evade police. Chief Finney blithely argued, "We shot at the suspect. Some bullets hit the house. . . . We don't always get to pick our backdrops when we are dealing with deadly force."[9]

CUCPJ exerted enormous effort with little visible impact on institutional power. Our eyes were opened to horrific human rights abuses by police and the brazen rejection of accountability, even when abuses were investigated, reported, and admitted to by police. We worked to expose the many contradictions that racial profiling and over-policing in minority neighborhoods represent, building awareness, and shifting the narrative around community safety and civil rights.

During these years, CUCPJ was essential to documenting and building the community's awareness and analysis of the problem. Tragically, our efforts were not enough. During the CUCPJ meeting just before police shot and killed Kiwane, Martel Miller spoke to our small circle: "The way police are showing up with guns out, I am afraid they're gonna kill someone." And they did.

Contradiction in Crisis

Just days after police killed Kiwane, we pulled out more chairs at our weekly CUCPJ meeting to accommodate the enormous crowd. We were joined by young friends of Kiwane, mothers terrified for their children, and some African American community leaders who, up to this point, had maintained that "kids just need to pull up their pants and learn to respect the police." We mapped out the problem on a huge whiteboard, while asking questions and discussing answers in turn:

"How is it that police can shoot and kill a kid outside his own home?!"

"Cause the cops are running around the North End all the time . . . guns out, blazing."

"Why did they have their guns out? No one was reporting a gun!"

"These were kids—not a hair on their face!"

"Yeah, Black kids. . . . This would never happen in a white neighborhood!"

[CHORUS: "Uh huh!"]

"How do we stop them from doing this?"

"The Council is ultimately the boss of the police."

"We have no friends on Council."

"We need more people speaking up, but they are afraid. If you get in the paper—you could lose your job."

"We do have people speak up, but Council doesn't listen."

"We need to run people for those seats."

[CHORUS: "Uh huh!"]

"Even if we elect new people—we need to change hearts and minds."

"When kids aren't at work or school, it makes them easy targets."

"They catch a case and end up in jail—or prison."

"The kids are not resisting arrest, they are resisting injustice!"

"People think to have safety, you gotta step on our rights—not true!"

[CHORUS: "Uh huh!"]

In this way, we formulated and reformulated—and reformulated again—the problems recurring over many years. This is how we connected the dots between stories, history, and data. We drew the picture of how the school-to-prison pipeline operates in our community, and how actions here feed growth in incarceration nationwide. Asking questions and discussing answers was how we articulated the systems in which our lived experiences of injustice were the "normal" and predictable functioning of fundamentally unjust systems. We worked together to build a shared analysis of some contradictions of the system that perpetuate the problem of police brutality.

Generate Desires

After Champaign police killed Kiwane, some community members expressed their desires interwoven with outrage: *Don't kill our kids. Don't pull guns on our kids. Don't make us trade our civil rights for your perception of safety.* As community organizer Terry Townsend shared: "Young people should know that we love you, and the question is not safe neighborhoods or civil rights, it is safe neighborhoods and civil rights." When we are stuck in an ongoing problem, and the pain and grief it produces, desire statements can grow our hope.

CUCPJ held an annual Unity March where hundreds of community members would march with signs emblazoned with problems and desire statements. After marching together, we opened up a People's Microphone and broadcast testimonies through our Indymedia channels. Aaron Ammons led us in chanting, "Tell me what community looks like! This is what community looks like!" We wanted to "make prisons obsolete," to borrow from the words of our guest, Angela Davis.[10] We wanted safety for our children. We wanted clean water, land, and air. We wanted health care and housing to be seen and provided as a basic human right. We wanted to redistribute wealth and end poverty. We wanted that, when harm is done, there is a process to bring people together to restore the community to wholeness. We wanted to build beloved community together, starting here and spreading everywhere. CUCPJ worked to transform these desires into specific, actionable demands that we built campaigns around. We sang, shared poetry, and played music together to illuminate the problem.

Formulate Contradictions

As CUCPJ worked to formulate the problems we faced, we focused on where there was friction between a stated principle and actual reality. Each time we thought we had dug out the root of the problem, we would see the problem sprout up again. Looking at the legacy of local police abuse, we dug further down to the roots, to this contradiction: *The public employees we pay and appoint to keep us safe, terrorize Black and Brown residents with impunity.*

"Public employees we pay and appoint" points to the fact that the public has two points of leverage in policing that occur every year: the budget process and the political appointment of the chief of police. "The police" often appears as an immutable institution. They are, in fact, how our local representatives are choosing each year to spend about a quarter of the city's budget. Here is a point of *decision* where we could design interventions.

"To keep us safe" points to the need to organize around beliefs and assumptions about what makes us safe, and how we know we are safe. Here was a point of *assumption* where we could intervene to try to shift public understanding. We held public forums, asking the questions: "What role do police play in the community's sense of safety?" "Can we contest the nonlegitimate safety roles of the police, and replace many of the legitimate ones with staff and programs better suited to handle the mental health and material needs of the community?"

"Terrorize Black and Brown residents" points to the fact that modern policing in the United States has roots in the seventeenth-century Slave Patrols and Town Watch groups tasked with monitoring and suppressing Black and Brown residents, immigrants, and "vagrants." We started a "New Jim Crow" reading group, to study the history of the modern criminal justice system.[11]

"With impunity" points to the systemic failure to hold police accountable for causing harm. People of every profession do harm, intentionally and unintentionally. The question is whether the profession holds them accountable and systematically learns and improves. Police defenders claim that holding the police accountable for civil rights and constitutional violations compromises both officer and public safety. No other profession, such as medicine or social work, argues this claim. CUCPJ explored why the police profession is treated differently. Looking back at my notebooks, I wrote this formulation of the contradiction in safety:

> *Suppressing crime by violating civil rights exacerbates the roots of crime: discrimination, displacement, disconnection, and poverty. In asserting a false contest between civil rights and safety, we make our community much less safe for some, and generally unsafe for all.*

In CUCPJ's weekly meetings, we grappled with how to use points of leverage to design interventions for change prior to taking action. We asked questions: "What is the problem?" "What are we trying to achieve?" "How can we be strategic?" "What are we well positioned to do right now?" "What other partners do we need?"

Use-of-Force Policy Change

When initial investigations into the shooting of Kiwane resulted in a finding of "no wrongdoing," we pushed on the contradiction of how a use-of-force policy absolved police who killed an unarmed fifteen year old in broad daylight, within seconds of police making contact. CUCPJ designed a campaign to change the use-of-force policy, including clear prohibition on a gun being drawn on an unarmed or fleeing suspect. During the back and forth attempts to change this and other police policies, the city administration argued that their hands were tied by their labor contract with the police. We reformulated the problem as a contradiction:

> *Police unions have extended their role past protecting the labor rights of their members, and are shielding members who commit human rights crimes from prosecution. In doing so, the police unions are contributing to the eroding public trust of the police, and compromising the safety of the same officers they are trying to protect.*

This contradiction points to the Fraternal Order of Police (FOP) contract as a further point of leverage.

A cadre of FOP lawyers from Chicago descended on our small town to conduct backroom conversations with elected leaders and to block these changes. CUCPJ united with the Graduate Employees Organization (GEO), which had just won a historic labor victory against the gutting of tuition waivers. The GEO lent their expertise in negotiating labor contracts, proposed revisions to the police union contract, and with CUCPJ's formulations, fierce tenacity, a broad coalition, and legislative champions, we won changes to the labor contract and use-of-force policy.[12] That we were able to win any changes at all to these "sacred" documents enshrining police power was the bigger victory.

Campaigning for a New Mayor and Police Chief

CUCPJ had been publicly calling for a new chief of police since Officer Finney pulled a gun on Kiwane in October 2009. In 2011, campaigns for mayoral candidates and the city council opened up points of leverage to secure new leadership.

Jerry Schweighart, a former police officer, was Champaign's mayor for twelve years. In 2010, a video of the mayor claiming that President Barack Obama was not an American citizen went viral. Pressing on the contradiction of a racist, Tea Party Republican leading an electorate that was majority registered Democrats, members of CUCPJ worked on the mayoral campaign to elect Don Gerard, a moderate white Democrat who beat Schweighart by a mere 232 votes. Within six months, Chief Finney announced his departure. Within nine months, Anthony Cobb, a well-respected Urbana police officer, became Champaign's second African American chief of police. Leadership matters. The change in Champaign was palpable, but not immediate.

The Assault of Calvin Miller

As we approached the second anniversary of Kiwane's death, in fall 2011, Calvin Miller, son of CUCPJ member Martel Miller, was beaten by Champaign police officers. Calvin was a friend of Kiwane and lived in terror of the police, so when police pulled behind his van, young Calvin panicked, jumped from his vehicle, and ran for his life. Assuming guilt, the police pursued Calvin on foot, and as his father Martel Miller testified: "He was knocked to the ground. He was beaten with a baton and then he was turned over, pepper-sprayed in the eyes, and punched while he was in handcuffs."[13]

Again, community members were activated. When Calvin bravely testified to the city council at their next meeting, on crutches and speaking with a blackened and swollen eye, he was accompanied by over one hundred supporters. Once again, dozens of Black residents shared their stories of police brutality, piercing the bubble of the white middle-class understanding of police as protectors. Martel Miller addressed the city council, listing seven police officers by name who were notorious for brutalizing Black and Brown residents. The week after Calvin Miller and his supporters showed up to speak, police advocates organized their own speak-out before the city council. One officer directed his comments to Martel, who was sitting nearby: "I hope all the thugs like your son are scared of the police. I have never seen anyone beaten or battered by the police department in twenty-three years. . . . If Miller wants to see racism, he should look in the mirror."[14] Officer Tim Atteberry, a white officer who regularly patrolled the historic African American neighborhood known as the "North End," also spoke out: "Race is not the problem. The problem is cultural issues, parenting issues."[15] His voice escalated as he spoke: "Don't tell me about culture. How dare you accuse me of racism! I have an appreciation of honest culture, *honest* culture."[16]

A system in contradiction attempts to obscure its weak points. A publicly funded and appointed police department that regularly violates the constitutional rights of due process and equal protection of citizens is fundamentally vulnerable. The more vulnerable it is, the more it will try to either hide or flex its power. When actors who maintain an oppressive system speak out, as these police officers did publicly, they often reveal unspoken premises of the system they maintain. CUCPJ members used independent media to amplify these moments and make the contradictions in systems visible. Many of these histories only live in the archive of the *Public i* newspaper hosted by UC-IMC, thanks to journalists like Brian Dolinar and Belden Fields. Meanwhile, the public tracks the ebb and flow of this conflict, working to make sense of it. This is how we shift culture.

There are times when you feel like you are sinking. In the end, Calvin Miller pleaded guilty to a misdemeanor to avoid a felony, and left town to avoid being continuously targeted by police officers. Officer Atteberry was recognized as Officer of the Year. The union organized a vote of no confidence for new Chief of Police Anthony Cobb. At the time when poverty rates were still climbing due to economic recession, the Champaign County Board proposed to spend $20 million in public funds on jail construction and expansion projects.

In response, CUCPJ opened up a second front to fight jail construction in addition to police brutality, as both continued to advance. Over the next few years, some of the police officers Martel named continued to assault residents. One of them was Officer Matt Rush—one of the officers who beat young Calvin. Rush punched a Black military veteran and traveling dialysis technician, nearly breaking his eye. He brutally beat a young Black man, requiring his jaw to be wired shut. Rush had once beaten a woman so badly she suffered a miscarriage. Rush had the most use-of-force incidents in the police department for three years in a row. Finally, in 2014 Chief Cobb fired Rush, but the Fraternal Order of Police appealed and Rush got his job back.[17] The city claimed it was unable to remove Rush again, as he had not been prosecuted criminally. In response, CUCPJ organized a petition of hundreds of names, marched to the courthouse, and personally handed it to the state's attorney, Julia Rietz. If she would prosecute Rush, the city would have the tool they needed to remove him after four lawsuits and $320,000 in payouts. Rietz stated that "his actions in using force to subdue resistive subjects are defensible under Illinois law."[18]

Qualified Immunity

We finally had found a policy taproot of police violence and were able to name it: "qualified immunity." Qualified immunity is a principle written into the Illinois Constitution that enshrines police immunity. It sets the bar unreasonably high for prosecuting police officers for human rights abuses, unless the acts are considered "willful or wanton conduct." Despite the twenty local cases CUCPJ documented of local law enforcement brutalizing civilians and sharing them with the county's state's attorney, mayor, and chief of police, we continued to see abuse. It continued despite multiple successful lawsuits against the city for police brutality and an unprecedented march on the city council to demand Rush be fired. And when the City of Champaign finally took its first, publicly visible step to hold an officer accountable, they were blocked by a forcefield of defense reserved only for police.

Qualified immunity meant that it was nearly impossible to remove abusive officers and police officers knew if they were wearing a badge, they could do anything to a Black, Brown, or poor person in Champaign County and get away with it. Professor Sundiata Cha-Jua wrote an editorial for the local newspaper about what needed to be done, as a community, to structurally intervene and transform the police force: "We have to dismantle the extra powers that police have [under the Uniform Peace Officers' Disciplinary Act]," . . . Until you do that, you're never going to have good police-community relations."[19] Yet in that moment, it was unclear what additional steps we could take at the local level to stop these human rights abuses at the local level. We felt defeated.

Running for the State House

In late 2013, I got a call from Carol Ammons: "I am thinking about running for state representative." We discussed the opportunities: imagine if we could take on criminal justice reform at the state level? We could take on qualified immunity for police, bail bond reform, the prison phone racket, and more. The opportunities outweighed the risks.

Carol Ammons was and is the hardest working, most visionary public servant I have ever had the opportunity to work with. With a toddler on my lap, I managed Carol's primary campaign for the Illinois House out of my living room. We pulled together a diverse, grassroots, all-volunteer dream team of seasoned organizers in the community. She faced off with an opponent handpicked by the state's attorney and lavishly funded by the Speaker of the Illinois House.[20] The political establishment lined up behind Carol's opponent: a white, male attorney. Our campaign was outspent ten to one. However, our Campaign to Elect Carol Ammons gathered over 250 volunteers, some who had never even registered to vote, and who were now helping us register 2,500 new voters in a race that could easily be decided by a few hundred votes. We turned out more voters in Black neighborhoods than during Obama's first presidential primary. Carol streaked past her opponent, in the end winning 61 percent of the vote.[21] We clapped our hands together and danced through the County Administration building, while chanting: "This is what democracy looks like!"

In the next eight years, Carol would champion the legislation proposed by our Campaign for Prison Phone Justice to cap the cost of prison phone calls, winning the lowest call rates in the country;[22] a raise of the minimum wage to $15 an hour; and in 2020, Representative Ammons worked with the Illinois Black Caucus to pass groundbreaking pretrial reform legislation that made Illinois the first US state to end cash bail. No longer would anyone be held in Illinois jails because they are too poor to bail out. Poor people would no longer lose their jobs, housing, and kids simply due to being locked up. Prosecutors would have less leverage to force defendants to take unjust plea bargains just because they are desperate to be released from jail and get their lives back. Jail populations would be cut, meaning more local funds could go toward anti-poverty and prevention programs and not jail building projects—not only here in Champaign County but throughout the state.

The Campaign to Elect Carol Ammons was a leveling up of our organizing and power. Although we had run campaigns before, the Campaign to Elect Carol Ammons sharpened our understanding of the radical premise of "one person, one vote." In our highly stratified society, we rarely count equally—which is why the conservative movement has continuously focused its energies on blocking ballot access for working, poor, and nonwhite people, paths to citizenship for immigrants, and paths to elected office for women and people of color.

CUCPJ Ends Meetings

In 2017, CUCPJ members decided to end our meetings as we pivoted toward working with Representative Ammons on state legislation. A smaller group created Build Programs Not Jails, a single-issue group that carried that portion of CUCPJ's work forward. Looking back on and assessing CUCPJ's victories over the past two decades: we stopped local police from acquiring taser stun guns for ten years, then helped pass one of the most restrictive taser gun usage policies in the country. We supported Forgiveness Weekend, turning it into an annual expungement and record-sealing fair that has sealed hundreds of criminal records to date. We started Community Courtwatch to put eyes and ears inside the courtroom, helped families navigate complex systems, and threw our efforts behind a number of cases of Black men who remain free as a result. We asserted the right for the public to record police activities, paving the way for a state constitutional change. We exposed and mobilized against local police assaults of numerous African Americans including youth, veterans, and mothers. We replaced Champaign's outwardly racist mayor, chief of police, and several notorious rogue officers. We secured structures for civilian pversight of police in Urbana and Champaign, although even now, a decade later, they remain compromised. We forced the county to investigate and interrupt the practice of selecting all-white juries. We supported dozens of progressive candidates who won public office. We stopped a massive jail building project three times; although it passed in 2021 under Democrat leadership, the overall number of beds was reduced as a result of our persistent efforts. We ran a prison phone justice campaign that resulted in Illinois having the lowest price for phone calls in the country, helping families stay connected as we work together to dismantle mass incarceration. We built knowledge, infrastructure, community connections, leadership, and power. Yes, we moved the needle of justice in Champaign County!

National Movement

When the police killed Kiwane in 2009, a movement against police harassment and brutality of Black and Brown residents had been building in small communities all over the country. This movement would continue to build over the next ten years as police killings of civilians escalated dramatically.[23] In 2013, Trayvon Martin was killed by a vigilante in Florida and #BlackLivesMatter was born. In the years that followed, police officers shot and killed hundreds of unarmed Black residents. Every one of these people loved and was loved. These horrific stories felt new, but they were not—they were part of a long-standing pattern, like what we observed in Champaign County. Thus began a national conversation, a rallying cry, about *why*. Why would it ever be the case that police would feel so threatened, or so shielded from accountability, that they would kill someone else's child?

Organizers studied the way racist fear is pressed so deeply into the white psyche that white police officers see African American boys as five years older than they really are.[24] They looked at why officers who commit such clear human rights violations are able to escape accountability and prosecution. They studied the way conservative white prosecutors are elected in uncontested races across the country;[25] the way use-of-force policies are written to legalize the killing of unarmed civilians; the way police labor contracts block cities from disciplining rogue officers; and the way qualified immunity is written into the founding documents of policing and government. This is what articulating a system looks like. Building an analysis of the system we are in is a process that starts with conversation, connection, and grows rhizomatically—like the roots of bamboo—quiet, underground, and interconnected in every direction, until it finds an opportunity to break to the surface and grow into a forest of loving affirmation of existence and resistance. We experienced this when the hashtag #BlackLivesMatter first circulated online in 2013, moving huge groups of protestors into the streets around the world to protest racialized police violence.

In 2022, the Illinois Black Caucus attempted to eliminate qualified immunity for police officers in their landmark criminal justice reform package. That portion faced fierce opposition by the police union and its allies, and it was cut as the rest of this historic legislation passed, ending cash bail and bringing pre-trial reform to Illinois. To date, this is the closest we have come to addressing the policy roots of police brutality.

Looking back, it is clear that power—both the kind built by the grassroots, and the kind the grassroots works to move—is contested and resilient. Sometimes when you are sinking, you don't see that you are actually part of a rising tide. CUCPJ made the most gains when our coalition was broadest and those most affected—the people our police force brutalized and tortured, and their families—were supported, centered, and heard by that larger coalition. When the coalition fell into disrepair, those most affected were re-isolated. We learned that the roots of policing as an institution are intertwined with the history of slavery in this country, and in the domination and exploitation of underclass and working-class people in US democracy. To stop police impunity, we must excavate the racist roots embedded in the founding of this country to remake our democracy in such a way that it refuses all logics of superiority.

CHAPTER 22

FORMULATION

The World Is Never Finished

We are beginning to understand that the world is always being made and never finished; that activism can be the journey rather than the arrival; that struggle doesn't always have to be confrontational, but can take the form of reaching out to find common ground with the many 'others' in our society who are also seeking ways out from alienation, isolation, privatization, and dehumanization by corporate globalization.

—Grace Lee Boggs, *The Next American Revolution: Sustainable Activism for the Twenty-First Century*

Now that you have designed your intervention, it is finally time to intervene! And as soon as you intervene, it will be immediately time to observe, reflect, learn from, and respond to the consequences of your intervention. Making social change is an iterative process happening on many scales simultaneously. A moment of intervention is only a brief, conspicuous moment, supported before and after by analysis, strategy, design, reflection, revision, and revisioning. This chapter details the work of turning actions into systems change. This includes responding to the backlash that arises when we perturb powerful systems, and foraging for consequences on the margins to move them to the center.

We began this section with the story of Champaign-Urbana Citizens for Peace and Justice (CUCPJ) as an example of a small group iterating the Spiral of Change over fourteen years, so that you would have events to reflect on as we share our formulations about this stage of the process. Learning from continual feedback brings us back around to the Gather People and Stories step on the Spiral of Change, which overlaps with Act and Reflect as you begin the cycle again. Repeating this cycle is how we increase participation and grow democracy. Every cycle of the spiral is an opportunity to grow participation.

Foraging for Consequences

Every good historian can trace fundamental changes in social systems to groups who planted the seeds of new ideas in fertile social conditions. Those seeds are being planted all around us, but without actively working to see, amplify and learn from them, they become drowned out by floods of distracting information.

Shortly after seeding our designs, we have to actively forage for their consequences, watching for tender shoots that show up, feeding them the nutrients of our attention, clearing the weeds of false narratives to give them sunlight, and watering the consequences we want. We can cultivate and grow small experiments into fields of various solutions that can build on each other and work together.

From the moment we act, we are in a time that is ripe with information and opportunity. After we design and intervene, we may want to retreat and rest, but the work is just beginning. After an action, its consequences ripple through the system it is working to change, and it is in these moments the cracks of the system may be revealed, as systems' actors rush to patch them. Our actions have perturbed the self-regulation of the system. We cannot control how the system will react, but we can observe its reaction and work to influence how it behaves. This is the cybernetic framework for making change. Through repeated strategic interventions, we may be able to influence the system toward a more just and desirable world for everyone. Or the system may fortify itself in response to the intervention, growing its resistance to change. Most likely, we will observe both and will become disoriented about whether we are making progress or not.

Foraging for consequences is a practice of action and reflection that grounds us amid this disorientation. To forage for consequences, we observe the effects interventions produce, both obvious and hidden. We monitor the system's response, looking for how we can make use of it. We overturn stones to see what is hard to see, reaching out to listen to a variety of voices. At this point, the intention behind our design is less important than its consequences. For example: what consequences do we observe from those positioned to defend the system? What consequences do we observe from audiences—those assembled and the bystanders? How was the action talked about? How did allies react? How about those within our own group?

Consequences may show up in storytelling: engagement in media; a shift in the way a problem is described; or new voices speaking up. There may be consequences in policy or power structures. It is helpful to follow the movement of resources, such as the hiring or firing of staff or the growing or cutting of funds. We may notice that pathways to power open or new roadblocks are put in the way. It is helpful to follow the movement of people. How do roles change? What kinds of friendships and connections form or fissure? Where do groups and alliances grow or break? Foraging for consequences is a practice of outreach, observation, curiosity—and often humility.

Foraging for consequences is an essential practice we need to build into our designs for action so that we can learn and make effective change over time. Too often we focus on the action and treat consequences as the natural unfolding of events. If we wait for consequences to be served to us, they will come as old narratives that replicate the status quo and erase our work. Instead, we must plan how we will discover and respond to the consequences of our actions as they unfold, emphasizing those consequences we want, and mitigating the impact of those that are harmful.

Designing for Backlash

Backlash is predictable. It often signals the contradiction becoming visible. This is the point and counterpoint of change: we highlight a contradiction, the system responds to cover it up, we expose it again, it reframes, we resurface it, the system goes on attack, we duck and find a way to keep pushing, and it looks for an exit through delay or appeasement. It is seductive to get caught up in the drama of this escalating fight, but doing so can be a waste of precious energy and time. As the staying power of an oppressive system is revealed, and the fight becomes protracted, emotions build. Distracted by the fireworks of the fight, burgeoning projects and social movements may lose control and discipline, stray from strategy, and splinter. We may compete over attention and status. We can lose our focus on attacking systems and their premises, and instead attack individuals or groups, perhaps because these fights are easier and closer to hand. All of these destructive tendencies are exacerbated, incentivized, and rewarded by social media and the individualism and narcissism they fuel. We must resist their pull and instead stay focused on learning from our disagreements, building power that will manifest our shared values in concrete ways.[1]

It is at times of backlash when the problem can feel the *most overwhelming*, but there is also the *most opportunity* for learning. As we learn, we can pivot to better strategies for change. As Saul Alinsky maintained in his book *Rules for Radicals*: "The action is in the reaction."[2] Alinsky was the son of Jewish immigrants who organized with residents in the poor communities in Chicago where he grew up "so that the most oppressed and exploited elements could take control of their own communities and their own destinies."[3] Alinsky, and the many organizers who studied his work, saw moments of conflict or system stress as opportunities to push forward, while reformers, fearing a change of system, often shouted "go slow."[4] These chaotic moments of crisis contain opportunities for greater justice—or for greater exploitation.

Here are four ways systems' actors typically react to contradictions to tame them into conflicts: denial, reframing, attack, and appeasement. Using these, systems' actors can push a contradiction back into its conflict cave where it growls and grows, but never resolves. Understanding these forms of backlash is helpful: we can see these as potential signs of progress and design to respond to them.

When using denial, systems' actors hide or lie about a problem. In reframing the issue, they spin and distort information to make the square peg of the problem appear snug inside the round hole of the system's response to it. When you encounter denial and reframing, it is helpful to have independent media outlets behind you. The contrast between denial or reframing against a well-formulated contradiction, informed by the experiences of those affected, makes great stories that educate wider publics about the system maintaining the problem.

Akin to reframing is "censorship by flooding," a phrase coined by Mark Enslin and taken up by Manni Brün to illustrate how in societies premised on freedom of speech, the press, and assembly, directly censoring or controlling these premises exacerbate contradictions and make systems of control more visible, and therefore, vulnerable. To avoid visibility, systems' actors may instead choose to drown out systems, challenging information flows with a glut of systems-maintaining information. Instead of canceling speech and creating silence, they insert noise, which makes it hard to find a meaningful signal. This is how censorship by flooding works. In the past, corporate media outlets would amplify a single (often remote and tragic) story, ignoring the myriad efforts to build alternatives in our own backyards. Censorship by flooding has become easier and more pernicious in the world of corporate social media, where investments in propaganda and fake news mobilize online mobs to deploy them. Methods of control have become more indirect, such as algorithmic hiding of inconvenient information from social media or a flood of disinformation pushed by artificial intelligence, as articulated by Safiya Noble.[5]

When our actions appear drowned in the information flood, it is time to put on our rainboots and wade into the water to find consequences that can carry us to dry ground. We can seek out community—those doing similar actions and those inspired by our actions—to link arms with, and communicate person-to-person about what is happening, so we don't get swept away. Here, again, independent media can help us. Exposing when those in power "flood the zone" makes a compelling story that can redirect attention back to our narratives.

When denial, reframing, and censorship by flooding don't work, the system often turns to direct attacks, as systems' actors try to control speech or bodies to hide a contradiction. For example, they may destroy a media outlet to muzzle information, such as when the US destroyed radio stations in Iraq to hide the consequences of their saturation bombing of civilian targets.[6] They may suppress statements of a protest, such as when police confiscated puppets in advance of global justice protests to eliminate the most eye-catching version of our messages.[7] They may pass bans on camping to move homeless residents out of public view, hiding the consequence of a system that maintains scarcity in a society of abundance.

As we grow our strength and outmaneuver these attacks, systems' actors may shift to appeasement. Meeting a fraction of a need is a form of appeasement; it ties up energy that could go toward resistance and redirects it to competing for scarce resources. It is essential to reject the false solutions the systems' actors propose, such as offering small present gains as appeasement for enormous future losses. It is important to distinguish between a compromise that brings a win at the cost of cutting off the path toward your desirable society and a compromise that leaves that path open.

Designing Solidarity

Predictably, the splintering of groups and movements for change often happens over the contested differences in our assessments of consequences. At a time when a strategy of solidarity and commitment to multitactical long-haul organizing is needed most, we may turn on each other in suspicion and accusation. Our culture of individualism—with its single issues and singular identities—threatens to tear through whatever solidarities we build. Systems' actors exploit these differences through a strategy of divide and control, manipulating our analysis and understanding of consequences.

We can, instead, build a united front by designing solidarity. In "Re-Designing the Character of the Care-Actor," Susan Parenti provides this distinguishing description: "Solidarity is when someone gives support to other people that cuts across the usual social power lines."[8] Solidarity requires listening, humility, and building trust. We act in solidarity when we listen and take care to respond to the requests of a multiplicity of impacted groups. We act in solidarity when we forge connections with those who have been working, often quietly and for years, on similar or linked problems. We act in solidarity when we stand against all logics of superiority, refusing dehumanization in all its forms.

Solidarity is not to be confused with unity. Unity can be important in moments of action, but we should build democratic cultures that embrace rather than ignore tensions between unity and difference, belonging and challenging, safety and risk. This approach allows our projects and movements to grow from the inside—such as with the voices of Black women inside the civil rights and women's liberation movements whose important critiques paved the way to intersectional analyses of power; or how the perspectives of queer, bisexual, and transgender people working toward gay liberation help us understand gender and sexual orientation as spectrums.

Reflecting

Reflection is arguably the most important, and most often overlooked, step in the Spiral of Change. We reflect not only on the systems we are trying to change but also, internally, on our own processes and dynamics. In our work we will—unwittingly, but inevitably—reproduce some of the undesirable dynamics of the culture and systems we are trying to change. How could we not? We should expect these dynamics and discuss how to better align our practice with our desires. Cultures of backlash, canceling, and disposability do not forward our goals. They are produced by pain and isolation, reflecting and propagating those negative dynamics outward. Instead, we work to redress trauma and prevent harm, fostering the conditions in which these harmful dynamics no longer arise. In the process of reflection, disagreements about the consequences, next steps, and group process inevitably arise. To benefit from this friction, we need relationships that hold both solidarity and difference. Reflection is our opportunity to heal ourselves and our world in tandem, thereby learning to use new means to achieve new ends.

In chapter 21, we discussed how Champaign-Urbana Citizens for Peace and Justice (CUCPJ), a multiracial group made up of unemployed, working class, and professional people, young and old, gay and straight, radically altered the community and all who participated in the process of making change. It is a model for the kind of "two-sided transformation" that Grace Lee Boggs describes as necessary for revolutions: change of ourselves and our institutions.[9]

CUCPJ members' commitment to attending in-person meetings to coordinate our actions, two hours a week for thirteen years, provided the necessary space and time to wrestle with the ways the contradictions in our society were maintained inside and outside of us. Time and again, as we went around the circle sharing our perspectives, there were frictions: someone would say something from a place of unacknowledged privilege, or assert their perspective as dominant, or speak with an ignorance of history. But instead of shutting down or blowing up, others would speak their truth to a rapt audience, and we could feel the process of liberation as old assumptions crumbled and new connections were born. Despite the ignorance we each exhibited at some point, our love and respect for each other, born from working together for so many years, carried us.

In CUCPJ, we walked the path of transformational organizing. In doing so we connected with the lineage of the "re-founding" of the country after the Civil War, leading to changes in the US Constitution, as a document of social premises for the country, to include African American men and later all women as participants in democracy. We struggled against dehumanization in many cumulative actions, observing and reflecting together, challenging our thinking, and building the power that transformed the political and social landscape of our community. The story of CUCPJ's transformative steps to act–forage–reflect–renew stands as a model for our praxis: the braiding of action and reflection through the contradictions in our work while being guided by our desires for the common good.

Changing Our Minds

Governing society together requires living with uncertainty. Cooperating with those we disagree with is the indispensable minimum of building community. It is uncomfortable to recognize that, in any project of governing ourselves, the allure of certainty is a liability. Working together often entails committing to work past the point an experiment fails, long enough to learn enough to design and try the next experiment, such that some success and a deeper relationship and wisdom can grow. Without making mistakes, we can't learn, but this is easier to accept with regard to our own mistakes than with regard to the mistakes of others. It's hard to open ourselves to others' mistakes and offer them grace and the chance to learn. Many of us have been indoctrinated to have no patience for this kind of generosity. When systems and cultures foreclose on the possibility of learning, they become dysfunctional.

Instead, we invite a process of balancing stability and change toward social evolution. What does it look like to lead in a way that leans into uncertainty? Can we cultivate leadership where authority floats between participants? We need relationships that can hold solidarity *and* difference in the face of a culture of backlash and disposability. We can do so through valuing relationships, planning for difference, and embracing heuristic, agile design.

A thought, project, or social movement that is unable to change is dead. In its death, it may be irrelevant, or dangerous, like a zombie. If our work is to be living, if our efforts to grow democracy are alive, then we must develop the ability to reflect on consequences and change our minds. We educate ourselves, and through repeated collective action and reflection, we cultivate wisdom: the intuition built through practice in how to apply experiences and knowledge in principled and effective ways.

There are challenges to changing your mind. When you learn new information and see a situation in a new light, it is important in such a moment to articulate both the outcome you want to avoid (that your old position would lead to), and the values and goals you share with your critics. The story of your vulnerability in finding yourself wrong, and your journey through uncertainty to your current position is compelling. Tell it well—and you will bring people with you. The more sympathetically you can articulate your opposition's point of view before moving away from it, the more you can create an inclusive approach to your work.

If we get too attached to a particular tactic or way of doing things, it becomes difficult to be strategic and evolve. At the same time that we build spaces of safety and belonging, we can't let ourselves become too comfortable within the confines of an old idea as it ossifies into a rigid identity and culture. We may find ourselves in the middle of a radical project, pushing up against the boundaries maintained by those who have found safety and belonging in the original formulation of the project, and are unwilling to continue to reformulate it in light of new information and reflection.

Repeating the Spiral of Change

Throughout this book we have walked the path of praxis—between theory, practice, and reflecting on interventions. Moving around the Spiral of Change, we come to voice about our experiences, understand them as shared problems in systems, formulate the contradictions in these problems that reveal points of leverage where we design interventions led by our desires.

Now that we have acted, foraged for consequences, and reflected on what we did, what happened as a result, and how we did it, it is time to begin the spiral again, guided by all we have learned this time around.

CHAPTER 23

ASSIGNMENT

Praxis Braids
Action and Reflection

Here we are, at what appears to be the last step—Act and Reflect—but instead of arriving at the end, we are just getting started. Our learning accelerates us into the next loop of the spiral where the outputs of our reflection become inputs to our contradictions, desires, and designs. In reflecting and reformulating, we take new action with renewed wisdom.[1] With reflection it is possible to make and remake democracies, premised on equity and living in balance with the earth. In the following assignments, we invite you to try out a variety of ways to act, forage, reflect, and renew.

Change-Making News

With a barrage of daily news stories that are big, scary, and hopeless, it is no wonder that we feel small, irrelevant, and distrustful of each other. When we are terrified, our brains are focused on surviving and not open to learning. We can practice foraging for consequences daily by locating change-making news stories. These stories suggest a strategy for tracking world events while resisting disillusionment.

We can find—and tell—the stories of the problem through the lens of a systemic analysis and what is being done about it.

Find the news story

Find the change-making news story. One that shows positive consequences of intentional actions or where a problem is highlighted through the lens of what is being done about it. Bonus points if it was done by a group. Extra credit if it happened within your community.

Foraging for Consequences Within Your Group

After an intervention, gather with your group and discuss:

What did each person see?

What new connections were made?

How did the target of your pressure or action respond? Did they try to turn contradictions into conflicts? How?

How did bystanders react or participate?

Ask everyone. In foraging for consequences, asking everyone is a golden opportunity to increase participation—especially if you have designed and built the capacity to both listen and respond to what people say.

Foraging for Consequences Outside Your Group

The more people you engage in these conversations, the more concrete and surprising consequences you will gather. Ask as many people as you can. Foraging for consequences is a golden opportunity to increase participation—especially if you have built a way to listen and respond to what people say. Figure out who it's important to ask and the best context for approaching them. A few suggested things to ask them about:

Their experience of the problem before the intervention.

Whether your formulation of the problem matches their experience.

Their experience of the intervention itself.

The consequences of the intervention they have experienced or observed.

What problems they see persisting and/or shifting and/or cropping up after the intervention.

What they think the best response to these current problems might be.

How they would like to be further involved in responding to these problems.

Who else you should be talking to about all of this.

Scrapbooking Consequences

For decades I, Danielle, have kept a scrapbook, with photos and journal entries that are traces of my foraging for consequences. Over time, I can follow the throughline of an intervention, which can sometimes take ten or more years. This has become an essential strategy to keep me motivated and always reflecting on next steps.

Collage a scrapbook

For your actions, or if seeking actions to inspire and inform you, keep a "consequences scrapbook" of news media, articles, feedback and responses to press coverage, art and media-making examples and experiments, thank yous, etc. and your own thoughts about them.

Reflect on Consequences

As a group or alone, gather your desire statements, designs, and the consequences you observed. For the **intervention** itself, its design and execution, ask the following five questions:

> In what ways did the action reflect and/or fulfill our desires?
>
> In what ways did it fall short of our desires?
>
> What do we want to do more of next time?
>
> What do we want to avoid?
>
> What new desire statements do we need to formulate as criteria for the future?

For the **consequences** you foraged, what happened after you intervened? In conversations held with many other people, ask and answer the same five questions. Then, looking at the **internal processes** and dynamics of your group, participants ask and answer the same five questions again.

Interview a Mentor

Conduct an interview in which you ask a mentor or elder: "Think of a time when you changed your mind about something that you felt was fundamental. What were the triggers for a change of mind? Who was involved? What were the circumstances? What did you observe?"

Revise Desires and Designs

Consider how, in the light of new information, you would repeat—differently—all the steps on the Spiral of Change:

Reconvene

Based on all your work acting, foraging, and reflecting, who do you want to work with around the next revolution of the spiral? Whose perspective do you want to consult in an ongoing way as you move forward? Who would you love to learn more from? What would be the most irresistible way to invite them to collaborate?

Tell the stories of what happened

What stories, and whose, have now come to your attention and need to be amplified? Where will you look for them now and who needs to hear them?

Reformulate the problem

Based on all the experiences and information you gathered and processed, how would you formulate the problem now?

Relook the system and its relations

Now that you've acted and the system has reacted, what have you learned? Do you look the system any differently? Are there new elements to include? New relations or shifted ones to describe? Have you witnessed dynamics you did not anticipate?

Reformulate your desires

Which of your desire statements remain the same? Which would you revise, and how? What new desires have arisen and require formulation?

Reformulate the contradictions

Taking into consideration the stories, formulations of the problem, system looks, and the reactions of the system to your last intervention, would you formulate the system's contradictions any differently? Have new vulnerabilities been revealed that you can target as points of leverage?

Design your next intervention

By this point, you have learned a lot. Put this learning into action in the design of your next intervention. Your learning constitutes new criteria to guide your decision-making. On the small scale, of course, it makes sense to do more of what works but in making social change, the context in which we are intervening is continually shifting. By intervening the first time, we changed the context ourselves, on top of all the changes we had nothing to do with. We cannot step in the same river twice, and we should not limit our imaginations by trying to do so, no matter how much we honor and seek to learn from the past.

From One No to Many Yeses

All that you touch, you change.
All that you change, changes you.

—Octavia Butler, *Parable of the Sower*

You are important, no person is dispensable, and we need everyone to work everywhere to build our participation. Capitalism and imperialism are running the planet out, requiring us to make the worlds we want through an abundant variety of interventions at every level. The road to our healing, justice, and thriving leads through our solidarity and language, analysis and strategy, action and reflection, over and over again.

In this moment, we need your expertise, your desires, and your designs—in your fields of concern—for increasing everyone's participation in the decisions that affect all our lives. To build participatory democracy, people need not only access and resources, but to feel safe, to belong, and to have purpose. To sustain the changes we long for, our designs must encompass healing and repair. We need to value our relationships across our differences with such high commitment that we stay connected through conflict, working to understand one another more deeply and supporting our healing and growth in its incompleteness. Our power to make change is an emergent property of our repeated participation, which transforms us as we transform the world. These are key points from this book we hope will carry you forward.

Organizing within Media Justice, Champaign-Urbana Citizens for Peace and Justice, and the Crown Heights Tenant Union has given us the experience of being transformed through working for equity across race and class. We continue to ask this legitimate question: "How do we continuously work to unravel unconscious bias and white supremacy while we build a world 'where many worlds fit'?"[1] Jeff Perlstein, co-founder of Seattle Indymedia, credits the Zapatistas with promoting "the whole idea . . . that we all can come together in these moments from one unified 'no' to globalization, 'no' to global capital, 'no' to power from above. The model and the process has to have ways for people to express their different yeses, their different identities, their different ways of expressing themselves."[2]

Teaching at the School for Designing a Society has given us a valuable set of tools for formulating and designing across domains that are normally siloed. Thinking together in a small group we can make use of our longing for what is missing by naming it and building toward it. Collaborating is a joyful experience. We are delighted to have shared these delicious ideas with you through formulations and assignments, and we hope that you play with them for hours or years . . . and make your own.

This is an uncertain and frightening time where we are given the near impossible task—one given to every society facing paradigm shift or perish—where we are simultaneously called to act *and* evolve. James and Grace Lee Boggs reflect on this dilemma in their book *Revolution and Evolution in the Twentieth Century*, where they present the overarching lesson learned from the shortcomings (or outright failures) of the revolutionary movements of the twentieth century as the inability of actors to reflect, learn, and change. Without reflection, efforts and movements for change become resistant to evolution. This historical pattern points out a contradiction inherent in democratic revolutions: *Revolution requires the consolidation of power and the assertion of certainty to overthrow imperial powers and dictators, yet democracy requires sharing power, reflection, and navigating uncertainty.* Resisting the status quo and seizing power require different skills and create a different culture than governing equitably and justly. A rebellion is a disruption of oppressive systems, but a revolution is a longer-term project to structure society more equitably to meet human and ecological needs.

In *The Next American Revolution*, Grace Lee Boggs describes a way to navigate this contradiction through a "two-sided" transformational organizing approach that changes us as we change institutions and systems, as we "reinvent revolution."[3] We contain within ourselves the cosmos of our society. Through transformational organizing we nurture a process and culture of participatory democracy that practices our desirable society in our everyday actions as we work to create it. This practice must be rooted in love and continuous learning to be effective. This is how we cultivate wisdom.

To root our work in love, we seek knowledge and desire for what is good for all. To root our work in continuous learning, we lead with curiosity, humility, and an openness to be transformed. How do we lead with love?[4] Here are some formulations Danielle uses to guide her organizing:

> *I lead with love when I act toward my social desires rather than merely reacting to problems, seeking to build and not only to fight.*

> *I lead with love when I seek to understand the systemic roots of problems rather than blaming and excluding those who manifest their symptoms.*

> *I lead with love when I recognize every human as a legitimate other and can articulate the position of my opponent in a fair way even while I disagree with it.*

> *I lead with love when I act in ways designed to carry everyone—myself, my community, and even my antagonists—to higher ground so that the community as a whole is better off because of my actions.*

We face these questions: will we lead with hate or love? Will we amplify logics of superiority or insist on logics of inclusion? Will we be swallowed by autocracy, or resist and deepen our democracy? As we write this, mechanisms of repression that have long targeted poor communities—whether Black, Brown, immigrant, or Indigenous—have rapidly scaled up to include more and more people, as our cities are becoming openly occupied. Injustices long in contradiction with our democracy make it vulnerable and call for repair and healing: colonization, rape, slavery, mass incarceration, and now, globalized capitalism. Corporate power has hijacked our means of self-governance to generate false scarcity and produce profit, when we want them to generate abundance and meet human needs.

At this crossroads, we must remake, reconstruct, and re-found our democracy. Democracy requires us to recognize everyone in their full humanity and to take pleasure in our true equality. In this way, the oppressed will liberate oppressors from their lonely, nihilist place of harming others and then claiming victimhood only to weaponize it against the most marginalized. When we refuse the disposability of anyone in our beloved communities—young Black men, poor rural workers, our migrant neighbors, trans folks, our elders, people with disabilities, women and femmes—we are remaking democracy. Democracy feeds on acts of solidarity—both large and small—when I will show up for your rights with the same ferocity as I show up for my own. It shows up in spaces of humility, when we cultivate curiosity and connection through asking legitimate questions and listening to one another. This is a time of bravery—to speak up, and hold lines—as well as humility, when we do not yet know how to make the next stage of history, or whether we will be able to have a planet viable enough to make it at all.

Democracy is something we can and need to do everyday, everywhere. How can we include our families in planning to boycott and divest from structures of harm? Find others working on similar issues and join with them? Ask whose voices are missing and find ways to listen to them and support their efforts? Together we can remake our democracy around the values we have long held but struggle to practice socially: care for each other and the earth, inclusion, respect, freedom, and responsibility.

Democracy dispels autocracy. Our participation is our power.

Afterword

How to read *Remaking Democracy: How We Make the Worlds We Want*? Especially considering that certain kinds of reading are part of its subject: reading a social situation, reading the results of one's actions, reading the face of the clock of the world? The *we* that brought forth this work consists of a duo of a composer and an activist. Keeping that in mind, however, becomes helpful only after spending some time with the reading, when it emerges that these labels are made to encompass more than writing music and organizing rallies. Also, it turns out that the composer of the pair has been involved in post-Occupy Wall Street housing activism, and the activist is also a sculptor, poet, organizer of infoshops, ex-school bus driver, and . . . elected public official. Over the course of the book, the terms composer and activist expand to the point that they begin to converge.

Other words surface in this reading that at first appear familiar but in their combination and insistence seem to mean something that requires explication. What is "desire" doing here? What must "participation" mean that it can be the antidote to fascism? Things are spoken of as the result of "design" that are usually held to be the work of chance or fate. I am called upon to "look a system" and "forage for consequences." If I formulate contradictions I might locate points of leverage. As I try out these phrases and their corresponding sets of actions, it occurs to me that each might warrant its own study, a book of its own. As I read, I find historical backgrounds, formulations, instructions, illustrations, assignments. Perhaps this is a textbook? But I'm also drawn into personal experiences and reflections of the authors that appear necessary not only for understanding where they are coming from, but also for knowing where the argument, and my involvement as a reader, might be going.

Certainly, the *we* of how we make and the *we* of the worlds we want must be larger than the duo. I read each *we* and consider whether I am meant to include myself in either. Gradually *you* joins in and comes to the fore. The social and political implications of inclusion and exclusion churn in the evolving foreground and background of this project—participation, decision-making, stake-holding, intervening. One of the refrains of bell hooks' article "Choosing the Margin as a Space of Radical Openness" applies here: "Language is also a place of struggle."

We want. In a way this book traces the history of a particular fifty-year effort in central Illinois to focus on this aspect of social change, in dialogue with related worldwide movements. Susan Parenti would say about the School for Designing a Society (SDaS): 'This is not an education in know-ing, but an education in wanting.' The political activism inside and outside college campuses has tended to focus, correctly, on what the "we" of the time were against. What we were for was mostly implicit. Occasionally this would come to the fore—"*Tell them about the dream, Martin*"—in renewed experi-ments in alternative education, alternative organizations of work, intentional communities, cooperatives, and ten-point programs. Still, the consciousness imposed by regimes of oppression tends to focus our collective resistance on what we wish to oppose, to counteract, to abolish. The space for discussing, figuring out, perhaps formulating what we, some we, might want instead, has been the explicit intention of SDaS.

I was present for and implicated in some of the projects cited in this hybrid account. Like Elizabeth Adams, I became interested in counterhe-gemonic art, particularly music, when I was a young person, and took this interest to college. In my first class in composition at the University of Illinois, I was confronted with Herbert Brün, who asked us to question the social assumptions of the language—even language about music—that we students used in daily life. He offered: "A composer is a person who brings about that which without them and without human intent would not happen." Hmm. So this could include not only, say, Michael Holloway, Sal Martirano, and Ron

Nameth bringing about *L'sGA for Gas-Masked Politico, Helium Bomb, 3 16mm Projectors and 2-Channel Tape*—devastating piece!—but also NON:op Open Opera Works' recent remix and expansion of this work, "L'sGA: Lincoln's Gettysburg Address," with Kao Ra Zen, A.J. McClenon, Ja Nelle Davenport-Pleasure, Willie "Prince Roc" Round, and Christophe Preissing—devasting update! Brün's formulation of composer could include Patricio Guzman and team making the film *The Battle of Chile* (1977), but perhaps also Marianne Brün ensuring that Herbert invited his students to the screening of *The Battle of Chile*. Marianne's construction of the artist-in-residence program at the Unit One/Allen Hall living-learning program, the classes she taught there: The Necessity of Art, Theater and Social Change, A Woman is Not a Sometime Thing, and Designing Society. Her way of coaching students in how to fail their draft physicals. Her presentation at a conference of the American Society for Cybernetics on the Designing Society course, and the "living book" brought about by Annetta Pedretti with Marianne and respondents. (Check out houseofannetta.org.)

Herbert also offered to the freshman class: "Composition creates a context in which a false statement turns true." Hmm. What might the false statement be of Ravel's *Piano Concerto for the Left Hand*? or Gil Scott Heron's *No Knock*? we asked ourselves. Only after a year of ensuing student-generated projects did I learn of the roots of this formulation in an assignment from a course Herbert taught collectively with Heinz von Foerster and others in 1968, at the request of students: "Write a paper entitled 'Right or Wrong: My Desires.' On no more than two typewritten pages state anything of which you wish to say: 'While it is not the case, I desire it to be the case.'"

Marianne's composition of her Designing Society course in 1981 and 1984 included a reprise of this assignment within a sequence: write lists of desire statements; gather in groups to look at implications and interactions of statements; segue to a study of the current society with the help of *The Capitalist System: A Radical Analysis of American Society* (1972); then take a breather to delve into a book cart of utopias to see if any might live up to the desires or address the problems of the first two sections; and lastly, a sort of social design charette involving the whole class. Around this time, Marianne began meeting with students to explore the possibility of starting a school. The community that grew around these courses formed touring performance groups: the United Mime Workers, the Performers' Workshop Ensemble (PWE). PWE defined ourselves as a project-based group, "project" meaning performance workshops, concerts, plays, house theaters, collaborative books, conferences, and eventually SDaS. PWE met Danielle during one of our residencies, at New College in Florida, which brought about her becoming a participant in the first SDaS and later one of the main organizers, along with her relocation to Urbana and instigation there and nationally of various projects, campaigns, and organizations. Champaign-Urbana Citizens for Peace and Justice (CUCPJ), a case study in this book, was a composition of Danielle, Carol Ammons, Aaron Ammons, and everyone who took part. Focusing on racism in local policing and injustices of the criminal justice system, CUCPJ explicitly combined activism and activist self-education. When someone came to us seeking help against their isolation in the hostile and confusing justice system, we would organize court watch for them but also encourage them to join court watch for others. Meanwhile, we would discover unexpected consequences of concerted showing up.

To appreciate an action as activism is to see how it may create an opening for people who have been closed off, how it may spark further organization toward justice, how it may reveal to us our power or clarify what we are up against, or help us define who we are. To appreciate an action as a composition is to see how its unique combination of elements may seem at first puzzling, but then to ask how the puzzling parts are functioning, what new sense they gain from the whole, to see them as contributing to a learnable moment, as possibly offering a new structure to build on, as possibly calling on me to change myself into the not-yet-existing reader/listener/viewer necessary to perceive it.

Remaking Democracy arrives at a time of increased persecution of people living on various margins, of contortions of legality, of US troops deployed in US cities, ongoing genocide under US auspices, global rightward political shifts, and new questions among us, whoever we may be, who wish to counteract some or all or any of this. New predicaments call for new compositions. The stakes—for us, for our family members, for members of our community and our twin cities, as well as the stakes for people under oppression around the world—are so vastly different from each other as to defy comprehension, description, and transformative action. This book (an action and a composition) offers some fresh notions of how to proceed. I am its student.

Mark Enslin
Urbana, October 2025

Notes

Introduction: "What time is it on the clock of the world?"

1. David Swain, Facebook message to Danielle Chynoweth, November 9, 2016.
2. Christina Dunbar-Hester, *Low Power to the People: Pirates, Protest, and Politics in FM Radio Activism* (Cambridge, MA and London: MIT Press, 2014), ix.
3. Cecilia Kang, "F.C.C. Approves Broadband Subsidy for Low-Income Households," *The New York Times*, March 31, 2016, nytimes.com.
4. For example, Alana Devich Cyril. See her short, documentary film on her experience, *My Life, Interrupted* (2018).
5. Even as our mentors cringe and tell us to reread Theodor Adorno's *Negative Dialectics*.
6. Herbert Brün, "The Need of Cognition for the Cognition of Needs," in *Cybernetics of Cybernetics, or, the Control of Control and the Communication of Communication*, ed. Heinz von Foerster et al. (Champaign-Urbana: Biological Computer Laboratory, University of Illinois, 1974).
7. "[T]he fully enlightened earth radiates disaster triumphant," opens *Dialectic of Enlightenment*. Theodor W. Adorno and Max Horkheimer, *Dialectic of Enlightenment*, trans. John Cumming (London: Verso Books, 2016), 3.
8. Belden Fields, "Remembering Manni Brün," *Public i*, March 27, 2014, publici.ucimc.org.
9. Heinz von Foerster et al., *The Cybernetics of Cybernetics* (Champaign-Urbana: Biological Computer Laboratory, University of Illinois, 1974). Also see Margaret Mead, "Cybernetics of Cybernetics," in *Purposive Systems*, ed. Heinz von Foerster (New York: Spartan Books, 1968), 1–11.
10. See Robert White Scott, "An Intellectual History of the School for Designing a Society" (PhD dissertation, University of Illinois at Urbana-Champaign, 2011), 140, hdl.handle.net/2142/24073; Marianne Brün, *Designing Society* (London: Princelet Editions, 1985).
11. *Patch Adams*, directed by Tom Shadyac (Universal Pictures, 1998). See also Patch Adams and Maureen Mylander, *Gesundheit!: Bringing Good Health to You, the Medical System, and Society through Physician Service, Complementary Therapies, Humor, and Joy* (Rochester, VT: Healing Arts Press, 1993).
12. Paulo Freire, *Pedagogy of the Oppressed* (New York: Bloomsbury Academy, 1970), 126.

Chapter 1

1. Grace Lee Boggs, "Radical Visions, Possible Worlds: A Panel Discussion with Grace Lee Boggs and Immanuel Wallerstein, Moderated by Scott Kurashige," *Race, Poverty, and the Environment* 17, no. 2 (Fall 2010): 75–8. Listen to the panel discussion on Radio Reimagine [aka Radio RP&E], a podcast series based on articles and interviews in *Race, Poverty, and the Environment*, radioreimagine.com.

2. Boggs, "Radical Visions, Possible Worlds."

3. See José Corrêa Leite, *The World Social Forum: Strategies of Resistance* (Chicago: Haymarket Books, 2005), 10–12.

4. For a primer on the global economy in this era: Sarah Anderson, John Cavanagh, and Thea Lee, *Field Guide to the Global Economy* (New York: New Press, 2005).

5. Boggs, "Radical Visions, Possible Worlds."

6. James and Grace Lee Boggs Center, "Our Mission," boggscenter.org.

7. Grace Lee Boggs, *The Next American Revolution: Sustainable Activism for the Twenty-First Century* (Berkeley: University of California Press, 2016), xv.

8. Karl Marx and Friedrich Engels, *The Communist Manifesto*, trans. Samuel Moore (London: Penguin Books, 2015).

9. Immanuel Wallerstein, *World-Systems Analysis: An Introduction* (Durham and London: Duke University Press, 2004).

10. Jerry Mander, "Economic Globalization: The Era of Corporate Rule," Nineteenth Annual E.F. Schumacher Lecture, Salisbury Congregational Church, Salisbury, Connecticut, October 23, 1999. Here, Mander is paraphrasing the work of Wolfgang Sachs. See Wolfgang Sachs, *Planet Dialectics* (London: Zed Books, 1998).

11. Mike Collins, *The Rise of Inequality and the Decline of the Middle Class* (Chicago: First Flight Books, 2016).

12. Kirsten Almberg and Robert Cohen, "Modern Coal Miners Have Higher Death Rates from Lung Disease Than Their Predecessors," *NIOSH Science Blog*, Centers for Disease Control and Prevention, February 27, 2023, blogs.cdc.gov.

13. James Fulcher, *Capitalism: A Very Short Introduction* (Oxford: Oxford University Press, 2004).

14. Bill Blackwater, "Why Capitalist Economies Need to Grow," *Monthly Review Online*, October 10, 2014, mronline.org. See also, the chapter entitled "Endless Compound Growth" in David Harvey, *Seventeen Contradictions and the End of Capitalism* (London: Profile Books, 2015).

15. Josh Ryan-Collins et al., *Where Does Money Come From?* (London: New Economics Foundation, 2012).

16. See the work of artist Eric Pickersgill, who has documented our social disconnection in photographs: ericpickersgill.com.

17. Harvey, *Seventeen Contradictions and the End of Capitalism*, 263.

18. Founded in 2017 in Albany, New York, Housing Justice for All is a statewide coalition of more than eighty grassroots groups representing tenants and homeless New Yorkers. See housingjusticeforall.org.

19. bell hooks, *Feminism is for Everybody: Passionate Politics* (Boston: South End Press, 2000), 46.

20. Michelle Alexander, *The New Jim Crow: Mass Incarceration in the Age of Colorblindness* (New York: New Press, 2010).

21. See Keeanga-Yamahtta Taylor, *From #BlackLivesMatter to Black Liberation* (Chicago: Haymarket Books, 2016); Patrisse Khan-Cullors, Asha Bandele, and Angela Y. Davis, *When They Call You a Terrorist: A Black Lives Matter Memoir* (New York: St. Martin's Press, 2018).

22. See Walter Nicholls, *The DREAMers: How the Undocumented Youth Movement Transformed the Immigrant Rights Debate* (Stanford: Stanford University Press, 2013).
23. See Nick Estes, *Our History Is the Future: Standing Rock Versus the Dakota Access Pipeline, and the Long Tradition of Indigenous Resistance* (New York: Verso, 2019).
24. See Barbara Ransby, "Ella Taught Me: Shattering the Myth of the Leaderless Movement," *Colorlines*, June 12, 2015, colorlines.com.
25. Sabina Alkire and Séverine Deneulin, *An Introduction to the Human Development and Capability Approach* (Ottawa: Human Development and Capability Association, 2009).
26. Malkia Cyril, "Shifting Culture, Making Change," *Convergence Magazine*, June 27, 2012, convergencemag.com.
27. Noam Chomsky coined the term "the manufacturing of consent" in the context of justifying the Vietnam War. See Edward S. Herman and Noam Chomsky, *Manufacturing Consent: The Political Economy of the Mass Media* (London: The Bodley Head, 1988).
28. This vision is central to the mission of Media Justice, mediajustice.org.
29. Alfredo Lopez, *The Organic Internet: Organizing History's Largest Social Movement* (Quetzaltenango: Entremundos Publications, 2007).
30. May First/People Link, "Statement of Unity" (2006), mayfirst.coop.
31. See Safiya O. Noble, *Algorithms of Oppression: How Search Engines Reinforce Racism* (New York: New York University Press, 2018).
32. Naomi Klein, *The Shock Doctrine: The Rise of Disaster Capitalism* (Toronto: Vintage Canada, 2007).
33. See Franklin D. Roosevelt, "Message to Congress on Curbing Monopolies," April 29, 1938, presidency.ucsb.edu.
34. Bertolt Brecht, in *Writing the Truth: Five Difficulties*, trans. Richard Winston, for the magazine *Twice a Year*. Collected in William Wasserstrom, ed., *Civil Liberties and the Arts: Selections from* Twice a Year, *1938–48* (Syracuse: Syracuse University Press, 1964).
35. Robert O. Paxton, "The Five Stages of Fascism," *The Journal of Modern History* 70, no. 1 (March 1998): 1–23.
36. See Alicia Garza, *The Purpose of Power: How We Come Together When We Fall Apart* (New York: One World, 2020).
37. Robert McChesney, "Making Media Democratic," *Boston Review*, June 1, 1998, bostonreview.net.
38. Garza, *The Purpose of Power*, 20. [Emphasis added.]
39. adrienne maree brown, "gifting my attention," *adrienne maree brown* (blog), August 9, 2012, adriennemareebrown.net.
40. Paul Celan, "Corona," *Poems of Paul Celan*, trans. Michael Hamburger (New York: Persea Press, 1972), 61.

Chapter 2
1. adrienne maree brown, *Emergent Strategy: Shaping Change, Changing Worlds* (Oakland: AK Press, 2017), 13.

2. bell hooks, "When I Was a Young Soldier for the Revolution," in *Talking Back: Thinking Feminist, Thinking Black* (Boston: South End Press, 1989), 10.

3. Susan Parenti and Willy May, *Playing Attention to Language*, unpublished booklet, 2003.

4. Herbert Brün, *my words and where i want them* (London: Princelet Editions, 1986), 22, 30.

5. Parenti and May, *Playing Attention to Language*, 7.

6. Stephen Sloan, "Doing the School for Designing a Society and Doing Cybernetics," paper presented at 32nd Annual Conference of the American Society for Cybernetics, Falls Church, Virginia, March 29–April 1, 1999.

7. Robert White Scott, "An Intellectual History of the School for Designing a Society" (PhD dissertation, University of Illinois at Urbana-Champaign, 2011), 69, hdl.handle.net/2142/24073.

8. Herbert Brün, *When Music Resists Meaning: The Major Writings of Herbert Brün*, ed. Arun Chandra (Middletown, CT: Wesleyan University Press, 2004), 226.

9. See Center for Story-based Strategy, "What is Story-based Strategy?" (nd), storybasedstrategy.org.

Chapter 3

1. Subcomandante Marcos, "Statement of Subcomandante Marcos to the Freeing the Media Teach-In," organized by the Learning Alliance, Paper Tiger TV, and FAIR in cooperation with the Media & Democracy Congress, New York City, January 31–February 1, 1997.

2. As of 2025, twelve Indymedia websites remain worldwide, down from a peak number of 210 centers, although some groups have transitioned into new organizations.

3. Feven Merid, "The Promise of IndyMedia," *Columbia Journalism Review*, November 22, 2024, cjr.org.

4. Joseph Torres and Juan González, *News for All the People: The Epic Story of Race and American Media* (New York and London: Verso, 2011).

5. Alfredo Lopez, *The Organic Internet: Organizing History's Largest Social Movement* (Quetzaltenango: Entremundos Publications, 2007).

6. David Solnit, "How We Created a Festival of Resistance in the 1999 Battle of Seattle," *The Indypendent*, November 19, 2019, indypendent.org.

7. Vandana Shiva et al., *Seeds of Suicide: The Ecological and Human Costs of Globalisation of Agriculture* (New Delhi: Research Foundation for Science, Technology, and Ecology, 2000).

8. Ike Okonta, *When Citizens Revolt: Nigerian Elites, Big Oil, and the Ogoni Struggle for Self-Determination* (Trenton: Africa World Press, 2008).

9. Todd Wolfson, *Digital Rebellion: The Birth of the Cyber Left* (Urbana: University of Illinois Press, 2014), 87.

10. John Tarleton, "Protesters Develop Their Own Global Internet Service," *Nieman Reports*, December 15, 2000, niemanreports.org.

11. Merid, "The Promise of IndyMedia."

12. Liam O'Donoghue, "85% Coalition Fights for 100% Equality Under Law," *Public i,* April 21, 2002, publici.ucimc.org.
13. Sascha Meinrath, "CUWiN: Wirelessing the Revolution with Open Source Mesh Wireless Technologies," *Government Technology*, August 3, 2010, govtech.com. CUWiN was primarily coded by Dave Young with support from Josh King, Dan Meredith, Zach Miller, and other technologists.
14. Xeni Jardin, "Getting the Gulf Back on the Grid," *WIRED*, September 7, 2005, wired.com.
15. See Kevin Michaels, "Arab Student Harassed," *News & Letters* 47, no. 6 (July 2002), marxists.org.
16. Evan Henshaw Plath, "Social Media, Digital Identities, and People's Platforms," *RevolutionZ Life After Capitalism* podcast with Michael Albert, episode 286, June 9, 2024, revolutionz.buzzsprout.com; Ignacio Siles, "Inventing Twitter: An Iterative Approach to New Media Development," *International Journal of Communication* 7 (2013), ijoc.org.

Chapter 4

1. Gwen Snyder, social media post, 2020, revised with permission.
2. Alfredo Lopez, *Democratize This! How We Make the World We Want*, webinar hosted by Danielle Chynoweth and Elizabeth Adams, July 22, 2020.
3. "Movements begin with the telling of untold stories," was the motto of the Media Mobilizing Project (now Movement Alliance Project, MAP), founded in 2005 to use community-based media production to develop a shared analysis and build the social and political power of poor and working-class people in Philadelphia.
4. This idea came to Danielle through nurse and healer Antonia Herbstreit and to Elizabeth through Anne Weiser Cornell and Barbara McGavin in courses on Inner Relationship Focusing, taught through Focusing Resources, focusingresources.com.
5. Jung scholar and Dreamwork Master Teacher Marc Bregman is the founder of North of Eden Archetypical Dream Work, northofeden.com.
6. Barbara McGavin and Ann Weiser Cornell, *Untangling: How You Can Transform What Is Impossibly Stuck* (Berkeley: Caluna Press, 2024), 125.
7. Mark Enslin, "Listening and Unentitled," *Cybernetics and Human Knowing* 20, no. 1–2 (2013): 23–9. The essay is a companion piece to a musical composition for a single pianist-speaker, who is forced to speak the words heard by thirteen different people being exploited while not being listened to. Mark explains that it is intended to "portray and embody, and to some extent analyze, the difficulties of listening, particularly in situations of social inequality."
8. Enslin, "Listening and Unentitled."
9. In-person interview, Danielle Chynoweth and Meadow Jones, Urbana, September 1, 2024. See also, Meadow Jones, "Archiving the Trauma Diaspora: Affective Artifacts in the Higher Education Arts Classroom" (PhD dissertation, University of Illinois, 2018), ideals.illinois.edu/items/109961.

10. Marianne Brün, "Paradigms: The inertia of language" (1980), in *When Music Resists Meaning: The Major Writings of Herbert Brün*, ed. Arun Chandra (Middletown, CT: Wesleyan University Press, 2004), 292–300.
11. Herbert Brün, *my words and where i want them* (London: Princelet Editions, 1986), 22, 30.
12. Brün, *my words and where i want them*.
13. Amy Goodman, "Right Livelihood Award Acceptance Speech," Swedish Parliament, Stockholm, December 2008, rightlivelihood.org.
14. Susan Parenti and Willy May, "Playing Attention to Language," unpublished booklet, 2003.
15. Carter Godwin Woodson, *The Mis-Education of the Negro* (Washington, DC: Associated Publishers, 1933), 21.
16. See Robert White Scott, "An Intellectual History of the School for Designing a Society" (PhD dissertation, University of Illinois at Urbana-Champaign, 2011), fn 105, hdl.handle.net/2142/24073.
17. Audre Lorde, *Sister, Outsider* (Berkeley: Crossing Press, 2007), 40–2.
18. bell hooks, *Talking Back: Thinking Feminist, Thinking Black* (New York: Routledge, 2015), 12.
19. Mariana Romo-Carmona, *Compañeras: Latina Lesbians* (New York and London: Routledge, 1994), xxi.
20. Sarah Peyton, *Your Resonant Self: Guided Meditations and Exercises to Engage Your Brain's Capacity for Healing* (New York: W. W. Norton & Company, 2017).
21. Mark C. Enslin, "Teaching Composition: Facing the Power of the Respondent" (DMus diss., University of Illinois at Urbana-Champaign, 1995).
22. Enslin, "Teaching Composition."
23. Larry Richards, "Connecting Radical Constructivism to Social Transformation and Design," in *Craft and Constraints, Clocks and Conversation: A Larry Richards Reader, 1987–2007*, ed. Ruth Marrero (Urbana: The School for Designing a Society, 2007), 88.
24. George Villanueva, "L.A. Eco Village: 20 Years as a Model of Sustainable Living," PBS SoCal, December 19, 2013, pbssocal.org.
25. Julie Bindel, "Obituary: Andrea Dworkin," *The Guardian*, August 29, 2013, theguardian.com.
26. Lorde, *Sister, Outsider*.
27. Laurence D. Richards, "Conversation vs. Communication: A suggestion for 'the Banathy Conversation Methodology,'" *Constructivist Foundations* 11, no. 1 (November 2015): 58–60, constructivist.info.
28. C. Wright Mills, *The Sociological Imagination* (Oxford and New York: Oxford University Press, 2000/1959), 5.
29. "The Beloved Community," The King Center, thekingcenter.org.
30. Martin Luther King, Jr., *Letter from Birmingham Jail* (London: Penguin Modern, 2018).
31. David Harvey, *Seventeen Contradictions and the End of Capitalism* (London: Profile Books, 2014), 263.
32. Grace Lee Boggs, *The Next American Revolution: Sustainable Activism for the Twenty-First Century* (Berkeley: University of California Press, 2016), 17. See

also Margaret Wheatley, *Leadership and the New Science: Discovering Order in a Chaotic World* (San Francisco: Berrett-Koehler, 1999), 44–5.

33. adrienne maree brown, *Emergent Strategy: Shaping Change, Changing Worlds* (Oakland: AK Press, 2017).

34. Scot Nakagawa and Sue Hyde, "Shifting the Narrative – Protecting our Futures, with Malkia Devich-Cyril," podcast, August 29, 2024, convergencemag.com.

Chapter 5

1. Barbara Ransby, *Ella Baker and the Black Freedom Movement: A Radical Democratic Vision* (Chapel Hill: University of North Carolina Press), 2003.
2. To learn more, see the Praxis Project, "Roots & Remedies," thepraxisproject.org.
3. "Composition for Hands" and "Odd-one-out" are adapted from exercises offered by Mark Enslin in his SDaS classes.
4. Burcu Yançatarol and Krzysztof Wodiczko, "Interview with Krzysztof Wodiczko," *m-est*, March 4, 2011, m-est.org; Ian Wojtowicz, ed., *Interrogative Design* (Cambridge: The MIT Press, 2024), 222.
5. Meadow Jones, "Archiving the Trauma Diaspora: Affective Artifacts in the Higher Education Arts Classroom" (PhD dissertation, University of Illinois, 2018), ideals.illinois.edu/items/109961.
6. Meadow Jones, "To Write What You Know: Embodiment, Authorship and Empathy," *Sensoria: A Journal of Mind, Brain & Culture* 10, no. 1 (Victoria, Australia: Swinburne University of Technology Press, 2014), 49–56.
7. "The Beloved Community," The King Center, thekingcenter.org.
8. Dr. Arthuree Wright, "25 Traits of the Beloved Community," *R-Squared*, General Commission on Race and Religion, February 1, 2025, r2hub.org.

Chapter 6

1. Zora Neale Hurston, *Dust Tracks on a Road: An Autobiography* (New York: Harper Perennial, 2006), 120.
2. There is mounting science-based evidence that children who have experienced childhood sexual abuse, or other "adverse childhood experiences" or trauma, have much higher incidents of cancer and chronic illness. In my case, I, Danielle, was diagnosed with a rare form of ovarian cancer when I was forty-five years old.
3. Referring to the United States' bombing of Hiroshima and Nagasaki, Japan in August 1945.
4. See Therese Pokorney, "Protestors rally in the publication of *News-Gazette* cartoon," October 2, 2018, dailyillini.com.

Chapter 7

1. "Sexual Assault Prevention Tips Guaranteed to Work," *No, Not You* (blog), September 24, 2009, tumblr.com.
2. Susan Parenti and Willy May, "Playing Attention to Language," unpublished booklet, 2003, 7.
3. Parenti and May, "Playing Attention to Language," 8.
4. In the 1980s, British Prime Minister Margaret Thatcher made famous her assertion: "There is no alternative [to capitalism]." The phrase "*¡Sí se puede!*" ["Yes, it can be done!"] comes from Dolores Huerta's leadership of the United Farm

Workers of America (later United Farm Workers Association) in 1972 and has been used widely ever since.

5. Favianna Rodriguez, live speech at Media Justice event, Oakland, California, April 8, 2016.

6. adrienne maree brown, *Emergent Strategy: Shaping Change, Changing Worlds* (Chico, CA: AK Press, 2017), 2. Also see her podcast, *How to Survive the End of the World*, with Autumn Brown.

7. See Margaret Mead, "Cybernetics of Cybernetics," in *Purposive Systems: Proceedings of the First Annual Symposium of the American Society of Cybernetics*, ed. Heinz von Foerster et al. (New York: Spartan Books, 1968), 1–11. See also Heinz von Foerster, *Cybernetics of Cybernetics*, ed. Stephen Sloan (Minneapolis: Future Systems Inc., 1976).

8. Stephen Sloan, "Doing the School for Designing a Society and Doing Cybernetics," paper presented at 32nd Annual Conference of the American Society for Cybernetics, Falls Church, Virginia, March 29–April 1, 1999.

9. See Kimberlé Crenshaw, *On Intersectionality: Essential Writings of Kimberlé Crenshaw* (New York: New Press, 2015).

10. From Herbert Brün, "Questions to Ask a Problem," unpublished teaching material, personal notes, nd. See also, the "Questions to Ask a Problem" assignment in chapter 8.

11. bell hooks, *Feminist Theory: From Margin to Center* (Boston: South End Press, 1984).

12. Parenti and May, "Playing Attention to Language," 22.

Chapter 8

1. See Stafford Beer, *Beyond Dispute: The Invention of Team Syntegrity* (Chichester: Wiley, 1994).

2. Herbert Brün, *Irresistible Observations* (Champaign: Non Sequitur Press, 2003), 207.

3. Stafford Beer, *Brain of the Firm: The Managerial Cybernetics of Organization* (New York: J. Wiley, 1981); Stafford Beer, *Designing Freedom* (Toronto: House of Anansi Press, 1993); Gordon Pask, *Conversation, Cognition, and Learning* (New York: Elsevier, 1975), 395.

4. Sloan composed approximately thirty texts between 1995 and his death in 2001, all with titles roughly approximating "My Current Self-Description of Manic Depression in a System," as ways to generate conversation within SDaS. See Robert White Scott, "An Intellectual History of the School for Designing a Society" (PhD dissertation, University of Illinois at Urbana-Champaign, 2011), 62, hdl.handle.net/2142/24073.

Chapter 9

1. See Wandjell Harvey Robinson, "Victory Video for Illinois Campaign for Prison Phone Justice," *Media Justice*, October 22, 2015, youtube.com; Jadlin Mendoza, "#Phone Justice Victory for Media Grassroots Action Network," *Media Justice*, October 22, 2015, youtube.com.

2. Brian Dolinar, "Securus is Charging Families Six Dollars for Phone Calls from Jail," *Public i*, November 18, 2023, publici.ucimc.org.

3. Ulandis Forte, "My Grandmother's 20-Year Fight for Prison Phone Justice," *Truthout*, June 21, 2019, truthout.org.

4. WMMT-FM is the noncommercial, community radio service of Appalshop, Inc., a not-for-profit multimedia arts center founded in Whitesburg, Kentucky in 1969 as an economic development project of the War on Poverty. In 2012, Sylvia Ryerson, a former DJ for the show, directed "Calls from Home," a documentary about the weekly radio program, distributed in short form by Field Notes recording studio, June 20, 2012, vimeo.com.

5. See Emmet Sanders, "Full Human Beings," People's Policy Project, nd, peoplespolicyproject.org.

6. Thanks to the years of advocacy by the Human Rights Defense Center and the Prison Policy Initiative, our campaign finally made national news: "Unfair Phone Charges for Inmates," *The New York Times*, January 6, 2014, nytimes.com.

7. Peter Wagner and Alexi Jones, "Timeline: The 18-Year Battle for Prison Phone Justice," *Prison Policy Initiative*, December 18, 2017, prisonpolicy.org.

8. Michelle Tauber, "Woman Who Grew Up with Both Parents in Prison Is Now Helping Kids Like Her Find Hope," *People*, June 10, 2021, people.com.

Chapter 10

1. Herbert Brün, *Irresistible Observations* (Champaign: Non Sequitur Press, 2003), 118.

2. See Sarah Peyton, *Your Resonant Self: Guided Meditations and Exercises to Engage Your Brain's Capacity for Healing* (New York: W. W. Norton & Company, 2017).

3. Founding principles of the National Playground Association, April 12, 1906, in the White House under President Theodore Roosevelt. National Recreation Association Records, University of Minnesota, Twin Cities, Social Welfare History Archives, Minneapolis, www.lib.umn.edu/swha.

Design Rondo

1. Proposal for design groups quoted in Stephen Sloan, "Doing the School for Designing a Society and doing cybernetics," paper presented at 32nd Annual Conference of the American Society for Cybernetics, Falls Church, Virginia, March 29–April 1, 1999, 50–1.

Chapter 11

1. This assignment was presented by Rob Scott, School for Designing a Society, 2005.

2. Herbert Brün, *When Music Resists Meaning: The Major Writings of Herbert Brün*, ed. Arun Chandra (Middletown, CT: Wesleyan University Press, 2004), 226.

Chapter 12

1. Made in collaboration with Matt Gray, udderbot.com.

2. Mark Enslin, in conversation with the authors, nd.

3. Dario Solina, "What's your excuse not to change your life?," TEDxLinz, November 26, 2024, youtube.com.
4. Herbert Brün, *my words and where i want them* (London: Princelet Editions, 1986), 49.

Chapter 13

1. Herbert Brün, *When Music Resists Meaning: The Major Writings of Herbert Brün*, ed. Arun Chandra (Middletown, CT: Wesleyan University Press, 2004), 226.
2. Mark Enslin, "Listening and Unentitled," *Cybernetics & Human Knowing* 20, no. 1–2 (2013): 25.
3. This is a combination of true stories, where names and identifying information have been changed to protect confidentiality.

Chapter 14

1. Mon Mohapatra, Victoria Law, Tracy Rosenthal, and Beatrice Adler-Bolton, "Carewashing: Carcerality Disguised as Social Welfare," panel discussion, Socialism 2024, Chicago, September 1, 2024.
2. The United States spends over $180 billion dollars to incarcerate almost two million people annually. See "United States Profile," Prison Policy Initiative, nd, prisonpolicy.org.
3. Wendy Sawyer and Peter Wagner, "Mass Incarceration: The Whole Pie," Prison Policy Initiative, March 11, 2025, prisonpolicy.org.
4. Angela Davis, *Are Prisons Obsolete?* (New York: Seven Stories Press, 2003).
5. "Story-based Strategy," Center for Story-based Strategy, storybasedstrategy.org.

Chapter 15

1. Chris Pullam, "Cunningham Township Board approves social service budget," *Daily Illini*, May 6, 2014, dailyillini.com.
2. Editorial Board, "Poverty isn't measured by feelings," *Smile Politely*, March 7, 2019, smilepolitely.com.
3. Alexa R. Yakubovich, Alysha Bartsch, Nicholas Metheny, Dionne Gesink, and Patricia O'Campo, "Housing Interventions for Women Experiencing Intimate Partner Violence: A Systematic Review," *The Lancet Public Health* 7, no. 1 (January 2022): e23–35; EL Bassuk, JC Buckner, LF Weinreb, A Browne, SS Bassuk, R Dawson, and JN Perloff, "Homelessness in female-headed families: Childhood and adult risk and protective factors," *American Journal of Public Health* 87, no. 2 (February 1997): 241–8.
4. Deuteronomy 15:11.

Chapter 17

1. Herbert Brün, *my words and where i want them* (London: Princelet Editions, 1986), 49.
2. Robert White Scott, "An Intellectual History of the School for Designing a Society" (PhD dissertation, University of Illinois at Urbana-Champaign, 2011), 43, hdl.handle.net/2142/24073.

3. Rachel Prizant Kotok, *Morpho Didius: Palindromic Poetry* (Worthington, OH: Armature Publishing, 2024).

4. Sarah Childress, "A 'Noble Experiment': How Solitary Came to America," *Frontline*, April 22, 2014, pbs.org.

Chapter 18

1. Rinku Sen, "How to do Intersectionality," *Narrative Initiative*, March 8, 2021, narrativeinitiative.org. Originally published in 2017 by Rinku Sen.

2. Herbert Brün, *Irresistible Observations* (Champaign: Non Sequitur Press, 2003), 118.

3. World Economic Forum, "Charted: How Have US Goods and Services Changed in Price Since 2000?," February 23, 2022.

4. For "prefigurative politics," see Wini Breines, *Community and Organization in the New Left, 1962–68: The Great Refusal* (New Brunswick: Rutgers University Press, 1989), 46–52. The phrase "build a new world in the shell of the old" is a well-known slogan of the Industrial Workers of the World (IWW).

5. See Earthaven, earthaven.org.

6. Quoted in Kenneth Cloke and Joan Goldsmith, *The Art of Waking People Up: Cultivating Awareness and Authenticity at Work* (San Francisco: Jossey Bass/ Wiley, 2003), 211.

7. Amy Rothstein and C.T. Lawrence Butler, *On Conflict and Consensus: A Handbook on Formal Consensus Making* (Portland, ME: Food Not Bombs Publishing, 1987).

8. See Herbert Brün, *my words and where i want them* (London: Princelet Editions).

Chapter 19

1. See "No Funny Business: Patch Adams on Health Care Reform," Aspen Health Forum, The Aspen Institute, 2009, youtube.com.

2. "Health Insurance Coverage – United States, 2008 and 2010," *Morbidity and Mortality Weekly Report*, Center for Disease Control and Prevention, November 22, 2013, cdc.gov.

3. Susan Parenti, "Re-Designing the Character of the Care-Actor," Gesundheit! Institute, 2007, patchadams.org.

4. Parenti, "Re-Designing the Character of the Care-Actor."

5. Parenti, "Re-Designing the Character of the Care-Actor."

6. John Glick, "We shape our future as we shape ourselves," TEDx talk, College of William and Mary, April 6, 2024, youtube.com.

Chapter 20

1. For examples, see: Brian Aubvine, Betsy Densmore, Mary Extrom, Scott Poole, and Michel Shanklin, Center for Conflict Resolution, *A Manual for Group Facilitators* (Madison: Center for Conflict Resolution, 1977); Amy Rothstein and C.T. Butler, *On Conflict and Consensus: A Handbook on Formal Consensus Making* (Portland, ME: Food Not Bombs Publishing, 1987).

2. Heinz von Foerster, *Cybernetics of Cybernetics*, ed. Stephen Sloan (Minneapolis: Future Systems Inc., 1976).

3. Bill Mollison, *Permaculture: A Designers' Manual* (Tyalgum, Australia: Tagari Publications, 1988).

4. adrienne marie brown, *Holding Change: The Way of Emergent Strategy Facilitation and Mediation* (Chico, CA: AK Press, 2021).

5. See Jo Freeman, "The Tyranny of Structurelessness," originally delivered at the Southern Female Rights Union in Beulah, Mississippi in 1972 and reprinted over the decades in publications like *The Second Wave* (1972), *Berkeley Journal of Sociology* (1972–73), and *Ms. Magazine* (1973). Multiple versions of the essay have been edited into a newer version on Jo Freeman's website, jofreeman.com. Howard J. Ehrlich wrote a response to Freeman's argument in *Reinventing Anarchy, Again* (Oakland: AK Press, 1996), 178–9.

6. Herbert Brün, *Floating Hierarchies* (Baltimore: Smith Publications, 1984/96); Herbert Brün, "A Longing for Links," *Sighs in Disguise* (Champaign: Non Sequitur Press, 2003), 152; Jude Lombardi, "Herbert Brün on Floating Hierarchies," Baltimore, 1994, youtube.com.

7. Barbara Ransby, "Ella Taught Me: Shattering the Myth of the Leaderless Movement," *Colorlines*, June 12, 2015, colorlines.com.

8. Charles M. Payne, *I've Got the Light of Freedom: The Organizing Tradition and the Mississippi Freedom Struggle* (Berkeley: University of California Press, 1995).

9. Ransby, "Ella Taught Me."

10. Heinz von Foerster, "The Perception of the Future, and the Future of Perception," in *Understanding Understanding: Essays on Cybernetics and Cognition* (New York: Springer, 2003), 199–210.

11. Andrew Boyd with Dave Oswald Mitchell, *Beautiful Trouble: A Toolbox for Revolution* (New York and London: OR Books, 2012), 318; "Dow does the right thing/How Dow did right for the people of Bhopal . . . for an hour," The Yes Men, theyesmen.org.

12. See Stacey A. Robinson's collage art works, staceyarobinson.com.

13. Bill Mollison, *Permaculture: A Practical Guide for a Sustainable Future* (Washington, DC/Covelo, CA: Island Press, 1990).

14. Mollison, *Permaculture*, 38.

15. In Robert White Scott, "An Intellectual History of the School for Designing a Society" (PhD dissertation, University of Illinois at Urbana-Champaign, 2011), 60, hdl.handle.net/2142/24073.

Chapter 21

1. CUCPJ's history is not a single story. In this case, I, Danielle, present one version of our fourteen years together. The author thanks Carol and Aaron Ammons, Martel Miller, Chris Evans, Belden Fields, and Sundiata Cha-Jua for their input and feedback on this chapter.

2. See Moon-Kie Jung, *Beneath the Surface of White Supremacy: Denaturalizing U.S. Racisms Past and Present* (Stanford: Stanford University Press, 2015).

3. Sean Crawford, "The Extent Of Segregation In Illinois," *NPR Illinois*, January 24, 2019, nprillinois.org.

4. Sundiata Keita Cha-Jua, "'We Believe It Was Murder': Mobilizing Black Resistance to Police Brutality in Champaign, Illinois," *The Black Scholar* 44, no. 1 (2014): 58–85.

5. Gabriel L. Schwartz and Jaquelyn L. Jahn, "Mapping fatal police violence across U.S. metropolitan areas: Overall rates and racial/ethnic inequities, 2013–2017," *PLoS One*, June 24, 2020, doi.org/10.1371/journal.pone.0229686.

6. Brian Dolinar, "Champaign Police Fatally Shoot Unarmed 15-Year-Old African American Youth," *Public i*, October 4, 2009.

7. Alicia Garza, *The Purpose of Power: How We Come Together When We Fall Apart* (New York: One World, 2020), 239.

8. Jon Yates, "Rights, eavesdropping law collide in filmmakers' case," *Chicago Tribune*, October 7, 2004, chicagotribune.com. Note that the legal change included an expansion of police powers to record without a warrant; see ACLU of Illinois, "Eavesdropping Bill Passes in Illinois," December 5, 2014, aclu-il.org.

9. Steve Bauer, "Community group leaders meet with police, homeowner," *News-Gazette*, July 14, 2007, news-gazette.com.

10. Angela Davis, "Beyond Mass Incarceration," public talk, University of Illinois YMCA's Friday Forum, September 27, 2013; Angela Davis, *Are Prisons Obsolete?* (New York: Seven Stories Press, 2003).

11. Michelle Alexander, *The New Jim Crow: Mass Incarceration in the Age of Colorblindness* (New York: The New Press, 2010).

12. Brian Dolinar, "Changes to Police Contract Come from 'The Work of the Citizen,'" *Public i*, January 20, 2013, publici.ucimc.org.

13. Tim Mitchell, "Miller calls for 'whole community' to speak at Champaign council meeting," *The News-Gazette*, October 27, 2011, news-gazette.com.

14. "Champaign City Council – 10/25/11," Champaign Government TV (CGTV), October 25, 2011, champaign-cablecast.cablecast.tv.

15. "Champaign City Council – 10/25/11."

16. "Champaign City Council – 10/25/11."

17. Danielle Chynoweth, "Prosecute Matt Rush for Brutalizing Black Residents," Action Network, February 2016, actionnetwork.org.

18. Mary Schenk, "Rietz: No charges against Champaign officer," *The News-Gazette*, February 23, 2016, news-gazette.com.

19. Sundiata Cha-Jua, "Police Brutality: what we should do," *The News-Gazette*, December 13, 2015, news-gazette.com.

20. The speaker, Mike Madigan, was later convicted on corruption charges. See "Former Illinois Speaker of the House Michael J. Madigan Sentenced to Seven and a Half Years in Prison After Corruption Conviction," US Attorney's Office, Northern District of Illinois, June 13, 2025, justice.gov.

21. Tom Kacich, "Ammons cashes in," *The News-Gazette*, March 19, 2024, news-gazette.com.

22. See chapter 9, "Campaign for Prison Phone Justice."

23. GBD 2019 Police Violence US Subnational Collaborators, "Fatal police violence by race and state in the USA, 1980–2019: a network meta-regression," *The Lancet* 398, no. 10307 (October 2021): 1239–55, thelancet.com.

24. Christopher Ingraham, "Why White People See Black Boys Like Tamir Rice as Older, Bigger and Guiltier Than They Really Are," *The Washington Post*, December 28, 2015, washingtonpost.com.

25. "Study Finds 95 Percent of Prosecutors Are White," Equal Justice Initiative, July 8, 2015, eji.org.

Chapter 22

1. See adrienne marie brown, *We Will Not Cancel Us* (Oakland: AK Press, 2020); Alicia Garza, *The Purpose of Power: How We Come Together When We Fall Apart* (New York: Penguin, 2020).

2. Saul Alinsky, *Rules for Radicals* (New York: Random House, 1971).

3. Eric Norden, "Playboy Interview: Saul Alinsky. A Candid Conversation with the Feisty Radical Organizer," *Playboy* 3 (March 1972): 59–78, 150, 169–79.

4. Nina Simone, "Mississippi Goddam," track 1 on *Nina Simone in Concert*, Philips Records PCC 608, 1964.

5. Safiya Noble, *Algorithms of Oppression: How Search Engines Reinforce Racism* (New York: New York University Press, 2018).

6. Aaron Glantz, *How America Lost Iraq* (New York: Tarcher/Penguin, 2005).

7. Starhawk, "Sunday, April 16, 2000 (The A16 Anti IMF/World Bank action in Washington DC)," self-published report, starhawk.org.

8. Susan Parenti, "Re-Designing the Character of the Care-Actor," School for Designing a Society/Gesundheit! Institute, October 7, 2007, patchadams.org.

9. Grace Lee Boggs, *The Next American Revolution: Sustainable Activism for the Twenty-First Century* (Berkeley: University of California Press, 2016), 39, 90, 100.

Chapter 23

1. Grace Lee Boggs underlines the dialectical aspect of progress: "These two notions—that reality is constantly changing and that you must constantly be aware of the new and more challenging contradictions that drive change—lie at the core of dialectical thinking." Grace Lee Boggs, *The Next American Revolution: Sustainable Activism for the Twenty-First Century* (Berkeley: University of California Press, 2016), 62.

Conclusion: From One No to Many Yeses

1. Todd Wolfson, "From the Zapatistas to Indymedia: Dialectics and Orthodoxy in Contemporary Social Movements," *Communication, Culture and Critique* 5, no. 2 (2012): 149–70.

2. Jeff Perlstein, interviewed by Miguel Bocanegra, Center for Labor Studies, October 15, 2000, depts.washington.edu.

3. Grace Lee Boggs, *The Next American Revolution: Sustainable Activism for the Twenty-First Century* (Berkeley: University of California Press, 2016), 39, 47, 90, 100.

4. Melanie DeMore, "One Foot/Lead With Love," January 10, 2017, youtube.com. DeMore sings: "*You gotta put one foot in front of the other and lead with love— put one foot in front of the other and lead with love . . . I know you're scared. And I'm scared too. But here I am, right next to you.*"

Acknowledgments

Susan Parenti said: "We need a new word added to the English language; a word that means 'Yes, I, myself wrote this piece, but in the company of a we.'" When we designed our Independent Media Center, Susan vehemently argued it should be called the "*Interdependent* Media Center." We wish to highlight the interdependencies that produced *Remaking Democracy* where "I" is nested in, and cares for, the "we." At a time of alienation and re-segregation, intergenerational collaboration and mentorship are what keep us alive, connected, and improving. This book is an emergent property of decades of conversations and relationships that have braided love, critique, and creativity. It is also the fruit of the biome of our communities of supporters, both near and far.

The work of Mark Enslin weaves through this book and makes it what it is, as we quote his formulations, strive to emulate his teaching, and stretch our brains to try to describe his compositions. Additionally, in his possibility-opening, silence-attending-to, ego-effacing mode of being, he was involved in the organizing of most of the interventions we recount.

We honor our intellectual influences and collaborators who passed during the writing of this book: bell hooks, who came to New College in 1991 inspiring our gender studies collective, Robert McChesney who applauded the vision of this book before he passed, Belden Fields who gave some of his last days to review book chapters, Elandria Williams whose presentation in our webinar was one of her last, the clown doctor who slayed hierarchy John Glick, poet Michael Holloway, organizer Brandi Collins-Dexter, and ecologist Dave "The Prairie Monk."

We honor our teachers within the School for Designing a Society (SDaS): Susan Parenti, Mark Enslin, Herbert Brün, Manni Brün, Steve Sloan, Carol Huang, Arun Chandra, Lori Blewett, Jeff Glassman, Lisa Fay, Larry Richards. Thanks to Rob Scott who pulled together the archives and intellectual history of SDaS in a dissertation that still wants to be published; to Jude Lombardi, Maria Silva, Koushalya Jeganathan, and Keith Moore for documenting our history; and to Dario Solina and Al Schneider whose enthusiasm for this book's contents buoyed us in difficult moments.

We are grateful for our partners Matt Zarnowiecki and Jane McClintock, children Astrid Adams, Orlando Adams, Ezra Shine Chynoweth, parents and grandparents Gloria and Dave Chynoweth, Leslie and Rob McClintock, Kathy and Van Bowersox, Connie Carden, Dinny Adams, Barbara Osborne, Nancy Hopkins, Jim and Susan Zarnowiecki, and many caregivers.

We thank our early readers and "Book Love" attendees: Carol and Aaron Ammons, Sundiata Cha-Jua, Chris Evans, Rohn Koester, Miriam Larson, Kate

McDowell, Jane McClintock, Copenhaver Cumpston, Meadow Jones, Stefan Brün, Michael Brün, Arun Chandra, Vita Wallace, Margaret Cuonzo, Orion Montoya, Al Schneider, Karen Emmerich, Kabir Dandona, Ida Hattemer-Higgins, Chiranuch "Jiew" Premchaiporn.

We applaud the 200+ people who showed up for our *DemocratizeThis!* webinar during the pandemic, and co-presenters Aaron Ammons, Safiya Noble, Alfredo Lopez, Ricardo Levins Morales, Susan, Mark, Elandria Williams, Michael Hollingsworth, Almah LaVon Rice, Lucie Vitkova, Andrew C. Smith, and David Kant; sponsors Media Justice, Highlander Research and Education Center, Urbana-Champaign Independent Media Center, Siebel Center for Design, and event support Brook Celeste and Jake Fava.

Our book midwives have our unending gratitude: Malav Kanuga who immediately and unwaveringly stood behind this book, our "embeditor" Erika Biddle who alchemizes encouragement and sharpening, stalwart supporter and designer Copenhaver Cumpston, super writing fellow Alice Boone, movement design guru Josh McPhee, and lightning typesetter Kirsten Dennison.

Our healers and Focusing partners helped us sync body and spirit together through this writing: Ann Chan, Nancy Melin, and Antonia Herbstreit; Sarah Peyton, Lily Revere, and Scott Scherer.

Thanks to our many mentors and supporters including Julie Harting, Coco Reed, Jacob Barton, Elizabeth Hoffman, Katherine Golub, Ann Weiser Cornell, Barbara McGavin, M. E. O'Brien, Anna Schriefl, Nancy Wallace, Ishmael Wallace, Free U NYC, and CHTU comrades. Malkia Cyril-Devich, Vina Kay, Roberta Rael, Brian Mercer, Ana Montes, Patrisse Cullors, Petridish, John Tarleton, DeeDee Hallack, Nan Rubin, Cheryl Leanza, Hannah Sassaman, Steven Renderos, Brandy Doyle, Joe Torres, Sascha Meinrath, Chris Ritzo, Ash-lee Henderson, Sage Crump, Dr. Artika Tyner, Jamie McClelland, Alfredo Lopez, and all our partners in media justice; Esther Patt, Ruth Wyman, Bernadine Stake, Benjamin Grosser, Sarah Roper, Emily McKown, Rachel Storm, Tomas Delgado, Don Owens, Aimee Rickman, Sam Smith, Karen Simms, Ben Joselyn, Traci Barkley, and so many working for change in our community; Father Joseph Merkt; Rebecca Ginsburg, Karen Linder, Charlotte Green, and all the Friends Meeting members; Augustus Wood, Dr. Reverend Evelyn B. Underwood, Barbara Kessel, James Kilgore, Brian Dolinar, Dottie and Brian Vura-Weis, Vaceilla Clark, DJ BJ Clark, Carol Inskeep, Sandra Ahten, the Kruses and Grandpa Wahlfeldt, the Storms, Deacon Clayborn, Byron Clark, E. Martel Miller, James "Tygar" Corbin, and all IMC/CUCPJ/Build Programs Not Jails members; Mary Lee Sargent, Kimberlie Kranich, and all the 85% Coalition members; Brandon Bowersox, Sigfried Gold, Lori Gold Patterson, and all the On the Job Consulting/Pixo members. To those gathering for Art Nights: elizaBeth Simpson, Emily and Azmi Fetterer, Lorene Anderson, Citlaly and Gabe Stanton. Thank you, Laura Haber, for conversation and dreamy writing retreat space.

About the Authors

Danielle Chynoweth is a media justice and housing rights leader, securing victories with low-income communities for over thirty years. She works to end homelessness and hunger as an elected official and public health board member in Urbana, Illinois. As Cunningham Township Supervisor she designed Bridge to Home, Solidarity Gardens, and CARES Alternative Crisis Response, combining direct service, mutual aid, and political organizing. As Organizing Director for Media Justice, she coordinated national victories for prison phone justice, net neutrality, and broadband expansion, after helping to pass the Local Community Radio Act. She co-founded the Urbana-Champaign Independent Media Center and was Vice-President of Pixo, a worker-owned technology company. She has led twelve successful electoral campaigns, including Carol Ammons for State Representative. As a city council member, she spearheaded public arts, community broadband, solar affordable housing, and police oversight in Urbana. Her work has been highlighted in *Columbia Journalism Review*, *In These Times*, and hundreds of local media pieces. She was recognized as a Women Making Waves in 2025 and awarded Woman of the Year in Central Illinois in 2011. She received her MA from the New School for Social Research and BA from New College of Florida, where she co-founded the Gender Studies Collective. She is a Field Instructor at the University of Illinois School of Social Work and teaches social change at the School for Designing a Society and internationally.

Elizabeth Adams, PhD, is a composer, teacher, and caregiver who has worked at the intersection of art, education, organizing, and care for over twenty years. She is a knowledge worker intent on creating the cultural change that will support social justice. Her compositions use sound to invoke social and political metaphors and have been performed throughout Europe and the United States. She produces anticapitalist music concerts with Julie Harting, created pop-up political education spaces with Free University NYC, and won historic rent laws with the Crown Heights Tenant Union. With the Orfeo Duo, she co-organized *Songlines*, a collaborative public mapping of over seventy NYC blocks through songwriting and parade. She has taught at Columbia University and teaches at the School for Designing a Society.

For speaking engagements, workshops, and press requests, contact the authors through: remakingdemocracy.org.

ABOUT COMMON NOTIONS

Common Notions is a publishing house and programming platform that fosters new formulations of living autonomy. We aim to circulate timely reflections, clear critiques, and inspiring strategies that amplify movements for social justice.

Our publications trace a constellation of critical and visionary meditations on the organization of freedom. By any media necessary, we seek to nourish the imagination and generalize common notions about the creation of other worlds beyond state and capital. Inspired by various traditions of autonomism and liberation—in the US and internationally, historical and emerging from contemporary movements—our publications provide resources for a collective reading of struggles past, present, and to come.

Common Notions regularly collaborates with political collectives, militant authors, radical presses, and maverick designers around the world. Our political and aesthetic pursuits are dreamed and realized with Antumbra Designs.

commonnotions.org
info@commonnotions.org

BECOME A COMMON NOTIONS
MONTHLY SUSTAINER

These are decisive times ripe with challenges and possibility, heartache, and beautiful inspiration. More than ever, we need timely reflections, clear critiques, and inspiring strategies that can help movements for social justice grow and transform society.

Help us amplify those words, deeds, and dreams that our liberation movements, and our worlds, so urgently need.

Movements are sustained by people like you, whose fugitive words, deeds, and dreams bend against the world of domination and exploitation.

For collective imagination, dedicated practices of love and study, and organized acts of freedom.
By any media necessary.
With your love and support.

Monthly sustainers start at $12 and $25.

commonnotions.org/sustain

STORY PROBLEM
SYSTEM
DESIRE CONTRADICTIONS
DESIGN
ACT REFLECT

Art by Christopher A. Evans